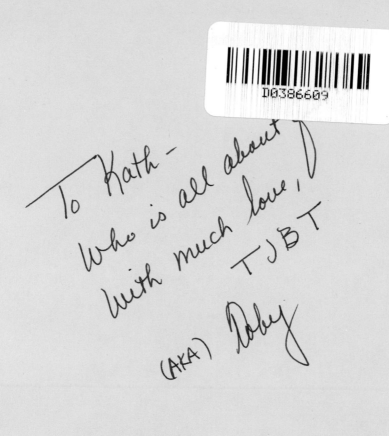

To Kath —
Who is all about
With much love,
TJBT

(AKA) Robby

The
Value-Creating
Consultant

The Value-Creating Consultant

How to Build and Sustain Lasting Client Relationships

Ron A. Carucci
and
Toby J. Tetenbaum

AMACOM
American Management Association
New York • Atlanta • Boston • Chicago • Kansas City • San Francisco • Washington, D. C.
Brussels • Mexico City • Tokyo • Toronto

Special discounts on bulk quantities of AMACOM books are available to corporations, professional associations, and other organizations. For details, contact Special Sales Department, AMACOM, an imprint of AMA Publications, a division of American Management Association, 1601 Broadway, New York, NY 10019. Tel.: 212-903-8316. Fax: 212-903-8083.

This publication is designed to provide accurate and authoritative information in regard to the subject matter covered. It is sold with the understanding that the publisher is not engaged in rendering legal, accounting, or other professional service. If legal advice or other expert assistance is required, the services of a competent professional person should be sought.

Library of Congress Cataloging-in-Publication Data

Carucci, Ron A.
     The value-creating consultant : how to build and sustain lasting client relationships / Ron A. Carucci and Toby J. Tetenbaum.
         p.   cm.
     Includes index.
     ISBN 0-8144-0502-9
     1. Business consultants.   I. Tetenbaum, Toby J.   II. Title.
HD69.C6C27   1999
001'.068—dc21   99–41185
                                                                    CIP

Printing number

10   9   8   7   6   5   4   3   2   1

For Barbara,
Matthew & Rebecca . . .

For Larry,
Hilary & Hank . . .

. . . relationships of immeasurable
lasting value . . .

Contents

List of Figures

Acknowledgments

Many people contributed their support to this project over the past five years. Our very special thanks go to all those who told us their heartbreaking and heartwarming stories reflected on these pages. To our colleagues who read the book prior to its final printing, we thank you for your insights and suggestions that helped refine our message, especially David, Karen, Linda, and Greg We are also deeply indebted to Andrea Pedolsky at Altair Literary Agency, without whose insightful criticism, risk-taking, encouragement, persistence, and strong advocacy this book would simply never have happened. Finally, we gratefully appreciate the efforts of the AMACOM staff, whose collective talents significantly enhanced the quality of the book. In particular, we would like to thank Ellen Kadin and Mike Sivilli. They helped bring five very long years to a happy ending! We also wish to thank Cathleen Ouderkirk, and her graphic design staff for making the insightful choice of the nautilus as our cover graphic, a long-time symbol of symbiotic relationships and growth. Additionally, we want to acknowledge the wonderful book by Anne Morrow Lindbergh, *The Gift From the Sea,* in which the nautilus shell, or argonauta, represents the healthy, long-developed relationship between two "persons as persons." This icon appears throughout the book as a reminder of the book's foremost purpose.

Finally, we are especially grateful to those consultants and clients with whom we spoke who are models of the principles and practices described in this book. Thanks for setting the example.

The Value-Creating Consultant

Introduction

"It is not the strongest of the species that survive, nor the most intelligent, but the one most responsive to change."
—Charles Darwin

Picture this. The grand ballroom of a huge downtown hotel in a thriving southern metropolis is teeming with sojourners on a pilgrimage. The pilgrims constitute a variety of consultant types: consultants from within organizations, consultants from firms, and consultants out on their own. There are renowned gurus, guru wannabes, second-tier gurus, and next-generation gurus. And there are searchers: corporate executives and employees from numerous industries, disciplines, and organizations from around the globe—all searching. One after another, the consulting pilgrims of all types stand before the crowds of mesmerized searchers proclaiming their transformational powers, telling grand stories of organizations once in turmoil, now prospering because of the application of highly sophisticated, cutting-edge solutions. It is perfect, because these are not just any answers. These are *the* answers. Precisely the answers being sought. Business cards are exchanged in a mad frenzy in hopes of securing the consultant or guru or guru wannabe of choice—a choice based on a precise match between the question being asked and the answer being offered.

The sun has set and the hotel's grand ballroom is now empty. Only the remnants of coffee left on tables, spilled water, and papers strewn about speak of the crowd that earlier filled the room to capacity. Staring at the room from the lobby lounge, we look at each other and think, "Something's wrong with this picture." The absolute correctness of the consultants' presentations and the righteousness conveyed in their deliveries, combined with the passive ingestion of the words and promises by the collected group of searchers, does not sit well with us.

That was five years ago. We now realize it was the birthplace of this book. We thought to ourselves, "What would happen if we went into the companies represented at the conference and found out what really happened in their efforts to transform their organizations. Would there be any distinguishing features between those consultants that truly created lasting value for the organizations they served and those that only believed they had? Is there any way to differentiate a genuine "consultant of choice"?

Five years of searching for the answers to these questions has led us to an unequivocal "Yes!" We studied consulting engagements of many sorts in over fifty-four organizations across a variety of industries. We interviewed clients, consultants, and staff people to understand both the productive and unproductive experiences they've had with consultants. What follows is a distillation of all our learning into what we believe will be a user-friendly, practical, and challenging tool to help consultants, old and new, rethink our profession. We begin with context, since there are important factors that have played a significant role in shaping the current dynamics of the consulting industry. We believe it is essential to view the current problems in light of those forces that have influenced, and will continue to influence, the consulting profession.

The Times They Are A-Changing

The booming post–World War II economy and a predictable environment made work in the 1950s and 1960s seem relatively simple and straightforward. Managers in those years could begin and end their careers without ever facing a major crisis. But the explosion of technology in the 1970s altered the face of the American workplace forever. It revolutionized the way business was conducted, accelerating the pace of change and making the entire world one highly competitive marketplace. Overnight, the simple world of yesterday became a highly complex and ambiguous place to navigate. The once-clear map to the future became buried in multiple options and excessive amounts of information and data, another consequence of emerging technologies.

For managers, who typically need to control their environment, today's workplace has become a sea of unstable performance pressures. In a chaotic world of relentless change and unpredictability, managers can no longer count on a copacetic tenure. Rather, they can easily expect two or more major changes over the course of their careers. Unfortunately, few of them are sufficiently "seasoned" to cope with large-scale change or even adequately prepared to make the rapid and complex decisions demanded of them daily.

Something to Think About . . .

What are the driving forces acting on you that are instigating the need to change the way you practice your profession?

Help Is on the Way

Fortunately for managers and corporate leaders, there is an abundance of help available to them in the form of management consultants, and they appear to be taking advantage of that help in record numbers. According to the Kennedy Research Group's (KRG) report, "The Global Management Consultant Marketplace," the global management consulting industry showed 21.6 percent in market growth in 1997. Approximately 360,000 consultants at 3,800 firms (with over three employees) and at least 3,100 firms (with three or fewer employees) generated nearly $70 billion in business. KRG predicts growth at an average per annum rate of 16 percent through the year 2000 when the market will exceed $114 billion in annual revenue. Management consulting firms sell advice on strategy, operations management, information technology, and human resources. With increasing demand, the biggest challenge to consulting firms at this time is to recruit talent from a diminishing talent pool. KRG estimates that industry growth and natural

attrition will drive the demand for more than 250,000 new consultants over the next three years. KRG predicts widespread opportunities, new markets, and rapid growth, more so by the turn of the
century. These researchers note that business schools cannot produce MBAs quickly enough to meet that demand, despite the fact
that consulting is the leading career choice among MBAs at such
schools as Harvard, Wharton, Stanford, and Tuck. As many as
25–35 percent of graduates from these programs went into consulting in 1998. It is not surprising that consulting has become the
hottest field for B-school graduates since those who attend top
schools can command an entry salary of $200,000 including sign-
ing bonuses, tuition reimbursement, and other perquisites.

   While we can all understand why people may choose consulting as a profession, it is less clear why there is such a strong demand for their services. Yes, the world of business has become
more complex, fast-paced, and competitive, but shouldn't managers be expected to handle the challenges of the workplace at least
as well as a hired gun? Shouldn't managers be able to set their own
goals and design strategies for achieving them without the advice
of an outsider? Shouldn't they be able to make decisions and implement them without relying on external support? Apparently not.

The Alleged Value Proposition: Concentrated Focus and Up-to-the-Minute Learning

The reality is that most managers arc so overwhelmed with their
day-to-day tasks that they are not equipped to take on an additional assignment, particularly of a major initiative. In the "lean
and mean" world in which today's managers operate, most have
an overly full plate that cannot accommodate a major add-on. One
manager at a large technology company whose strategy was driven
by acquisitions was asked to develop a human resources schedule
that would be used during the due diligence phase of the process,
and then to see that all HR and line managers were trained to use
the schedule and to understand the company policies and philosophy underlying the schedule's elements—no small task. She spoke
of the assignment as what she did in addition to her "day job."
Most major change initiatives absorb far more of a manager's time

and attention than anyone anticipates. Consultants have the luxury of being able to devote the time and their full attention to a single issue; they can set strategy *or* design an information technology (IT) system *or* integrate two companies following an acquisition. If the assignment grows, they are able and, in fact, delighted to add more people to the team, something managers cannot do as readily.

Time-pressed managers also do not have time to advance their learning. In an information/knowledge age, where human intellect is the most valued asset a company can amass, intelligence, creativity, and problem-solving skills are critically desirable capabilities. It is not that American managers lack these traits, but their day-to-day functions frequently prevent them from finding the time for the reflection and learning required to be cutting edge. It is for this reason that many managers look to consultants. These are the individuals whose profession demands up-to-the-minute, in-depth knowledge of and experience in particular industries and their problems. Corporate clients expect consultants to use their considerable knowledge base and experience, their intelligence, and even their intuition to help solve the organization's problems, provide strategic advice, and alert them to potential opportunities. *Business Week* (July 25, 1994) noted, "In the next ten to fifteen years, the leading management consulting firms could well see their influence and power increase exponentially. That's because the top consulting groups, almost all of them American, probably control the deepest reserve of knowledge on how to manage globally and build worldwide networks of information technology." Many managers will admit to not having the time to read the newspaper, much less a book that might inform their work. In contrast, most consulting firms provide their employees with ongoing education. According to *The Economist* (March 22, 1997), Andersen Consulting spends a whopping 10 percent of its revenues on training. McKinsey and Company invests $100 million annually in training and research, and $50 million annually in formal training (*The Wall Street Journal*, September 8, 1993).

Insufficient time to focus on a major initiative or to be a continuous learner is not the only reason managers call on consultants. Another is consultants' ability to climb the learning curve more rapidly than managers can. By virtue of the number of different companies to which consultants have access, and the pooling of knowledge among the consultants within a firm, they are able to develop a competence in an emerging technique, strategy, or system more rapidly than the lone manager tackling it from the get-go in his or her own company. One of today's major issues, for example, is how to manage growth. Most managers climbed their career ladders during the decades of downsizing and cost cutting, in which everything focused on shrinkage. Managing growth is a new and different experience calling for a radical shift in mind-set and behaviors. Consultants can bring managers up to speed, having garnered their learning in the laboratory and the field.

Finally, most of us have had to deal with the fact that we sometimes cannot be a prophet in our own land. An oft-cited definition of a consultant is, "Someone who says what you've been saying all along, but comes from fifty miles away." No matter how smart a manager, how in tune he or she might be with exactly what is needed and how to implement it, it can be difficult to have influence or to impact one's own organization. In that case, the manager might look to a consulting firm to bring credibility to the project. What managers need to be mindful of, in this case, is that credibility is not synonymous with an insightful point of view. Buying a name, a firm, a pedigreed degree does not guarantee added value.

Something to Think About . . .

> How do you add value to the companies you serve?
> What efforts do you make to maintain your viability through knowledge and reflection?

A Dubious Track Record

With consulting on the increase, the obvious question is whether companies have received value for services rendered. Results are mixed. Unquestionably, the ideas generated and promoted by consultants helped America to become the most productive and efficient economy on earth. The impetus for business process redesign, for identifying and developing core competencies, for time-based competition, benchmarking, logistics, supply chain, project management, and other approaches to increasing efficiencies, improving quality, increasing speed, and generating innovation—all originated with consultants.

Yet there is mounting suspicion and skepticism about the value consultants can deliver. Total quality management (TQM) and reengineering were two programs marketed by many firms in the 1980s and 1990s that, in retrospect, earned disappointing results. For example:

- A study conducted by Ernst and Young found that, in many of the 584 companies it surveyed in the United States, Canada, Germany, and Japan, total quality management (TQM) programs did not lead to improved performance—sometimes TQM hindered it (Woolridge in *The Economist*, March 22, 1997).

- A McKinsey and Company study found two-thirds of the companies that joined the TQM bandwagon failed (Fuchsberg in *The Wall Street Journal*, October 1, 1992).

- Arthur D. Little found that only about one-third of 500 U.S. firms believed their quality programs had a significant impact on their competitiveness (*The Economist*, April 18, 1992).

- Reengineering did not fare well either, despite the fact that American businesses spent $7 billion on reengineering efforts in 1994 alone, with more than $1.5 billion going to consultants and other experts (*Fast Company*, April-May 1998). According to Adrian Woolridge (*The Economist*, March 22, 1997), consultant Michael Hammer, one of the two leading proponents of reengineering, admits most attempts at reengineering have ended in failure. James Champy, the other leading proponent, said in his book *Reengineering Management* (1995), "On the whole . . . even substantial reengineering payoffs appear to have fallen well short of their potential. . . . Although the jury is still out . . . (our) study shows participants failed to attain these benchmarks by as much as 30 percent."

- Only 16 percent of 250 executives interviewed by Arthur D. Little reported full satisfaction with their reengineering projects (Micklethwait and Woolridge, *The Witch Doctors*, 1996).

Failed efforts such as these are costly to companies, as the following examples demonstrate:

• Between 1989 and 1994, AT&T paid approximately one-half billion dollars to management consultants, trying scores of different strategies and change programs, without obtaining the desired excellent performance (Micklethwait and Woolridge, *The Witch Doctors*, 1996).

• Figgie International, a manufacturing conglomerate in Ohio, spent more than $75 million for advice, but barely escaped bankruptcy (O'Shea and Madigan, *Dangerous Company*, 1997).

Backlash in the Press: Consultant Bashing

Results such as these have led to a recent spate of newspaper and magazine articles as well as books that are severely critical of consultants' efforts. In *Dangerous Company: The Consulting Powerhouses and the Companies They Save and Ruin,* two *Chicago Tribune* reporters, Jim O'Shea and Charlie Madigan, document how some of the biggest firms in consulting conduct their business. They describe the outrageous fees charged, the minimal benefits produced, and the inept efforts of frequently unqualified consultants. In another book, *The Witch Doctors: Making Sense of the Management Gurus,* John Micklethwait, business editor of *The Economist,* and management correspondent Adrian Wooldridge debunk the purported gurus of management, their theories, and the fads that have overtaken business. Publications such as *Business Week* ("The Craze for Consultants," July 25, 1994), *The New York Times* ("Consulting: Don't Lose It, Improve It," January 4, 1998), and *The Puget Sound Business Journal* ("Consulting Isn't Just Insulting," January 30, 1998) have taken consultants to task. The magazine *Fast Company* has a regular column entitled "The Consulting Debunking Unit." Scott Adams has made best-sellers out of his Dilbert and Dogbert books, which poke fun at consultants.

While consulting firms are receiving a beating in print for having made a fortune selling advice regardless of the outcome, clients are increasingly expressing their displeasure through the courts. The authors of *Dangerous Company* tracked several of the more high-profile cases. In one example, they document the background leading up to lawsuits filed by Ohio manufacturer Figgie International against Deloitte and Touche, as well as Boston Consulting Group, with Figgie citing fraud and incompetence. The authors concluded, "The consultants created as many problems as they solved." They also describe the work Andersen Consulting performed for UPO, a leading licenser of petroleum and gas process technologies. UPO's president, Michael D. Winfield, is cited as saying, "The difference between what Andersen promised at the outset and what it delivered is staggering." The company charged Andersen with "fraud, incompetence, and neglect." In another suit, these same authors note that the British government made Andersen Consulting pay an $18 million penalty fee for not delivering a new social security system on time. There are many more lawsuits, most of which are not known to the general public since it is in the best interest of the consulting firms to settle out of court and to have the documents sealed. What is clear is that the incidence of clients who are dissatisfied with consultants' performance is growing as rapidly as the consulting industry, and that's not a good thing. Figure I-1 shows the current trajectory on which we believe today's consulting industry is careening.

A Precarious Lack of Accountability

Consultants consider themselves professionals. Yet, unlike most professions, consulting has no certification or licensing board to

Figure I-1. The consulting industry's negative direction.

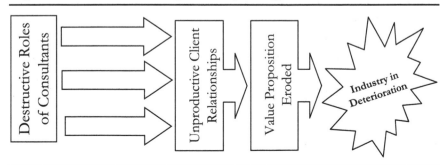

monitor entry into the field. In fact, anyone can put out a shingle and call himself a consultant. In the United States, everyone from doctors to hairdressers, lawyers to realtors, must pass an examination to practice and, in many states, must demonstrate their continued education in order to renew or retain their license. Not so with consultants.

There are also heavy sanctions in most professions against wrongdoing. Consulting, on the other hand, has no agreed-upon standards of practice, nor watchdog organizations to monitor its practice—either the promises made against the results obtained or the professional ethics of the participants. John Peet in *The Economist* (February 13, 1988) advises the field to be vigorous about upholding ethical standards and punishing lapses, exposing wrongdoing and opening itself to external inquiry. It is ironic that consulting firms are frequently brought in to identify a company's core competencies, to evaluate its workers and monitor their performance, yet consultants do not have any agency do the same for them, nor do they do it themselves.

At the current time, evaluation of consultants and their firms is occurring in the courts, where companies are extracting their pound of flesh for failed initiatives, and in the press, where exploits such as CSC Index's book-buying scam are promulgated for all to see. Consulting is currently a perfect example of the saying, "The cobbler's children have no shoes." The painful question being avoided is, "On this trajectory, what kind of imposed scrutiny are we inviting?"

A recent stroll through a local bookstore led us to discover thirteen books, all published within the last six years, on the field of consulting. Titles such as *How to Become a Successful Consultant, High-Income Consulting, How to Make It Big as a Consultant, Six-Figure Consulting, Start and Run a Profitable Consulting Practice,* and *Consulting for Dummies* were among the collection. We certainly think that understanding the "business" of consulting is important, and that a profitable business is absolutely more desirable than an unprofitable one. But these books, and many others like them, have conditioned this generation of consultants to focus on the highly lucrative and notoriety-building parts of consulting at the expense of truly understanding what it takes to be good at the work of the profession. There should at least be a balance between the need to be successful for one's self and the need to be successful for one's client. We believe it is important to replace the current mental model with a totally overhauled approach. We must be more thoughtful and comprehensive in preparing people to enter the field of consulting and not just bait them with the allure of riches and fame. In doing so, we can spare the next generation of consultants the consequences we are otherwise destined to suffer.

Something to Think About . . .

> How did you prepare yourself to be a consultant?
> What do you do to ensure you are a true professional?
> What ethical issues have arisen for you and your colleagues? How were they resolved?

Detergent Wars: Distinguished Service Turns Commodity

Call a consultant in to discuss a possible project and the consultant is likely to emphasize how his or her firm is different from and infinitely better than any other firm. The conversation is almost guaranteed to include some mention of "maximizing" profits, efficiencies, or performance (whatever the client's needs may be) in a "unique" manner. The reality is that there is truly minimal uniqueness among consultants' offerings. Bumping into one another at the same client sites, consultants learn what their competition is doing and they pick and choose what they like to add to their own repertoire. Just as Tide differs minimally from Cheer (they both get the wash clean), strategy firm A differs minimally from strategy firm B, much as they would like to think otherwise. Even Andersen Consulting, which is the behemoth of all and which bills twice as much as the next two earners, is losing its differentiation by moving from IT—whose star is fading—to general management consulting. Gary Hamel and Linda Yates, in their article "The Cobbler's Children" (*Consulting Magazine,* July, 1999), write, "Consultants often find it easier to preach change to others than to practice it themselves.

Visit the Web pages of the top ten consultancies and read what they have to say. The words are virtually interchangeable. If the managing directors of any of these firms swapped jobs tomorrow, they'd quickly find the levers and the place would run, more or less, the way it did the day before.''

Consulting has its roots in "counsel," but advice is ceding center stage to billable hours. The consulting field has grown so rapidly and the competition has become so intense that the once-honorable and distinguished service profession has lost its way. It now focuses its efforts on growing its own business—building people and dollars—rather than on developing products and services that genuinely aid the client.

Three examples are very telling: On March 11, 1997, *The Wall Street Journal* wrote an exposé of Towers Perrin, which was providing service to several companies in the area of diversity. Following a typical consulting process, Towers Perrin conducted interviews at each company, reviewed staff records, and eventually made recommendations, which its consultants would help to implement for additional fees. What the newspaper discovered was that eleven companies received identical or almost identical advice, despite the fact that the consulting firm was purportedly doing individualized analyses with unique recommendations suited to the individual company. It is difficult to believe all eleven warranted the same report given that the companies were widely disparate in industry and culture, ranging from Nissan to Thomson Consumer Electronics, Inc.

The second example comes from Oren Harari, who recounts in his column in *Management Review* (October 1996) how an acquaintance of his asked for his assistance when she decided to become an independent consultant. He went to his files and pulled out a report he had done several years back when he was consulting, thinking a model might be informative. The woman went off, did her consulting, and sat down to write her report. Her recommendations were the same as those in Harari's report! Was she influenced by his findings? Did things not change in the five years between his report and hers? Do all organizational problems boil down to a handful of repeated issues? Do consultants tend to share the same narrow lens in looking at an organization? A "yes" to any of these questions is somewhat frightening.

The final example was told to us in an interview with a woman who was a senior vice president at a Fortune 100 consumer-products organization. The only female at that level of the organization, she became the focus of the sales pitch for a consulting firm whose entry strategy was to build a huge retainer. She told us, "I was wined and dined, my opinions were valued, my suggestions were applauded . . . I never realized that I was being seduced. I'm embarrassed now when I look back on it, but I opened the door for a hundred-million-dollar initiative, which, in the end, produced nothing. They were like predators and I was their meal ticket, only I never saw it. They were so smooth." These consultants, members of a firm considered premier in the field, not only cost the company a bundle of money and diverted the energies of the workforce into a nonproductive initiative, they also damaged the self-esteem and confidence of a capable woman, who still has not recovered psychologically or professionally from the experience. After eighteen months of work, there was no evidence that the consultants added significant value. When the contract was finally terminated, it was learned that the firm was facing several malpractice suits for leaving behind similar debris at other companies.

If consultants continue to use the bait-and-switch sell, followed by a canned diagnosis and a flawed execution of an off-the-shelf solution that has been "customized" merely by putting the client's company name in the header of all documents, then consulting will continue to be perceived with disdain. Already consultant jokes are replacing lawyer jokes.

Despite the predictions for continued double-digit growth in the consulting field, the spate of consultant bashing is making managers leery of hiring consultants and cautious about stipulating contract and budgetary terms. Companies are increasingly asking consulting firms to quantitatively justify their services and requesting contingency fees. It should seem apparent that firms no longer merely want advice and attractively bound reports. They want the advice implemented and will pay only for results. Yet consultants seem strangely unaffected by the move to accountability, denying the changes that are in the wind and blithely going about "business as usual." Perhaps the lead consultant apologizes more profusely for the failures of a fledgling consultant, or adjusts fees more rapidly upon receiving a client's complaint, or offers more sophisticated excuses when the engagement fails to live up to expectations. But basically, consultants continue to push the same "hard sell" with the same earnest promises, despite the fact that such promises are leading to increasing numbers of court cases when they are not kept. We wouldn't be surprised to see consultants include a "no harm, no foul" clause in future contracts! What we're not expecting in the immediate future is a dramatic difference in consultants' attitudes toward their profession and a radical change in their consulting behaviors. We hope we're wrong, because not to change is to signal the demise of an industry we love and that we believe can provide genuine service that creates lasting value.

Where Value Gets Created

Throughout all of the organizations and engagements we studied, we were most surprised by what clients described as the greatest benefit of having consultants in their organizations. We presumed we would hear stories of great results, overhauled performance, and transformed organizations. Indeed, some did tell very positive stories of the outcomes their consultants helped them to achieve. But the predominant reason cited regarding why clients were "glad the consultants had been there" all centered around the relationship formed with the client. Getting results and having the talent to get the results were givens. Consumers of consulting services viewed the results and the required talents to achieve them as very important, and these factors certainly helped to distinguish consultants from those that were big talkers but couldn't perform. However, the defining characteristics that separated consultants who "did a good job" from consultants who "we definitely want to have back" focused on the experiences that resulted from the *relationship* established with clients. Here are the kinds of things clients said to us:

> "I could think out loud—test my own hypotheses and assumptions with a safe sounding board."
> "My consultant helped me understand and more precisely define the problems in my organization, and helped me accept

that there was more [to the problem] than just the symptoms I initially wanted to address."

"I learned things about myself that were key in helping me change with the organization."

"I know more now than I did when we started; I'm more capable."

"This was a hard project. Looking back, I can see how my view of the organization, and the world around it, has changed."

"I felt like I had a strong ally in the face of a lot of resistance."

"I feel more confident now to tackle even bigger problems on my own."

"Not only did I get what the contract said I would get, but there's been a sustained improvement in performance. We learned things we didn't anticipate learning."

"My staff noticed that I got smarter!"

Additionally, those consultant experiences that led clients to conclude "we would never have them back again" were less about unachieved results and more about negative relationships. Let us be clear, though—consultants who failed to perform as expected were usually dismissed or written off as a loss (as they should be). Our conclusion, therefore, is this: Having talent and producing expected results are necessary but insufficient to create lasting value for clients. Relationships deepen over time, and it is in the context of those close working relationships that opportunities to influence positive change for clients and their organizations appear. Such opportunities rarely occur in brief project stints. "Over time," in this context, should not be confused with "extended engagements." Merely prolonging the billables deteriorates value for the client. Investing in a deeper relationship with clients creates value. Figure I-2 demonstrates the process of how consultants create value during engagements.

There is also an important benefit to the consultant if this relationship building is done well. In an increasingly cluttered consulting market, more deeply embedded relationships in client organizations will inevitably be a source of growth. And that deeper penetration will be a direct result of the relationship formed with that client. Having the talent and getting the results merely gets you invited on to the playing field—with all the other talented, results-

Figure I-2. How consultants create value.

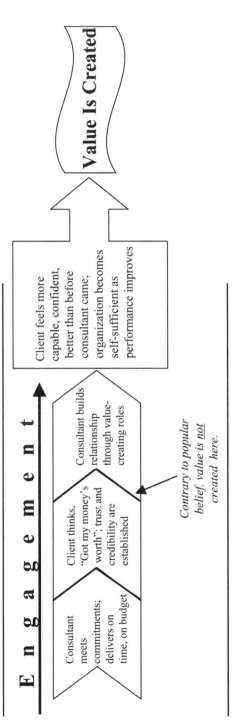

Value Is Created

Client feels more capable, confident, better than before consultant came; organization becomes self-sufficient as performance improves

E n g a g e m e n t

Consultant meets commitments; delivers on time, on budget

Client thinks, "Got my money's worth"; trust and credibility are established

Consultant builds relationship through value-creating roles

Contrary to popular belief, value is not created here.

producing consultants. Forming healthy, productive partnerships with clients who value the relationship they have with you will keep you on the playing field while others eventually limp to the sidelines. Figure I-3 shows our view of how consulting's current negative trajectory can change.

The High Risk of Value Erosion

Continued mediocrity in consultant performance, coupled with increasing cynicism in the market, will eventually force prospective clients to conclude that the best way to get help is on their own. In larger numbers, businesses will turn to the old adage, "If you want something done, it's better to do it yourself." In fact, many have already arrived at this conclusion. Several CEOs we spoke with made statements such as, "I don't use consultants. I hate them. They can't be trusted, and besides, I pay my people hefty salaries. They should be able to solve whatever problems we face."

While becoming more self-sufficient is certainly positive, the absence of an external point of reference against which to test one's thinking can also be dangerous. It can promote insular thinking and result in the loss of competitive advantage as market trends and shifts go unnoticed. But if prospective clients don't believe they can find a reliable, credible external source, they will tire of searching—at least in the consulting industry.

One risk might be that clients, viewing consultants as merely

Figure I-3. The consulting industry's positive change in direction.

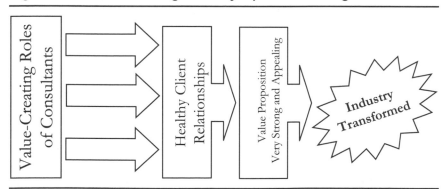

cheap, unreliable "middle men" will begin to turn directly to one another across industry boundaries for help in solving tough business problems. And they'll pay each other for it! Some companies are already doing this. Think about it. Cynics believe that all consultants do is transfer solutions from one company to another without adding value. So, if a company in the hospitality industry cracked the code on a complex problem that a company in another service industry was facing, why wouldn't the hospitality company be willing to send in people to help the other business solve the problem, in exchange for a fee? A business would be happy to have the additional revenue, and if the solution were really transferable, the recipient would be happy to pay for it—especially if it had already tried and failed using consultants. Far-fetched you say? Never happen? Doomsday soothsaying from the authors? Well, when people first began benchmarking, people said companies would never share their best practices—until they realized the value of the publicity. General Electric has gotten enormous value from the public attention received from selling its change methodologies to its own customers, without consultants in the middle. These are just a few examples of a trend happening more and more.

Does it mean the demise of the industry is just around the corner? Of course not. The point is simply this: If consultants become viewed as an unnecessary link in the value chain between problem and solution, the market will simply force the collapse of the value chain. It's happened in numerous facets of retailing, automotive manufacturing and sales, consumer electronics, and travel. Non-value-adding middle people are being eliminated between buyers and sellers. What's to prevent this from happening, in some fashion, in the consulting industry? Only a dramatic shift in how we think about and create value.

A Tour of the Book

When we began our research into the consulting field, we wondered whether the profession at large was being tarnished because of the greed or incompetence of a few rotten apples, or whether, in fact, the industry was in need of a major overhaul. Sadly, we found considerable evidence of abuse that suggests the negative perceptions of the field as a whole are warranted. The good news is that it is correctable. We have opted not to focus on the sizable fees, since we view them more as a symptom than as a root issue. Again, we believe value is created in the relationship between the consultant and the client, not in an economic equation. In fact, it is probable that, if true value is received, fees would most likely be a nonissue. Instead, we have looked carefully at the consulting relationship to understand where value is lost and where it can be enhanced, and to differentiate those consultants who provide value from those who do not. We believe the time has come to reinvent consulting. Our combined forty years of consulting experience, alongside our five years of focused research on the use of consultants, has given us a unique perspective on the effective and ineffective approaches consultants use. We have learned first-hand—from the client's point of view—those behaviors and characteristics that are destructive and those that create value.

Part One: Bad Habits and the Challenge of Differentiation

In organization after organization, engagement after engagement, our research repeatedly uncovered three consistent patterns perpetuating the negative trends, which are described in Part One. We begin with three negative roles consultants play. In Chapter 1, we first describe the *messiah,* the consultant who enters the organization as the white knight come to rescue the poor, ignorant people from the trap of poor performance and who thinks, "Thank God I'm here to save you!" We then describe the *dependency builder,* the consultant who enters the organization believing his or her expertise to be far superior to the client's, with solutions far too sophisticated and complex to be implemented without his or her help. This consultant thinks, "Don't even try this without me." Finally, we describe the colluder, the consultant who enters the organization, often as a political rubber stamp, to validate conclusions already drawn by the client and to repackage knowledge the organization has already gained. To feel secure about ongoing revenue and to avoid rejection, this consultant thinks, "Tell me what you'd like to hear."

Chapter 2 describes the character of consultants who fail to add value. These consultants take on the characteristics of *mis-*

sionaries, individuals who zealously proselytize their ideas and solutions, regardless of whether they fit the needs of the organization, and *mercenaries,* individuals who act as "guns for hire," providing whatever service the organization requests, right or wrong, while focusing on building billable hours. This first part of the book ends with a look at the nonproductive, potentially dysfunctional symbiotic relationship that can develop between the consultant and client.

Part Two: Becoming the Value-Creating Consultant

In writing this book, our goal was to identify ways in which the wrongs perpetrated by the consulting industry might be righted. We focused more on solving the problem than on merely adding another voice to the litany of complaints. Thus, while our research informed us about those consultant behaviors that attract the resentment and bitterness of clients, we spend the bulk of our time exploring those behaviors and characteristics of consultants that win their loyalty and respect.

Chapter 3 describes the value-creating consultant. This consultant rolls up his sleeves to work alongside the client, pushing against the grain in the uphill search for deeply embedded insights to problems that have eluded the client's organization. Value-creating consultants advocate a client's pursuit of improvement while ruthlessly inquiring into and dismantling those flawed patterns of thinking and acting that have blinded the organization.

The value-creating consultant can take on three roles: The first is the *partner,* or the consultant who works collaboratively with the client out of a philosophy that says, "We both have questions; together we'll find the answers." The partner has the humility to be able to make others successful. Next we describe the *capability builder,* the consultant who works with the client to share his or her expertise and to transfer skills and knowledge over to the organization. This consultant's philosophy is, "You're going to learn from this situation, so that next time a similar one arises, you won't need me." The capability builder has the generosity to give. Finally, we describe the *truth-teller,* the consultant who works with the client in an open and honest manner, providing continuous feedback that the client may or may not desire to hear. This consultant's philosophy is that the organization can't resolve its problems by continuing to ignore the fact that sometimes the "emperor really has no clothes." The truth teller has the courage to be authentic.

In Chapter 4, the discussion turns to the character of the value-creating consultant. It describes three operating principles demonstrated by consultants whose actions and beliefs model superior commitment to clients. These principles are self-reflection, gutsiness, and tough love. These three principles form the basis of the key defining feature of value-creating consultants—their ability to be irreverent. Among the many consultant engagements we observed, these three characteristics appeared over and over, serving as the guardrails that helped guide the actions and decisions of the more effective consultants. They also provide a credible and compelling foundation from which irreverent consultants influence their clients to consider significant change.

Part Three: The Partners and the Partnership

Chapter 5 focuses on the client and the characteristics that constitute a client of choice. We discuss the behaviors that make for a good client and the role of the consultant in helping to develop those behaviors in the client. The profile of a client of choice focuses on five characteristics that enable their success or, when underdeveloped or overextended, disable it. These characteristics are a results orientation, intellectual curiosity, optimism, self-confidence, and ambition.

Chapter 6 explores the messy, often intangible conflict inherent in the working relationship between external consultants and the client, as well as the client's staff. The subtle competition, threat, and undermining behaviors among these participants in a change effort often emanate from misunderstood roles, misguided assumptions, and the ill-conceived motives and roles described in Part One. We offer the EARTH model—equality, advocacy, respect, trustworthiness, and hope—as a guide to establish and enact meaningful and productive partnerships between consultants and clients. We believe that these principles are essential elements for effective consulting relationships.

Chapter 7 takes a special look at internal consultants, those professionals inside the organization who frequently participate in the change initiative and whose cooperation and collaboration are critical to the client–external consultant relationship. We discuss the ways in which the relationship between internal and external consultants can be managed to be positive and productive.

Part Four: Conquering the Engagement From Hell

Finally, Part Four presents a simulation that serves as a culminating activity for readers to reflect on their learning and to practice their skills. It is based on an amalgamation of both our experiences and those provided by our interviewees. The reader has the opportunity to analyze data, make decisions, determine interventions, and critique the decisions, behaviors, and communications of the characters in the case. At the end, we raise questions to challenge the reader's assumptions, analyses, and intentions to further extend and reinforce learning.

Who Should Read This Book

This book will be of paramount interest to independent consultants as well as consultants in small, medium-size, and large practices, from those just starting out to seasoned veterans. Managers of consultants who are responsible for developing consulting talent as intellectual capital in large consulting firms will also find this book valuable. Internal consultants within organizations, working in functions such as information technology, human resources, strategic planning, and quality, will find this book highly useful in improving their offering. This particular population remains frustrated by the irony that they are paid sometimes-substantial salaries, often only to be ignored. They long for useful guidance on how to play a more influential role in the countless strategic initiatives under way around them. Wanting more than a spectator's spot, they make earnest attempts to be recognized as more than just an extra pair of hands.

　　The need to import specialized expertise from outside the organization will increase as companies continue to struggle to find and maintain competitive advantage in fiercely competitive and global markets, many of which are undergoing consolidation. As this demand increases, so will the pressure on consultants to deliver sustainable value to clients and their companies. This is likely to spawn a ravenous appetite on the part of consultants for insightful guidance on how to respond to this pressure effectively, avoiding the stereotypical pitfalls for which consulting has now become infamous.

In writing this book, we attempted to blend the practical and profound into a new roadmap by which consultants can redirect their careers and, cumulatively, their profession. Using stories and examples that anyone who has worked as or with a consultant will relate to, this book challenges the reader to test personal assumptions and beliefs. It gives clear-cut direction and ideas for developing and maintaining effective, productive client-consultant relationships in a down-to-earth way. *The Value-Creating Consultant* turns a complex combination of relationships and tasks into actionable ideas any consultant will feel confident using repeatedly.

A Final Word Before We Begin

Neither of us want to be part of an industry about whom jokes are made, or to have people roll their eyes and snicker when they learn we are consultants. But, like it or not, that is where our industry is headed. We believe it can change. We offer no silver bullet, but we do hope that our book can help to ignite a dramatic change in an industry we are passionate about.

There is a story about a boy walking along the shoreline during low tide, picking up starfish and throwing them back into the ocean. A man walking on the beach stopped him and asked, "What are you doing?" The boy said, "I'm throwing the starfish back into the ocean. If they stay on the beach, they will die." The man scowled. "Don't be ridiculous." Pointing up the beach, he said, "Don't you see there are thousands of starfish on the beach. If you stayed here all week you couldn't possibly make a difference." The boy bent over, picked up a starfish, and threw it into the ocean. He proudly looked at the man and said, "I made a difference for that one!"

If the Kennedey Research Group's projections are correct,

there are going to be 250,000 more of us doing this work in the next few years. Imagine the difference we could collectively make if the majority of us decided to reject some of the industry's destructive current practices in exchange for a better choice. If you are more of a realist than idealist, then ask yourself, "When I'm not in the room with my clients, what do I want them saying about me?"

"What are they saying about me now?"

Part One

Bad Habits and the Challenge of Differentiation

"Progress has no greater enemy than habit."
—Jose Marti

A consultant is a consultant is a consultant (to paraphrase Gertrude Stein) . . . or is he? Today's consultants are largely viewed as interchangeable and, in the consultant-bashing books and magazines, virtually all are being tarred with the same brush. Clients have come to expect that most, if not all, consultants manifest the same undesirable behaviors. Yet the nearly $80 billion that the Kennedy Research Group reports was paid to consultants worldwide in 1998 would suggest otherwise. How can one argue that consultants are bad when they earn fees so exorbitant it suggests they are good? This dissonant situation was expressed by a client cited in *Consulting News* (June 1993): "We hate management consultants, and we still spend about $2 million a year on them." At a minimum, there's a strong ambivalence that surrounds consultants and the consulting profession.

Consultants are human and, as such, manifest most of humanity's foibles. In the extreme, they can create problems that eventually torpedo company projects, destroying good intentions and hard work. At a time when consulting is booming, when thousands of new entrants are flooding the field, it is becoming increasingly difficult to separate the good from the bad, the effective from the merely mediocre consultants. Clients have become so inured to bad practices, they no longer see them as bad; they accept them as the way things are and move forward with increasing cynicism and resignation. This is unfortunate, since good consultants—those who perform their work with integrity, professionalism, and effectiveness—must work five times as hard to distinguish themselves from the herd.

We don't believe bad consultants are bad people. They are just people who seem to have lost the essence of the profession they represent; namely, service to others. Instead, they begin to serve themselves and their firms. That self-interest can cloud their judgment and lead to unintended consequences. While human frailty may explain the negative behaviors manifested by some consultants, it doesn't excuse them, nor does it absolve us from our obligation to do everything possible to change them.

In the first part of this book, we look at those value-depleting behaviors and characteristics we have seen ruin consulting engagements time after time. These bad habits fall into three categories:

1. The destructive roles consultants play
2. The character and motivations that shape negative consulting behavior
3. The unhealthy relationships consultants form with clients

It should be noted that we did not find significant correlation between the size of the consulting firm and the degree or form of "bad habit" behavior. Our examples come from a range of firms spanning individual practitioners to the largest global consulting enterprises.

The first two chapters are not meant to be a condemnation of the profession. Rather, they are meant to intensify awareness of some of the less attractive practices of our profession and to challenge ingrained assumptions about what is and isn't helpful to those who pay our bills. They are meant to provoke personal reflection and, perhaps, even change.

1

Three Destructive Roles of Consultants

"You will always find some Eskimos ready to instruct the Congolese on how to cope with heat waves."

—Stanislaw Lec

Despite the bull market of the past several years, the accelerating rate of change and its complexity have created a palpable state of tension and anxiety among the world's corporate leaders who are responsible for leading their companies into an uncertain future while maximizing shareholder return. To seek relief from these pressures, business leaders have turned to consultants whose numbers multiply to meet the demand. This quick and significant growth in the consulting industry has led to an acceptance of mediocrity, sometimes incompetence, when it comes to quality outcomes.

In our research, we repeatedly confronted three value-depleting roles, depicted in Figure 1-1, that stand out as critically in need of correction: Playing the Messiah, Creating Dependency, and Colluding with the System.

Destructive Role One: Playing the Messiah
Thank God, I'm here to save you.

"Like clouds and wind without rain is a man who boasts of his gifts falsely;
The way of a fool is right in his own eyes."

—King Solomon

Figure 1-1. Bad-habit consultants.

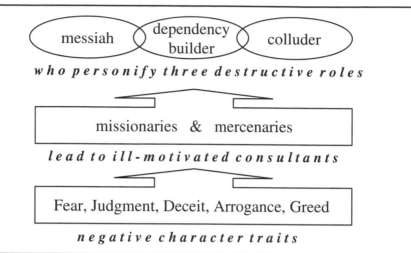

It is a natural phenomenon of group behavior that individuals in a group look to the alleged "expert" for answers. The phenomenon is heightened when the expert purports to actually have the answers and enacts the role of sage, prophet, or messiah. This dynamic is continually played out between consultants and organizations. Some consultants, eager to receive some of the wealth pouring into their field, as well as the idolatry accorded a self-proclaimed expert, promote themselves as the leaders of the next coming. They view themselves as being hired for the expressed purpose of providing the organization with the answer to whatever problem it is facing and charge fees commensurate with their status as an expert. Not only will the organization be unable to survive without them, they reason, it will be incapable of even the minutest progress without their sage advice. Messianic consultants are easily recognized by their position at center stage. Once hired, they write, direct, and produce the script, treating the company's managers and staff as mere actors in their play.

Senior managers within the organization hiring the consultant are not blameless. They contribute to the dynamic by craving the magic answer that will put their company ahead of the pack and raise to an exalted position anyone who promises to supply the secret answer. Having committed a huge sum of money to be allocated over a considerable amount of time, they view their destiny as inextricably linked to the consultant they hire. An abundance of wishful thinking bordering on outright fantasy surrounds their perceptions of the individual whom they endow with divine qualities and whom they anoint a guru.

Employees, highly anxious in these days of downsizings and mergers, play a role as well in holding the expectation that the consultant will lead them to the promised land. Although somewhat jaded by a string of unsuccessful consultants who have preceded the current messiah, a piece of them still holds out the hope that this one will be the one to save them.

When the consultant's importance becomes inappropriately amplified, he or she takes on the aura of an omniscient being. We saw just what an unfortunate situation this can be, as we watched it play out in one organization.

In describing a recent client addition, a consultant we know said to us, "They were actually lucky to get me to come and work with them. I turned down other big assignments because I know how much they need me, and I know I can do a lot for them."

Astonished by his arrogance, we arranged to talk with his clients about their new "messiah." We spoke with the vice president of quality assurance, who had hired him.

"So, of all the consultants you could have chosen, what distinguished him?"

Eagerly she replied, "He's absolutely incredible and passionate about his work. When he presented his proposal, my team fell in love with him."

"What did he do to foster such immediate bonding?" we asked.

"He made us promises and guarantees! And that's what we wanted," she declared. "He said to us, 'I'm going to turn your group into a world-class operation and make you industry leaders.' We loved hearing that. It was very inspiring."

Trying not to be surprised by her reaction, we asked, "And exactly how did he say he was going to do this, and how long did he say this transformation would take?"

"Well, he didn't get into specifics like that. He just said we were going to work hard, and that we had to believe it was possible." At this point, immediate images came unbidden to mind: We were reminded of Aladdin rubbing the genie's lamp three times, and the more nefarious image of the Reverend Jim Jones convincing his followers to drink the grape Kool-Aid.

Undaunted we continued. "So what results have you seen so far?" Proudly she told us, "He's working his tail off for us. He's gathered some very insightful data and presented it back to our senior leaders. My team is in contact with him every day, responding to all his requests for information so that he isn't delayed. I know it may not look like it, but I believe we're making great progress."

It seemed obvious to us that there were no results to report. "Do you have any concerns at all so far with the project?" we asked.

"Actually I don't. But I know some people on my team have been complaining. They feel like they're doing the grunt work while he gets all the credit. But I told them that we have no prima donnas here. We're all in this together. I won't tolerate people jockeying for center stage in my organization."

"So you don't believe your team's concerns have any validity?" we challenged her.

"I certainly don't!" she responded quickly. "We were very fortunate to be able to get this consultant. I had to work hard to convince the management committee to free up the money for the project. They need to be a little more grateful."

When we met with the consultant again, we said, "Boy, it sounds like you've made quite an impression on your clients. They were very enamored with the promises you made them about becoming world-class and industry leaders. How do you plan to revolutionize their performance?"

"Well, I see great potential in them. I know if I drive them hard, they'll rise to the occasion. It may not happen overnight, but Rome wasn't built in a day, either. Besides, I like them. They're nice people and they deserve a chance to find their potential greatness. That's kind of one of the reasons I took this assignment. I like to help good people achieve greatness."

Listen closely to the beliefs operating in the thinking of both the client and the consultant. Both have come to believe that the consultant is the almighty change agent come to rescue the organization from its mediocrity and transcend it to the outer limits of preeminence. Both actually believe the consultant has the capability and responsibility to do it. His need to be a sovereign help is buoyed with the illusion of omnipotent power he has created in his client's mind. Her need to detach from accountability and create the appearance of transformation is met because she was able to attract a high-priced, famous consultant who generates a windstorm of activity and paper.

Unfortunately, while not always this extreme, many consultants have difficulty conceiving of their role as one-half of a partnership. They too easily assume the messiah role and create imbalance, forgetting that they have been brought into the organization to help or assist in problem solving, teaching, designing, or implementing, not to take over and provide answers from on high. What often lies behind this "lapse" is the fact that people in the organization try to force the consultant into the omniscient leader role, expecting the consultant to have the answers to their questions and to solve their problems. They find it a relief to be able to turn over the problem to someone else and convenient to have another person to blame when things go wrong. Consultants who assume the role of messiah, accepting responsibility for giving all the right answers and finding all the best solutions, dilute organizational ownership, weaken the organization, and reduce its effectiveness. Not surprisingly, consultants end up becoming the most visible scapegoat when fingers start being pointed when things go wrong.

The organization that searches for the divine answer and discovers a consultant or a consulting firm who promises to deliver it often finds that, in the end, the man behind the curtain wasn't the great and powerful Oz after all. When expectations are unrealistically high, it is almost impossible for anyone to meet them. It is predictable that consultants who enter the organization under the delusion that they are messiahs who can save the organization from its competitors and put it into a leading position are destined for disaster.

Anyone who conveys to members of the organization that the consultant has all the answers is grasping at simplistic solutions in order to deliver on what was an impossible promise. Worse, it reinforces the norm that the consultant is the leader and the person who will do all the work—identify and analyze the problem, design and implement a solution, evaluate and report back at the end—which is not an effective long-range strategy for the organization.

The Need to Be Revered

Desiring respect, seeking approval, and enjoying attention are natural human motives, but in the consulting profession they can get pushed to an extreme. A consultant's success resides largely in her expertise, ideas, and opinions. This can create an inextricable connection in the consultant's mind between the expertise, ideas, and opinions and the consultant's sense of self. Given that the consultant's every word and action is judged and evaluated, and that her ideas are always assailable, the consultant's ego is continually open to potential assault. Differences of opinion or opposition to ideas can become a threat. When this happens, the consultant reacts to protect herself. Suddenly her contained need for respect, approval, and recognition runs amuck, and an insatiable appetite to be worshipped overtakes her ability to balance self-confidence with humility.

In addition, the outrageous fees paid to consultants, coupled with the reverence once awarded only to doctors and the freedom to make pronouncements for which they are rarely held accountable, provides the perfect environment in which to develop an inflated ego and to liberate a narcissistic personality. In short order, consultants see themselves as the next recognizable icon in an industry of people who have made a fortune from their views. The result is consultants stricken with the messiah syndrome. They compensate with self-exalting behavior and become even more hooked on their own wonderfulness. Their ego needs manifest themselves in unattractive, unprofessional, and unproductive behaviors: seeking center stage, posturing to attract people's adulation, credit-grabbing, deflecting blame to others, intimidating those who have the audacity to disagree. They shut out feedback or reinterpret it in a self-serving manner. Thus, when people fail to see eye-to-eye with them, rather than display an openness to an opposing or alternative view, they discount the other person's input, interpreting it as a form of resistance to a good idea or to the need for change.

It takes a rare individual to remain centered and not sucked in by one's own hype in an era when consultants are America's heroes and heroines. Sadly, consultants who play the messiah out of a need to be revered eventually fall from grace and face the exact failure they sought to avoid with their arrogance. When the client becomes frustrated with the lack of results, becomes aware she is losing control, sees the energy of her organization depleted with little to show for it, she suddenly turns around and blames the consultant for poor advice. The consultant's ideas and plans are publicly rejected, which is traumatic for the consultant, who views it as a personal rejection.

Figure 1-2 is a summary of destructive role one, playing the messiah.

Something to Think About . . .

> What solutions have you been sure are *the* answers in your practice?
> How have you fed into your client's fantasies and wishful thinking?
> How carefully do you monitor your need for approval and recognition?

Destructive Role Two: Creating Dependency
Don't think about trying this without me.

"Modern neurosis began with the discoveries of Copernicus. Science made man feel small by showing him that the earth was not the center of the universe."

—Mary McCarthy

It is frightening to see how quickly and deeply people throughout an organization can develop a dependency on a consultant. One senior vice president of human resources at a large financial services organization told us with vehemence in his voice, "I just got into this assignment and I'm astonished at how many consultants this division uses. There's one consultant wandering around this

Figure 1-2. The Messiah: "Thank God, I'm here to save you."

Symptoms	How the Consultant Feeds the Role	How the Client System Perpetuates the Role	How Performance Is Undermined
• Over-scrutinizing internally generated ideas. • Naming the initiatives after the consultant. • Routinely quoting the consultant/firm as leverage. • Delaying decisions until the consultant's input is received. • Consultant's/firm's influence becomes pervasive.	• Uses dogmatic, highly directive language. • Takes a dominant position in meetings. • Assumes a leadership role in projects. • Is evangelical about his/her position. • Uses intimidation when confronted with opposing views.	• Manifests high degrees of deference. • Accepts consultant's point of view without question. • Easily impressed by consultant's capabilities.	• Decision making criteria become faulty ("What would the consultant do?"). • Risk aversion increases. • Ownership of outcomes is diluted. • Unhealthy political agendas emerge and impede progress.

Consequence: Results not achieved.

place who's been here for years that I'm determined to get rid of. He has created so much dependency with users around here. I know of one department who can't even hold a [expletive] staff meeting without him there. It makes me sick."

Dependency is a strong dynamic, but what lies behind it? On the consultant's end, there are two powerful motivators:

1. *The need to help.* Underlying the choice to become a consultant is a genuine desire to help people or organizations. At the core of many consultants is a need to help. Helpers can have their

psychological needs met by playing enabling roles—making people happy, showing off expertise, controlling others, creating obligation, and giving meaning to one's own life. Not all of these motives are conducive to growth on the part of the person or persons being helped. The recipients of the assistance may be grateful and may admire the helper, but they may also resent the help, feeling obligated, helpless or dependent on the helper.

2. *Fear of losing the ability to help.* This second motivator is a consequence of the first—namely, that the psychic gain in being a helper can be so gratifying that the consultant begins to fear losing it. At some level, the consultant realizes that if the client becomes too self-sufficient, too "healthy" or too knowledgeable, he won't need a consultant anymore and the good feelings generated by helping (not to mention the financial benefits of recurring revenue streams) will disappear. Consciously or unconsciously, consultants recognize that sharing too much knowledge will take the mystique out of their business and they will no longer be needed. "Because the projects are bigger and longer, you're getting so close to your clients that they come to know all your tricks," says Fred D. Wiersema, a vice president at CSC Index. "Familiarity can breed contempt. You're no longer the guru with all the clever ideas."

Although it is human nature to want to feel needed and important, consultants can fall victim to this need at great expense to the client. In addition, the belief that "giving too much away" will lose a consultant revenue and respect as an expert is completely antithetical to the truth. Organizations now expect consultants to transfer their expertise to employees and are even writing it into contracts. The cliché that consultants should "work themselves out of a job" is becoming a required practice.

While the motives underlying the consultant's need to keep people dependent is fairly apparent, it is less clear why members of the organization succumb. Senior managers, in particular, should be impervious to the arrogance of consultants and their desire to withhold information and knowledge, yet they, too, get seduced into dependent roles. The inflated compensation packages senior managers command today presumably "buy" an incomparable skill set that includes cutting-edge knowledge of the industry, leadership capability, and an outstanding ability to identify and solve problems. This exchange misses an important element. Apparently the big bucks are paid to individuals who have the ability to identify and hire a consultant to whom more big bucks can be paid; in essence, senior managers subcontract the most critical and difficult work of the organization. Their greatest concern, then, focuses on whether the right consultant has been chosen. Ironically, rather than work alongside the consultant to ensure the right thing is being done, many senior managers literally leave the organization to the consultant, abdicating any responsibility for the outcome. It's as though the distancing will protect the manager should things proceed poorly. It represents, however, the ultimate in dependency.

Dependence on the consultant is not a phenomenon unique to senior managers. Two types of employees are easily hooked by consultants who foster dependency:

1. *Individuals anxious about changes and stressed by over-work.* In an environment in which people have more on their plate than they can handle, and where there are more project teams than there are people to serve on them, anyone who offers relief is seized upon. People who feel overwhelmed are more than willing to foist their problems and abandon their responsibilities to some-one willing to take them on.

2. *Individuals who are dependent-personality types.* Some people prefer to operate in a parent-child mode, being told what to do, when, and how. Their reliance on a consultant can be one manifestation of an unresolved authority issue stemming from their youth.

Senior managers and employees alike lose something valuable when they depend entirely on the consultant; they lose their ability to cope and to adapt. They become more dependent and helpless, more apathetic and passive, less willing to take risks, and less able to solve problems, make decisions, or initiate action. Worse, when they turn their problems over to someone else, they fail to learn how to solve them for themselves. When consultants engage in the process alone, they alone make mistakes and learn from them.

Those not involved in the process are deprived of the learning that goes along with it. Add to this the fact that dependency begets dependency. As one manufacturing company executive told us, "It's like an evil cycle. The more confidence managers lose in their ability to make decisions and solve problems, the more consultants are able to convince them that only they can do it for them. You'd think after four tries they'd take a hint." So often we hear managers complain about consultants who left them with plans they were unable to implement or a solution that created more problems than it solved. One manager, veins popping in his neck, face flushed with anger, said, "That firm got a multimillion dollar contract out of this company and left us worse off than when we started. Nobody knows what in the hell they did or what we're supposed to do now." Something is terribly wrong here. Unfortunately, it is not an isolated incident.

The Need to Be Needed

Several years ago, I was working in a consulting capacity on a high-profile project for the CEO of a major corporation. Months of research and design had gone into crafting a comprehensive solution for this rapidly growing organization. The day before the "big presentation" to the CEO and his staff, one of the project team members called and said, "Ron, we were thinking that maybe we could present this to the management committee by ourselves instead of having you with us. That way, we could gain some credibility in their eyes, and show them that we played a significant role in this, and that it wasn't just the consultant's work. How do you feel about that?" There aren't words to describe the size and intensity of the knot in my stomach. A windstorm of conflicting emotions surged through me. I was angry and resented the apparently well-plotted timing of the call. I was paranoid, thinking that this was the intricately schemed overthrow of my influence with the CEO, and of course, the beginning of the end of my work with the organization. I felt duped and rejected. I was frightened by the fact that I had missed the signals of their need for stronger independence. I was furious about being backed into a corner, not feeling a part of a decision but rather being handed a decision. And I was thrilled that the project team members had developed the confidence and commitment to take such a strong degree of ownership and risk for the project. It was a tough moment. Unfortunately, I made the wrong decision. I told them that I really thought it was better that I be there in case questions came up they might not be prepared to answer.

In hindsight, I realize my response was born from my need to alleviate the rejection I felt. Their newfound confidence and independence signaled to me a shift in my role and relationship with them. And while I did feel genuine excitement about it, I wasn't able to translate that into productive behavior. Instead of taking the opportunity to strengthen our relationship, I ended up bruising it by expressing what they heard as a lack of confidence in their ability.

In a profession such as consulting, a "helping" profession, one's need to be needed is indulged in a significant level of gratification. There is a natural tendency during the helping process for the helpee to depend on the helper while gaining new knowledge and skill. While the ultimate goal should always be to terminate the helping relationship once the helpee is able to solve problems on his own, it can be a source of comfort to both parties to prolong the relationship indefinitely. The helper's contribution to perpetuating the relationship is frequently rooted in the need to be needed. When one's natural desire for significance swells to a gluttonous need to be indispensable to others, this consultant has become a dependency builder. He has forfeited the opportunity to create lasting value because he has obstructed the client's opportunity to become self-sufficient. This consultant operates under the assumption that the stronger and more capable the client becomes, the less useful and important he becomes. To avoid such a state, the consultant indulges his need to be needed by prolonging the relationship beyond what is really useful. Unfortunately, as with the messiah, this consultant usually winds up expelled from the client organization because too much time passes without achieving any tangible results. Ironically, a desperate pursuit to be needed leads to the ultimate in being considered extraneous.

Figure 1-3 is a summary of the destructive role of dependency builder.

Figure 1-3. The dependency builder: "Don't even try this without me."

Symptoms	How the Consultant Feeds the Role	How the Client System Perpetuates the Role	How Performance Is Undermined
• Decisions require consultant's approval. • Leaders increasingly question their own abilities. • Deeper levels of the organization begin to resent consultant's/ firm's presence. • Consultant appears to know/care more about the initiative than the client. • Consultant recommends numerous postponements, citing "insufficient readiness" on the client's part.	• Uses condescending language that infers client inferiority. • Spoon-feeds information to the client. • Speaks in complex "jargon." • Continually draws attention to flaws in the organization.	• Allows the consultant to take on critical responsibilities. • Takes on a passive role in the initiative. • Seeks the approval and affirmation of the consultant. • Looks to the consultant for direction in areas consultant doesn't have expertise.	• Learning is significantly decreased. • Managerial self-confidence wavers. • Resource expenditures increase as time lines are expanded. • Resistance to change increases as organization cannot distinguish between the resented consultant and the initiative.

Consequence: Results not achieved.

Something to Think About . . .

> How do you monitor whether the help/advice
> you give your client is too much, too little, or just
> enough?
> Have you missed opportunities to create
> greater independence in your clients? Why?
> How carefully do you monitor your need to be
> needed?

Destructive Role Three: Colluding With the Organization
Tell me what you'd like to hear.

"He who winks the eye causes trouble, and a babbling
fool will be thrown down."

—King Solomon

Most of the people in a company perceive consultants to be truly
free agents, independent of the organization and therefore free to
speak their mind. Consultants, however, argue that this is only true
in the ideal world and not in reality. They understand that although
senior managers may purport to value open communication, including confronting unpleasant issues, they don't mean it. In fact,
any attempt to lay bare genuine feelings and emotions are threatening and thus taboo if the consultant wishes to stay employed.
Ever-protective of their own livelihood and looking forward to future work from the company, consultants are likely to protect
themselves by "playing it safe." Thus, they become a rubber stamp
for the projects sponsored by the people who hired them. They
become yes-people to the prevailing belief system operating in a
given culture. Although they may see barriers to achievement and
identify the hidden agendas of different groups within the organization, they often choose not to disclose them. They fail to fulfill
the opportunity to use their objectivity and to voice their differences in perspective, caving in instead to the pressures within the
system and the lure of future work. Unfortunately, when consul-

tants become inauthentic, they lose credibility and the confidence of employees and become viewed as a tool of management. At that point, the consultant might as well pack up and go home.

It is no feat to be a consultant when things go well and everyone is in sync. The true test of a consultant is when the consultant's findings and recommendations conflict with something senior management has said, is doing, or plans to do. This is where the rubber hits the road and the true test of the consultant's mettle lies. Conventional consultants take the easy way out, endorsing what they know is wrong, focusing only on building more billable hours, or on not threatening the future of the revenue stream or the relationships with fellow colluders.

Not providing honest feedback, difficult as it admittedly is, has led to some of our nation's greatest fiascoes. Consider, for example, the horrible tragedy of the Space Shuttle Challenger. The engineering firm hired by NASA made strong recommendations not to launch duc to concerns over the temperature's potential effect on erosion of the primary O rings. NASA, facing intense public scrutiny and a media lashing, scorned the firm for reporting such data the night before the scheduled launch. In an offline dialogue about NASA's wrath, managers of the engineering firm pressured the concerned engineers into "agreeing" to retract their concerns and to recommend the launch. The cataclysmic result speaks for itself.

More common is the tendency of consultants, especially large consulting firms, to deeply embed controversial issues into massive tomes spanning multiple volumes of data. One prominent firm we observed on an engagement presented its standard multiple-binder report in which it chose to obscure controversial issues. Their hallway rationale went something like this: "They're just not ready to deal with it. Besides, nobody ever reads these reports in such great detail; our retainer will be renewed by the time they discover it; and hopefully they'll be more receptive to the issue by then," as though the renewing of their high-priced retainer was magically going to produce a greater level of openness.

Many consultants argue that when they do express a contrary point of view, senior managers don't listen. They complain that their candid feedback falls on deaf ears and that the recipients really don't want to hear anything but good news and opinions that support the viewpoints they already hold. At this point they yield.

"You have to go where their energy goes" is one euphemism we've heard, meaning, "Don't make anyone uncomfortable."

Collusion isn't only the result of undisclosed feedback or controversial viewpoints. It also happens when consultants overextend advocacy to their clients. While it is important that we provide advocacy and hope to our clients (refer to the EARTH model in Chapter 6), overextension of these ingredients can lead to clients developing a false sense of well-being. In observing one consultant acting as a coach to her client, we asked, "Why such an enthusiastic cheer-leading approach?" She said, "I have to build up the manager's confidence. He's not ready to face the bad news yet, he's too fragile. Once I've got him where I need him to be, I'll start spoon-feeding him the hard stuff." Ugh! The rationale for collusion can be so seductive. Meanwhile, in conversation with her client's boss (and the approver of a potential bigger project), this same consultant would comment, "You were so right about your manager. He does need someone to hold his hand. I'm glad I got your input before I started working with him." Needless to say, her client knew nothing of her conversations with his boss. She has led the client to believe everything is going fine while confirming his boss's conclusion that he needs help. Everybody is happy.

The Need to Be Accepted

The unconditional acceptance of others is something each of us naturally desires. It's factory-installed DNA. And it's natural to conclude that the most logical way to gain such acceptance is to ensure we never do anything that angers, hurts, or disappoints those from whom we are seeking acceptance. This belief is then only a step away from believing that doing or saying anything that would anger, hurt, or disappoint someone forever risks their acceptance. A false belief, but a commonly overpowering one nonetheless.

The need to gain acceptance by keeping peace, harmony, and agreement drives many consultants to aggressively avoid the very conversations and actions their clients need to achieve the sought-after results. These consultants deceive themselves into thinking that "keeping a positive attitude" will help things work out for the best, and they believe that it is better than adding distress and discomfort to an already troubled organization. These consultants are chameleons, adapting their opinions and perspectives to the situation at hand. Their desire for acceptance has clouded their judgment and eliminated the possibility of creating the value they were hired for—to offer a point of view that didn't already exist. Eventually, someone in the client organization concludes, "If we always have the same thoughts as the consultants, one of us isn't necessary." As with the other unhealthy roles, the colluder's relentless pursuit of acceptance leads to what he most fears—rejection.

Figure 1-4 is a summary of the final destructive consulting role: the colluder.

Something to Think About . . .

Reflect on the times you found it easier to "go along" with your client, despite your personal misgivings. What rationalizations did you use to excuse your behavior? What was behind the behavior?
How carefully do you monitor your need to be liked and accepted?

Now that we have explored the three negative roles of consultants with bad habits, Chapter 2 will turn to the motives and character traits that underlie these roles.

Figure 1-4. The colluder: "Tell me what you'd like to hear."

Symptoms	How the Consultant Feeds the Role	How the Client System Perpetuates the Role	How Performance Is Undermined
• Clients' decisions "coincidentally" seem to coincide with consultants' recommendations. • Clients and consultants parrot each other. • Changes focus on form over substance. • "Camps" emerge as people hire their own consultants to augment the defense of their position. • Conflicts are fueled, but not resolved. • Rumor mill becomes a reliable source of information.	• Affirms client's actions. • Speaks in "reassuring" language to build up client's ego. • Tends to hang around with key "power players" in the organization. • Quotes the client in meetings ("As Judy said yesterday . . ."). • Gets in the middle of organizational conflicts and sides with the client.	• Asks binary questions that have obvious answers. • Inappropriately shares sensitive information with consultant. • Solicits input on decisions that have already been made. • Uses the consultant as a rubber stamp.	• False confidence emerges as arrogance increases. • Insularity can set in as outside points of view are rejected. • Speed hampered by unresolved conflicts and competing points of view. • Paralysis due to competing and conflicting agendas. • Critical organizational relationships hurt. • Innovation is stalled as people become averse to offering dissenting points of view.

Consequence: Results not achieved.

 2

A Relationship Gone Wrong: The Dark Side of Consulting

"The best way to see divine light is to put out thy own candle."
—Thomas Fuller

Most of us prefer equity in our relationships with others, a balance in what we give and what we receive. Client-consultant relationships are no different. We expect clients to pay in receipt of advice that adds value to their company, and we expect consultants to provide the advice in receipt of payment. It is the essence of a symbiotic relationship: two different organisms coming together for mutual advantage. What we discovered in our five years of research and the many articles and books that bash consultants is that the relationship is far from symbiotic and is much more parasitic—a case of one organism feeding off another and giving nothing in return. So many of the stories our interviewees related fell into this category that we feel compelled to share what we heard. Our purpose is not to build on the bashing, but to help consultants and their clients avert these dysfunctional relationships. Beyond Chapter 2, we will spend the remainder of the book exploring alternative approaches to consulting.

The Motivation of the Consultant: Mercenaries and Missionaries

"We may give advice, but we cannot inspire conduct."

—La Rochefoucauld

"For greed all nature is too little."

—Seneca

All consultants are not alike. They have different reasons for select-
ing the profession of consulting—differences that manifest themselves in different behaviors and attitudes toward their practice.
These, in turn, affect the client-consultant relationship, which in
turn has a direct bearing on the outcome. Some consultants are
motivated more by giving (advice), some in receiving (payment).
Enacted to the extreme, consultants' motives produce negative results, as illustrated in Figure 2-1.

In Figure 2-1, the one axis defines the mercenaries—individuals who, like professional soldiers, work for payment only. These
consultants are motivated solely by the desire for money or other
gain (e.g., notoriety). They see the profession as a means to a financial end in a field that provides maximum autonomy and economic gain. They view every engagement as a percentage of their
expected revenue goal and are less concerned with the nature of
the assignment than with its scope: How many team members can
this project bear? How many elements can we identify for billing?
How long can we extend the engagement? As the client presents
the problem (or, hopefully, from the consultant's perspective, multiple problems), the consultant is mentally preparing the budget. A
company that calls in a consultant thinking the problem is roughly
equivalent to a bad bruise or, at worst, a deep cut that might need
stitches should not be surprised to find that the consultant may
view the organization more like a patient near death. The mercenary-type consultant will advise multiple major surgeries conducted by a team of talented physicians if the organization is to
survive. Larry Farrell, ex-president of the consulting firm Kepner-
Tregoe, views consultants as "experts at packaged solutions (who),
once inside the door, are off on a billable witch hunt to find some

Figure 2-1. Negative motivations of consultants.

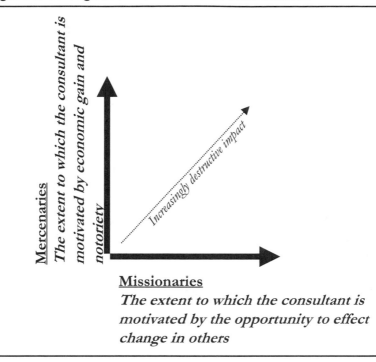

<u>Mercenaries</u>
The extent to which the consultant is motivated by economic gain and notoriety

Increasingly destructive impact

<u>Missionaries</u>
The extent to which the consultant is motivated by the opportunity to effect change in others

problems—problems you usually don't even know you have" (*Across the Board,* May 1993). Despite his cynicism, Farrell believes that "consulting is a great job, a giant ego trip, and the pay is outrageous." It would seem Farrell is familiar with the mercenary-type consultant.

In their extreme, mercenary consultants can be morally corruptible and without integrity about the work they do. They agree to do whatever the client wants even when they believe it's wrong, inappropriate, or a lost cause. Not having strong belief systems built around their work, they are the quintessential "guns for hire." If the wind blows toward globalization, they will sell globalization as the best thing since sliced bread. If the wind shifts toward a new technology platform, they shift with it. If the client wants X, they will deliver X, despite the fact that X might not be an appropriate solution. In the mercenary's view, arguing with the client who is set on a particular approach, technique, or tool is not the wisest way to build business. Better to give clients what they want, and if the client is unsure, sell what's "hot."

We were approached by a major telecommunications company that had acquired another telecommunications firm, which sought our "involvement in the integration" of the two companies. When we met with the client to clarify the company's needs and goals, we learned that the client believed the integration could be accomplished by "running everyone in the organization through a one-day values workshop." Unable to persuade them that this would not accomplish what they desired, we declined the engagement. To our amazement, one of our colleagues heard us discussing the incident and, almost dumbfounded, cried, "You're crazy! You should have taken the job and once you were in, you could have built it into work for life. Don't you know, they have really deep pockets." He then walked away, shaking his head in total disbelief at what he perceived to be a missed opportunity.

The underlying motivation to a mercenary-type consultant's side of the relationship, then, is solely avarice, leaving little reason to expect a successful outcome to the engagement.

The other axis of Figure 2-1 defines the missionaries, or consultants who see the profession as a means to transform organizations. Much like evangelists everywhere, they arrive on the scene prepared to save the natives from themselves, help them to see the light, and convert them to the right way. These individuals zealously proselytize their ideas and solutions, whether their opinions are needed or not. Like the mercenary, the missionary fails to listen to the real problems and needs of the client, but whereas the mercenary focuses on the bottom line, the missionary focuses on a very strong belief system that denies objectivity and brooks no variations or differences. In their heart, missionaries believe they are doing only good for the organization. They are blind to the dogmatism of their position. Should the missionary's program match the requirements of the organization, it is purely serendipitous. It is much more likely that there will be a mismatch destroying any chance of a successful outcome.

A consultant we interviewed once worked at a paper-goods manufacturing firm that became heavily involved in the quality movement during the 1980s. At one point, he led the company's quality teams, became certified as a Baldrige Award evaluator, and presented papers on total quality management (TQM) at professional meetings. He became an expert and a believer, which rapidly metamorphosed into a proselytizer for TQM. Thereafter, every problem at his organization, and in his new career as a consultant in other organizations, was defined in terms of quality. Every organization was encouraged to strive to achieve a Baldrige Award. While quality is clearly a desirable goal, and while changes driven by the Baldrige process can improve the way in which a company functions, it is not the answer to every issue. Unfortunately, this man sang only one note, but he did it with such passion and so convincingly that many companies bought his song.

Characteristics of Mercenaries and Missionaries

Asked to describe the consultants with whom they worked, our interviewees used different characteristics to describe what we would portray as either mercenaries or missionaries versus the "irreverent consultant," the effective consultant we will describe later in the book. Five particular characteristics were repeatedly cited as most problematic—the sources of value erosion. We believe these five negative character traits give rise to the motives of missionaries and mercenaries, which, in turn, produce the three destructive roles of bad-habit consultants (see Figure 1-1 in Chapter 1).

Deceit

Both mercenaries and missionaries misrepresent themselves. Acting in the guise of helping the client, both are self-serving. The mercenary, in pursuit of ever-greater fees, misleads the client by insisting there are still more problems to be solved and asserting that if the client does not pursue fixing these new and emerging problems, all of the preceding work will have been for naught. The missionary, in pursuit of converts, misleads the client by cunningly conveying that the organization is improving because it is following his lead. However, he makes certain his clients understand that they aren't there yet—and won't be without his guidance. Both types of consultants put a "spin" on the current situation and the state of their work that encourages the client to see the work as yet incomplete and still in need of consultant input.

One of the most insidious forms of deceit we heard about continuously is how engagements are sold. Mercenaries have become infamous for the "bait and switch" approach to luring in their prey. With clenched fists and tense jaws, one woman told us the following story:

> I have now begun to insist on interviewing the engagement team that will be assigned to my projects in my office before I sign anything. I've been burned too many times by the articulate senior consultant with just the right touch of gray on his temples telling me everything I need to hear, and winning my trust and confidence in his firm. Then, after the deal is signed, Wham! In walks a bunch of kids barely out of diapers claiming to know something about a world they've never experienced, and I'm supposed to pay for what they line-item on the bill as intellectual capital? Who are they kidding? Down goes my confidence and up goes my blood pressure. Now I hand-pick the engagement team. If they don't meet my standards, they don't come. It's like jury selection in a trial. It's time-consuming, but I'm not risking my budget and my organization anymore. It's a shame that it has come to this, but you simply can't trust what they tell you up front.

While it is unfortunate that bait and switch occurs, it is commonplace. And once the consulting firm employs it, clients remain distrustful throughout the entire engagement, flinching at every meeting, expecting the next "gotcha" to rear its ugly head. It seemed to us that the clients we talked to were mentally cutting their losses long before engagements ended, expecting to be disappointed by consultants who only wanted their bills paid despite saying all the right things.

Missionary consultants also have their own form of deceit at the start of engagements. They sport clever forms of manipulation and guilt to goad clients into signing on the dotted line. Think about it. Even the most confident of leaders is in a vulnerable place turning to an outsider for help when their personal resourcefulness and ideas run dry. What better time to cast a spell of doom and gloom while claiming to have the keys to unlock the shackles that hold the organization captive? Here is a portion of a conversation we heard repeated in different ways many times:

Client: I honestly can't figure this one out! We've tried everything we can think of. But the numbers just aren't moving.

Consultant: Believe me, you aren't the first person we've heard this from. Many of my clients are telling me that the tried-and-true solutions aren't cutting it anymore. I'm actually surprised you waited as long as you did before looking for help.

Client: I really thought the new technology we spent a fortune on would speed things up and motivate the regions to step up to the plate, but . . .

Consultant: But no go, right? It's natural to think our own solutions are perfect. Anybody in your shoes would probably be in denial about what was really going on. The regions probably think you are out of touch with the real issues, am I right?

Client: You should see the nasty-grams I get in my e-mail every day. You'd think I was out to get them on purpose!

Consultant: You probably haven't done a very good job of listening to them, have you? I mean, have you really spent time out there in the regions to understand what's going on? It's common for busy executives, like yourself, to get steeped in the day-to-day crises and forget about the people on the front lines.

Client: Well, I don't know if I'd say . . .

Consultant: Sorry—I didn't mean to make you defensive. It's just that I've seen this scenario dozens of times. You shouldn't feel badly. The good news is that it's very correctable. The real question is, how committed are you?

Client: Committed? Are you kidding, I'm desperate! The CEO is giving me hell about next quarter's forecasts.

Consultant: Excellent. I find pain like this to be an excellent motivator. It's important for me to know you'll stick it out once we begin and not cave in when it gets tough.

Client: I don't have any choice. So, what would you suggest?

Consultant: Well, as a matter of fact, a client of mine on the West Coast is facing a very similar problem. They are geographically dispersed, just like your organization, and are striving for ambitious growth, just like you are. Let me tell you what we've done for them that's working quite well. First, we . . .

You can just guess where the rest of the conversation is headed. It's the classic story of the wolf in sheep's clothing. There are few things more dangerous than turning over control to the deceitful wiles of a consultant come to rescue you.

Greed

Both mercenaries and missionaries are avaricious, but in pursuit of different ends. The mercenary seeks financial reward from the present assignment and the worldwide recognition that can bring future monetary payoff. A successful record combined with good PR can be parlayed into speaking engagements at $30,000 to $50,000 per three-hour session. Thus, the mercenary consultant takes credit for all successes and distances herself from all failures. She helps no one and only provides service that is itemized in the contract and tied to billable hours. The missionary seeks an expanding audience to convert to her beliefs. Thus, she hogs the limelight, grabs airtime from others, and roams the organization, ferreting out new acolytes. She is willing to help anyone who agrees to follow in her path.

Of the many, one particular downside to both forms of greed is that, for missionaries and mercenaries alike, learning stops. Because in both cases, they are willing to spare nothing to sell their existing offering to whoever will buy it, they develop a shtick that they milk as much as they can. The fierce attention paid to duplicating and extending the success of one offering cannibalizes time and energy needed to stay current and gain new knowledge for new offerings. This, of course, brings significant risk, as the following examples illustrate:

> The VP of a large marketing department hired the same consulting firm that the engineering department was using. The marketing department wanted help to conduct an audit of its function. This consulting firm had no more of a marketing background than did the engineers in the

engineering department , but the principal of the consulting firm was an old friend of the chairman's. The helpful thing to do would have been to recognize that the marketing VP was being politically opportunistic and either turn down the work or recommend that a more qualified consultant take on the project. The employees in the marketing department were outraged and pleaded with the VP not to conduct the audit, or at least to let them do it themselves or find a consulting firm whose specialty was marketing. The employees even spoke directly with the engineering consultants, who said, "What are we supposed to do, say no? If we turn it down, it may be seen as a reflection on our competence or our willingness to get involved. It may suggest we aren't confident in our own work, not to mention the loss of revenue the project could generate. Don't worry. An audit is an audit. It's not going to be as bad as you think." The consultants conducted the audit and the marketing VP paid $170,000 for a study that six months later he called "worthless." True, the client shares in the complicity here. But consultants such as these just can't control themselves when it comes to opportunities to promote their name and get paid for it.

Of the more than three dozen independent consultants or consulting firms we spoke with, more than two-thirds of them were delivering the same product or service that they had delivered for the past five years or more. Some even admitted, "Oh, I know I should probably get out there and learn more of the current stuff, but who has the time? Anyway, as long as there's a market for what I've got, what's the difference?"

One consulting firm showed us several proposals it had submitted to prospective clients. One proposal was to a large automobile manufacturer to conduct all of its first-line supervisor training, another was to conduct a benchmarking study on service for a fast-growing print/copy franchise, and a third was to conduct a series of workshops on workforce diversity for a retail electronics organization. The contents of the three proposals were so indistinguishable, we wondered if the consultants were even aware of how vastly different the three requests were. So we asked them.

"The only thing that seems to be different in these proposals is the header with the company name, the order in which you present the pages on the same four-quadrant model, and the names of the workshops. The content all seems to be the same—one personality assessment and its accompanying exercises, and a set of generic principles about management. Do you feel that these tools apply to any situation?"

The consultants confidently replied, "Yes, of course we do. It's the application of the information that makes it customized for the client. We've seen lives changed with these tools. They work. Besides, let's be real. If we started every client interaction from the ground up, we'd never make any money. We have to make a living you know."

Greedy consultants only learn the hard way. It usually takes dramatic failure before the light bulb starts to go on for them. When last we spoke with these consultants, they were in the process of dismantling their practice. Another consultant, who charges $30,000 for a half-day engagement told us, "I knew the client only wanted some high-priced entertainment and wasn't really serious about changing, but we went in anyway. I know which of my clients mean business and which ones don't. And my staff knows too. But, hey, if the market will bear it!"

One very large consulting firm, which purports their specialty to be strategy, information technology, and merger and acquisition integration, uses the same set of "fill-in-the-blank templates" on all of its engagements. They form teams within the client organization and have two or three of their consultants sit on each team. They launch the information hunt to populate blank lines and boxes in a ten-inch high pile of pro-forma templates. When the pile is completed, it is probably twenty inches high. One client of this firm, engaged in an acquisition integration, told us, "If I had known I was going to pay nearly $3 million just to have my people do the work for them, I'd never have hired them. And now that the deal is done, I've handed off the pile of data to my integration manager who basically feels the data are weak, and insufficient for making good decisions."

While we would encourage consultants and consulting firms who create valuable intellectual capital to leverage it as relevant opportunities arise, milking a well-worn two-by-two matrix beyond its usefulness or relevance is utter greed, and simply invites trouble.

Fear

Fear is a powerful driver of human behavior and a fairly prevalent emotion in today's workplace. Employees fear losing their jobs in an era of mergers and acquisitions where "redundancy" has replaced "downsizing" as a cost-cutting strategy. Conversely, and counterintuitively, employees even fear keeping their jobs in this fast-paced, technological business environment. Daily changes in the way work is done, new technologies, new structures, and new reporting relationships, all can be frightening to workers who are neither adventurous nor motivated by a challenge.

Consultants experience similar fears to employees. Here are some comments we heard when we spoke with colleagues during breaks at professional meetings:

Consultant 1:	"If I don't make my expected revenues, the firm may let me go."
Consultant 2:	"I used to be light-years ahead of the clients I work for, but no more. I don't know when it happened, but they've suddenly caught up. I hope they never find out we're pretty much neck and neck."
Consultant 3:	"The new technologies my clients are messing with really throw me. I worry about understanding what they're doing or, worse,

what those new systems can do. I don't always understand their capabilities, but I'm
afraid to ask too many questions or they
might not see me as an expert anymore. I
sure know I wouldn't pay anyone the fees I
get if they asked as many questions as I do.
My big fear is that they may catch on to
me."

Fear of inadequacy or of being released from an assignment
haunts consultants' day-to-day performance. Both mercenaries
and missionaries manifest fear—the mercenary fears that any misstep will put her revenue at risk, and the missionary fears that her
message will be contradicted by other consultants' messages or by
actual data obtained by the company. Thus, both types of consultants become risk-averse, mercenaries to delivering bad news and
missionaries to opening their beliefs to testing. They both live in
dread that one misstep may cause their gravy train to disappear.
The bigger their respective stakes, the greater their timidity.

In a recent engagement, our client's direct reports each
independently told us in one-on-one interviews of their
leader's abusive behavior in meetings, his inability to re-
frain from harshly and publicly criticizing their work, and
the almost Jekyll and Hyde nature he manifested. They
also told us that we were the third set of consultants to
whom they had given this feedback. We asked our client
if any of the previous consultants had given him any feedback on his leadership behavior that expressed the concerns of his team. He said no. Not certain whether his
blindness to his own behavior may have just blocked it
out, we asked to see any of the written reports to compare them with our findings. They contained no reference
to his behavior. One report actually painted quite a rosy
picture of how things were going in the minds of the
team members. Our diagnosis was that his behavior was
a major factor in the performance problems his business
unit faced. Whether or not he was willing to accept this
hypothesis was something else. But we believed he

played a significant role in impeding results. We did get to speak with one of the previous consultants to ask why she had omitted the data documenting the concerns of the team. She said, "Well, you catch more flies with honey than with vinegar, I've always found. Besides, there's always going to be a certain degree of whining from people. I don't think it helps to subject the client to all of it. It gets our relationship off to a much better start to just leave that stuff out." It didn't seem to dawn on her that he was no longer her client.

Arrogance

Both mercenaries and missionaries manifest an overblown sense of self-importance. Mercenaries gain their sense of conceit from the exorbitant fees paid for their services. They begin to believe they might really be worth the outrageous amounts they receive, a belief reinforced each time they earn a new assignment. We listened to consultants say things such as, "Boy, wouldn't you love to tell your clients what you really think?" and "I tell you, if it wasn't for the money, I'd never work with that client. I'm the only prayer they've got of surviving, although I certainly don't want to be associated with a flop of an organization. But I'll keep trudging along, propping them up and telling them how wonderful they are as long as they're willing to pay me $4,000 per day plus expenses."

Missionaries gain their sense of conceit from the rapt attention paid to their beliefs. The signs of megalomania in these types of consultants include conversations and speeches peppered with sarcasm, ridicule of the competition, and disdain for their own clients. Their message is clear: Do it my way or you will fail.

The senior management team of a large hotel chain was off site at an "executive team building" with a consultant that had been working with the hotel for almost a year. The intent of their work together was to help prepare the executive team to better lead in a global environment—clearly an important change in the organization. During a break, we happened to overhear part of a conversation among some of the managers. It went something like this:

"Do you believe these people? They've asked us to do some weird stuff before, but this takes the cake." Others jumped in, saying, "Yeah, and what's with this relay-race crap. I could be back in the office doing something worthwhile instead of out here playing." Another person said, "She reminds me of one of those TV exercise show hosts. Lots of pizzazz, but doesn't really say anything."

At this point, we couldn't resist joining in the conversation. "Sounds like your team building isn't going too well. How come?"

"Did you see what she had us doing out there? I just pray nobody I know was watching."

Curiously, we asked, "Why do you keep using her?"

"Beats me. Ask him," one participant said, pointing to his general manager.

We knew him, so we thought this would be an opportune time to say hello. He was standing near the buffet chatting with a few others. "Hi, Bill, how's it going?" He shook our hands—we hadn't seen him in a while.

"Well, you know how these things go."

"What do you mean?" We couldn't resist probing.

"You know, a little time away from the office to boost morale and energize the troops."

Innocently, we asked, "Do you think it's working?"

He smiled, hesitated, and said, "Well, I guess we'll have to wait and see."

Closing our brief conversation, we said, "You know, Bill, you might want to ask your team at the end of the day how they felt about it without the consultant around."

He said, "Good idea, I think I'll do that."

Extremely curious, we called him the next morning to see how his debrief went. "So, Bill, did you get a chance to talk with your team and find out how they felt about the team building?"

He exclaimed, "Boy, did I, and was I in for a rude awakening."

"What happened?"

"They hated it."

"Are you surprised?"

"No. I hated it too! I've been using this company for about nine months to try and get a little more of a broad focus—you know, now that we're moving into Europe, we need to be less parochial in our views. When she first came in, I thought she was, well, different, but I just wrote it off as our not knowing each other. She was just too outlandish for us. She reminded me of someone who'd dropped too much acid back in the sixties."

"Why didn't you end the relationship with her sooner if you didn't think it was going to work?"

"Well, to be honest, I thought my staff liked her, she came well recommended, and I didn't want to hurt her feelings. Well, now I know better. I put a call into her office this morning. I think it's time."

"Bill, if you don't mind us asking, approximately how much money have you spent with this company since you began using them?"

"Oh, I'd guess somewhere around $300,000."

We called the consultant to ask her what it was like to work with this company from her perspective. She said, "Well, frankly, I don't think they were ready for team building. My approach and techniques were more sophisticated than they could tolerate. They were very frustrating to be with. They resisted every suggestion that could have helped them. I'm not sure they are the 'brightest lights,' if you get my drift. I warned them from the beginning about the need to be open-minded, but they're too enamored with themselves. (Deep sigh.) But I guess it was a valuable learning experience for all of us."

"What did you learn about yourself as a consultant?" we asked.

"Well, nothing I didn't already know. I know that for some people, this work can be very threatening. It requires strong commitment and fortitude. Some have it, and some don't."

"Would you do anything differently if you had the chance?"

"No, I don't think so."

Arrogance leaves a bad taste in clients' mouths for a very long time. It doesn't matter how "right" arrogant consultants actually are, or believe they are. Clients are still the ones to pull the trigger.

Judgment

Both mercenaries and missionaries manifest a need to judge others while rejecting judgment of themselves. It is a form of control that enables both types of consultants to forestall others' judgments that might prove harmful to them. It's a form of self-protection that emanates from the belief that it is better for me to throw the first stone . . . before you do. Therefore, I condemn the work of others, denounce their beliefs, and lay blame at the feet of inadequate and incompetent company managers for all failures. In all judgments rendered, I am blameless.

Being judgmental is one of the most pain-inducing weapons consultants can use on their clients. Facing what seem to be insurmountable challenges, clients often start off consulting relationships somewhat defensively. Fearing failure, they seek the confidence of the consultant. But for missionaries and mercenaries to acknowledge any competency in their clients is to risk being less needed or revered, and to potentially forfeit maximum revenue. Better, instead, to draw attention to client's shortfalls, mistakes, or goofy idiosyncrasies so that their confidence dwindles and their desperation intensifies. Consultants who have mastered the art of being judgmental can do this in the subtlest of ways. They can be just obvious enough to push that insecurity button in their clients without having them feel overtly insulted. Off-handed comments in jest, subtle comparisons to "successful" leaders, backhanded compliments that end with "if only," and those notorious conversations that begin with, "Can I give you some feedback?" One senior executive told us this story:

> I was always fine except when he (the consultant) was around. I got knots in my stomach on days I knew we were meeting. He had the oddest way of making me feel incompetent. I found myself bracing for impact when he walked into my office with that week's list of my "screw-ups." Sure, some of what he had to say was useful and

accurate, but I got the impression that my feeling badly was his goal. After a few months, I just couldn't take it anymore. I started "postponing" our meetings, and eventually phased out his work. It wasn't worth the pressure. I was starting to think I had to please him instead of being the client and making sure he was getting done what I needed. It would have been easier to listen to, and accept, his feedback had he appeared equally interested in my priorities. He enjoyed feeling superior more than he enjoyed rolling his sleeves up and working. Frankly, that's not what I want in a consultant.

Consultants who are judgmental have greatly contributed to the coining of the phrase, "Here comes another *insult*-ant from another *insult*-ing firm."

These five characteristics of bad-habit consultants—deceit, greed, fear, arrogance, and judgment—are lethal to the health and well-being of the organization and the client-consultant relationship, and need to be eradicated. Clients need to be alerted to them so that they can recognize them early on before they work their evil.

Something to Think About . . .

> Has a desire to build your business or a passion to transform an organization led you to make the mistakes of a mercenary or missionary?

In light of the previous discussion about the characteristics of mercenaries and missionaries, ask yourself whether you have ever:

- Misled a client? Did you use the bait-and-switch sales approach, or become a wolf in sheep's clothing?
- Been opportunistic in dealing with a client? Did you build unnecessary business, or sell unvalidated shtick?
- Acted out of fear? Did you behave in ways to minimize losing work, or losing your reputation?
- Exhibited arrogance, conceit, or self-absorption?
- Judged others in ways that make you look better than them?

If you have committed any of these mistakes, ask yourself how these behaviors felt at the time. How do you feel now, looking back on them?

The Other Half of the Relationship

In a symbiotic relationship, clients have an equal role to consultants. How does that relationship play out? Our own research, along with consultant-bashing literature, suggests that the answer is, "Poorly." While the examples discussed in the previous section portray destructive consulting behavior, it isn't hard to see, in some instances, how the client contributes to the situation.

Two main criticisms can be leveled at clients. First, having hired one or more consultants, they abnegate responsibility for the success or failure of the initiative. How else do you explain data reported by O'Shea and Madigan in *Dangerous Company:* The $75 million spent by now-bankrupt Figgie International for no results, or the $100 million spent by a Fortune 500 company in our own study that also saw no results? This money was not spent overnight. There was plenty of time for the client to intervene, redirect, and/or pull the plug. Incidents such as these leave us totally astonished as well as confused. Where were the clients when the money was being spent? What kind of accountability measures were in place? Who was in charge? Did the client totally cede ownership to the consultant?

In addition to abnegating responsibility, we fault clients for "silver bullet" thinking. We believe the scenario plays out as follows: A problem arises and the client attempts alternative approaches to solving the problem himself. He fails and, realizing he has consumed precious time and resources in the process, moves into panic mode, launching a search for a "silver bullet." He is easy prey for a consultant who offers to provide one. The consultant, anxious to gain entry to a company, presents a panacea, the very thing to "fix" the manager's problem.

The symbiosis then escalates, becoming parasitic. To increase the odds of finding the silver bullet, the panicked manager brings in several consultants, often from different firms, and embarks on multiple initiatives simultaneously, creating an overload in which employees get bounced around from one activity to another in a steady stream of episodic interventions.

Let's look closer at the case of Figgie International (described by Jim O'Shea and Charlie Madigan in their book *Dangerous Company*), which supports this scenario. Andersen Consulting had three teams at Figgie. Deloitte & Touche had three projects in progress. Boston Consulting Group, Price Waterhouse, and Pritsker each had one project at Figgie. In all, there were twenty different major undertakings occurring simultaneously. The authors' comment: "Chaos reigned. One consultant's goal often clashed with another's. . . . no one seemed to see the big picture. . . . Figgie projects that had sounded simple on paper had become complex in practice, adding hours and costs to the bill." This is not an isolated example. In *Consultant News* (January 1995), KPMG Peat Marwick noted that one of its clients had thirty-five concurrent change initiatives spearheaded by multiple consulting firms with no orchestration of the various efforts.

Strafing the organization with a barrage of bullets can have serious consequences. It may mean that the positive effects of one program are canceled out by the negative effects of a different program. It may also mean that any change that does occur is likely to be superficial and cosmetic. Meaningful change won't occur merely because employees are too overloaded, reaching the state of future shock where changes come too fast to be assimilated. Like a sponge, people can only absorb so much before they become saturated. When this occurs, they become jaded, exhausted, and increasingly engage in dysfunctional behavior. When clients seek a silver bullet and consultants offer to provide one, failure is inevitable, because there are no magic solutions, no matter how many consultants are brought on board.

Something to Think About . . .

Think about a time you offered a client "silver bullet" advice.
Were the results what you expected?
How might you have handled the same situation differently?

If consultants engage in faulty roles and display bad-habit characteristics, we must all acknowledge that clients are not blameless. They, too, contribute to unsuccessful engagements. In Chapter 5, we discuss those attributes that make for excellent clients and how, when carried to an extreme, these same attributes can assist in derailing consulting engagements.

Our desire in Chapters 1 and 2 was to shed light on the negative behavior and habits of consultants that we heard spoken of with such contempt from our interviewees. We don't believe consultants who display these behaviors do so intentionally, or on every engagement. But the frequency of occurrence that has attracted the condemning, public criticism of many in the business community suggests intolerance for such consultants will only continue to escalate.

Part Two focuses on the alternatives. Becoming the value-creating consultant really begins by scrutinizing those choices we make with regard to how we practice our profession. It means reconsidering those assumptions about our clients that we have long accepted as true. And it starts by being willing to take a hard look inward to identify which of the bad habits discussed in this chapter might be leaking into our behavior. Once we can do that, we are ready to abandon them in exchange for those behaviors and characteristics that make one a value-creating consultant.

Part Two

Becoming a Value-Creating Consultant

"We are so happy to advise others that occasionally we even do it in their interest."

—Jules Renard

Well, that's it for the bad news. Now it's time to focus on the opportunity—how to change the long-accepted, unproductive behaviors to those that can distinguish truly gifted consultants from the also-rans. For some, this next section will serve as an affirmation—acknowledgment of having adopted an approach to consulting that both creates lasting value for clients while providing healthy gratification and rewards. For others, this next section will be a challenge. Some of what we suggest may seem foreign, perhaps even absurd. We encourage you not to throw out the baby with the bath water too quickly. Remember, these are recommendations that come primarily from clients, the bill payers, regarding ideal consultant-client relationships. We've tried to present the information in a logical and simple model, but the origin of the concepts is the scar tissue of leaders in organizations who've been burned by painful experiences, and the excitement of leaders in organizations who've had successful experiences working with consultants to effect change.

While Part One was intended to challenge readers with a compelling "why" to pay attention to negative behavioral trends in the consulting profession, Part Two is intended to provide some compass headings on "how" to actually change. We explore value-creating consultant practices in two categories:

1. Three value-creating roles consultants play
2. The character and motivations that shape value-creating behavior

Throughout the many organizations and consultant relationships we studied, we came across several examples of superior client-consultant relationships in which successful outcomes were achieved. We heard accounts of exciting relationships between consultants and their clients together searching for solutions to complex problems and breaking innovative ground in their pursuits. Our attempts to codify the patterns among these consultants resulted in the chapters that follow.

3

Three Value-Creating Roles Played by Consultants

"Without consultation, plans are frustrated, but with counselors they succeed."

—King Solomon

As the three destructive roles discussed in Part One share a common pattern (namely, the pursuit of gratifying the consultants' needs at the expense of the client's), so do the three value-creating roles. Inherent in these roles is the notion of service, a concentrated pursuit of outcomes that will primarily benefit the client. Whereas consultants enacting the destructive roles subvert necessary and productive change with their behavior, value-creating consultants fight mightily against taking on any roles or behaving in any way that may lead to maintenance of the status quo. They recognize the strong pull toward homeostasis and fight it, using every skill available to support the client while pushing the client forward often against great resistance. Value-creating consultants don't believe they are messiahs, don't foster dependency in clients, and don't collude with or against anyone in the organization. Instead, they insist on a balanced relationship, share unstintingly in the desire to build organizational capability, and tell the truth regardless of the discomfort it may cause. They never forget that they have been hired to help the organization and to move it forward. Figure 3-1 displays the model for describing the value-creating consultant.

Figure 3-1. Value-creating consultants.

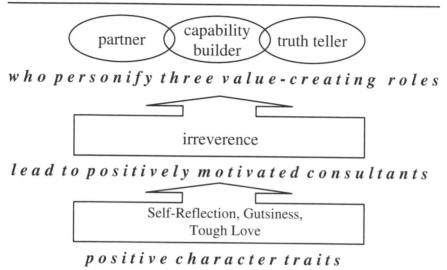

Value-Creating Role One: Being an Equal Partner
We have the questions, and we find the answers.

> "Joint undertakings stand a better chance if they benefit both sides."
>
>   —Euripides

The value-creating consultant establishes her relationship with the client by explicitly requiring an equal investment in the process and by maintaining the balance whenever it seems to tip too much in either direction. Much has been written in the past several years about the need for partnerships—be they between union and management, employee and boss, or members of a business alliance. Yet relatively little has been written about the need for consultants to partner with their clients, despite the increased appearance of consultants in the workplace and the fact that relationships between consultant and client would be more productive were they to be viewed as partnerships. While many consultants and consulting firms tout "partnering" in their pitches to prospects, their lack of supporting behavior has rendered the concept of partnership a cliché.

A true partnership is an interdependency, an exchange between equals. The consultant provides the organization with needed expertise and, in exchange, receives pay and an opportunity to test his models, apply his theories, and challenge his thinking in real time and space. A partnership is an agreement to work cooperatively and collaboratively in a common quest. It connotes a mutual belief in the initiative and a commitment to work together to effect its implementation. It's an understanding that participants will learn from each other; work together, take risks together, make mistakes together, and, if all goes well, succeed together. In a truly participative group in which discussion and decisions are shared, there are no "stars." Each person contributes to the best of his or her ability. The conversation needs to be, "It's our problem," not "It's your problem" or "It's the company's problem" or "It's their problem." Until you begin to hear the words *us, we,* and *our* in conversations, the partnership probably does not exist. Only egocentric consultants can object to such a collaborative arrangement. At some level, the consultant should understand that without the knowledge, skill, and expertise he provides, the group would not produce as effective a product as it will with him present. That internal satisfaction should be enough to make the consultant feel valued both personally and professionally.

There is a substantial benefit to the consultant as well as to the organization in a successful partnership. If the consultant comes into the organization as a prophet, promises to do wonders, sets up hopes and expectations, and then fails to meet these, she faces personal and professional disaster. Sharing the responsibilities for creating change with those who will be living with the consequences takes some pressure off the consultant. It is doing the consultant and the organization a favor.

The story of a consultant we know, who went into a consumer-products company to help manage a culture change and almost fell on his face, is highly persuasive. For a few weeks this fellow operated in his typical Lone Ranger mode, but found he couldn't make any headway. He rationalized the lack of progress in various ways: The executives weren't sufficiently involved, the employees were too overworked to contribute their time to the project, the technologies were ancient and incapable of providing the necessary data, and so forth. Having made little to no progress and with a project update due, he had visions of this project drifting into oblivion. Inspired by this prospect, he went and spoke with several key people, laid the situation out as honestly as he could, and asked for their help in understanding why he wasn't making progress. Each contributed a different but helpful suggestion about where the process was breaking down. He was astounded by how much good information he obtained and how many productive suggestions he was able to elicit and extract assistance on. The project turned out well in the end, and he has become a strong proselytizer for collaboration, cooperation, teamwork, and every form of working partnership possible. He learned that being handed a predetermined problem to solve is not a prelude to a successful outcome. However, when enjoined in the discovery process by those who must share in the outcomes, the needed information surfaced and ownership for the implementation of the solution was broadened.

Recently, one of us was making a presentation at a conference at which there were many other consultants joined by their clients in co-presenting the story of a specific project completed together. I, too, was with a client. But after watching several other joint presentations, I began to feel anxious. Each of the presentations, polished and slick, was primarily given by the consultant, with an occasional chime-in from the client. My client and I had planned to speak equally. We had little of our presentation scripted and no polished handout, except an outline we had prepared detailing our experience together. I worried that among my peers I would appear inferior, unprepared, and would embarrass myself and my client. We proceeded with our presentation as planned. Our different approach turned out to prove beneficial to those watching, as well as to my client and me. Afterward, someone in the audience complimented our presentation, saying, "It was hard to tell which of you was the consultant and which was the manager." Turning to me, she said, "Toby, you're not like other consultants. You're more like one of us." It is probably one of the greatest compliments a consultant could be paid.

Partnership: Nurturing a Long-Term Relationship

In a long-term relationship, the importance of maintaining the health and vitality of the relationship takes precedence over the needs of the transaction at hand. If you think about the way people tend to behave in healthy long-term relationships, it is very different from how they behave in a relationship comprised only of a series of transactions. Figure 3-2 details the contrast between long-term partnerships and transactional relationships.

Let's look at each of the characteristics of long-term partnerships one at a time.

• *Maintaining trust.* Partnerships established to endure over time require those in the relationship to continuously do "routine maintenance" on the relationship. That means having candid discussions about what aspects of the partnership are going well and what areas might need to be adjusted. It also means raising sensi-

Figure 3-2. Long-term partnerships vs. transactional relationships.

Focus of Long-Term Partnerships	*Focus of Transactional Relationships*
• Maintaining trust	• Maintaining courteous and pleasant demeanor
• Meeting the needs of both partners	• Meeting own needs
• Completing tasks while strengthening the relationship	• Completing the transaction
• Mutual ownership of outcomes	• Minimal ownership of outcomes
• Deep personal investment in the relationship	• Limited personal investment in the relationship
• Commitment to partner's development	• No sense of reciprocal development
• Building common ground from shared values	• Working on parallel ground

tive issues or concerns about behaviors that may inadvertently be impeding the continued development of trust. Partners work to address issues that may impair the relationship rather than avoid them out of fear of unpleasant conflict.

• *Meeting the needs of both partners.* For partners in a long-term relationship to feel that their partnership has been a beneficial and positive experience, it is essential that they not feel their needs have gone ignored or unmet. Beyond the usual "give and take" of a healthy relationship, long-term partnerships require members to actively pursue deeper understanding of their partner's needs and options for meeting those needs. While it is always helpful to have someone respond well to a request, it is even better to have someone take the initiative to both uncover and meet needs we haven't voiced.

• *Completing tasks while strengthening the relationship.* Individuals engaged in long-term partnerships are likely to participate in a nearly infinite number of tasks. Smart partners realize that ending one task with the relationship not only intact but even stronger than when they began will probably make the next task even more successful. As such, they look for opportunities to enhance the relationship while working on a particular task—for instance, always speaking with candor; praising an exceptional talent that genuinely contributes to the overall effort; sending a note of thanks for going the extra mile; looking for ways to unburden one another during high-stress times; and celebrating successful outcomes when tasks are done. These actions not only strengthen the partnership, but they help make the work more fun.

• *Mutual ownership of outcomes.* When labor is divided in a long-term relationship, neither partner worries that she will get "stuck" doing more than her fair share. As the rhythm of the partnership evolves, a natural gauge emerges that ensures all the weight is being pulled equally by both partners. Because each individual has unique gifts and knowledge, there is an understood "ebb and flow" from one to another that may not require both partners to run on all cylinders all the time. While one is working at full capacity, she is not looking over her shoulder keeping score to make sure her partner will eventually perform an equal amount of work. She simply trusts that when the task is completed, both partners will have contributed their fair share. The thrust is on being equal contributors in a common endeavor, not on being the score-keeper of another person's efforts.

• *Deep personal investment.* Productive long-term partnerships can't afford superficiality. Both partners know that it takes moving beyond shallow, rote interactions to establish a relationship that can withstand the test of time. It requires both members to be vulnerable and to disclose personal emotions and thoughts that enable new insights about one another to surface. It requires emotional perseverance during rocky parts of the ride, when withdrawing from the relationship might be tempting.

• *Commitment to partner's development.* Members of a long-term partnership are gratified watching their partner learn and grow. They look for opportunities in the context of their relationship to facilitate one another's growth and learning. From swapping stimulating articles to direct coaching, long-term partners search for ways to continually help each other stretch. Not looking to be the smartest kid in the class, nor practicing one-upmanship, they each enjoy the opportunity to challenge the other to "raise the bar" in pursuit of new capabilities and knowledge.

• *Building common ground through shared values.* Any enduring relationship requires its members to find reasons to stay connected over time. Usually, the reason stems from an initial attraction based on mutual beliefs, aspirations, and ideals. Finding out what these are for each relationship takes time, patience, and the willingness to explore. From basic issues of integrity to views on social concerns and spiritual issues, each relationship is shaped by a unique set of commonly shared values. When explicitly identified, these shared values can serve as an important source of motivation, inspiration, and insight into challenges partners face over the course of their relationship. Moments of their appearance are what usually precede sentences such as, "That's why I like you so much." It may mean knowing that each partner holds a deep respect for individuality, a particular view of God, a passion for helping others, ambition for greater influence, a "work hard, play hard" approach to life, a deep need to ensure fairness, a commitment to family—the list could be endless. Such shared values enable long-term partnerships to sustain the many inevitable changes and tran-

sitions they will undergo. These values serve as anchors that stabi-
lize partnerships and give them roots.

Key Ingredient: The Graciousness to Let Them Shine

The common denominator in the previously listed attributes is
summed up in a word: *other.* Being oriented toward the success
and well-being of the "other" person in the relationship, at least
as much if not more than one's self, is what primarily distinguishes
long-term relationships from transactional relationships. That's
really the essence of the consultant's side of the partnership.
Sometimes that may mean deflecting attention and credit away
from one's self toward one's clients. Sometimes it may mean
choosing to recede into the background when you have the chance
to look good in front of really important people. It certainly doesn't
mean adopting a posture of extreme deference or false humility.
True partnership from the consultant means not being consumed
with opportunities to gratify your own ego at the expense of opportunities to make your clients look good. Recognizing and taking
such opportunities requires graciousness. Watch closely—if you
look for them, they will frequently present themselves. You simply
have to want to see them. Figure 3-3 outlines this partnership philosophy.

Something to Think About . . .

> Have you ever had the urge to play Lone
> Ranger in an engagement? What happened?
> What characterized your interactions?
> How did the outcomes of that engagement
> compare with the outcomes of an engagement
> in which you might not have focused on build-
> ing the relationship?

Think about an engagement in which you worked to develop
a long-term relationship with your client, then ask yourself the
above questions.

Figure 3-3. The partner: "We have the questions and, together, we find the answers."

Characteristics	How the Consultant Enacts the Role	How the Client System Sustains the Role	How Performance Is Enhanced
• Joint problem solving, especially in definition and root-cause phases. • Testing of each other's assumptions. • A sense of mutuality and shared ownership. • Clearly defined accountabilities. • Routine, shared maintenance of the health of the relationship.	• Is generous with praise. • Looks for opportunities to make client look good. • Lays down clear ground rules for the engagement. • Initiates and maintains shared understanding of roles. • Treats the client as an intellectual equal. • Engages client in joint decision making. • Holds client and self accountable for agreed-on outcomes.	• Involves consultant in complex decisions about the engagement. • Maintains visible involvement beyond the project inception. • Ensures resources are deployed to maintain viability of engagement. • Treats consultant as an organizational equal. • Holds consultant and self accountable for agreed-on outcomes.	• Decisions are grounded in well thought-through, sound judgments. • Ownership of project spreads faster throughout organization. • Organization's leadership and problem-solving abilities are strengthened. • Collaboration is openly modeled for and adopted by client staff.

Consequence: Sought-after results achieved.

Value-Creating Role Two: Building Capability
*You're going to learn this time, so next time
you don't need me.*

"Give instruction to a wise man, and he will be still wiser,
Teach a righteous man, and he will increase his learning."

—King Solomon

The value-creating consultant believes she has an obligation to
help the organization to stand on its own without her help. She sets
as a primary goal helping the organization to solve its problems in
such a way that its employees develop as individuals and become
more competent in solving problems without help from consultants. To accomplish this, she must share her knowledge, skills,
ideas, thinking, and processing. She cannot hold back in an attempt to leverage another assignment. In fact, the value-creating
consultant sees her job as putting herself out of work. What is interesting is that consultants who subscribe to this school of
thought never seem to lack work. One story from a senior manager
in a pharmaceutical company may explain why:

> What really impresses me about George is how open he
> is, not only about sharing what he knows, but sharing
> the credit. When he and I did a presentation to our legal
> department, not only did he do the research on the legal
> issues, but he shared it with me beforehand so I could
> learn it and so I wouldn't be left out. That's a really
> decent consultant. It's a real partnership. I was so im-
> pressed with him I recommended him to others, and two
> people I know have already used him.

Value-creating consultants believe it is critical to always have
a learning objective that develops their client's capability. Solving
a problem is only one-half of the consultant's responsibilities. The
other half is ensuring that clients have not created a dependency
on a consultant to do their thinking and problem solving, so the
individuals in the company can solve similar problems themselves
the next time. They believe the old Chinese proverb: Give the man

a fish and you feed him for the day. Teach him to fish and you feed him for life.

As a capability builder, this consultant facilitates, coaches, or supports, but doesn't do the work for the people in the organization. She gets satisfaction from seeing them do things for themselves that a conventional consultant would normally do for them. Geoffrey Bellman, in *The Consultant's Calling,* advises consultants to get out of the client's way and let them run their own organization. He writes, "It means celebrating their accomplishments. It means keeping your mouth shut while they learn. It means helping them learn rather than doing their work." Following Bellman's recommendation, the value-creating consultant involves people as much as possible, holds working sessions with the people who will be implementing the program, and involves them in deciding what to do, who to involve, and when to do what. The value-creating consultant moves control to the members of the organization who will do the work whenever the opportunity allows. She prepares them to handle the responsibility. When her assignment begins to wind down, she reduces her involvement and weans away any residual dependency. She gently tests whether the client is able to function in the new situation with the new relationships and processes that emerged during the engagement. She asks herself whether she is leaving a secure leadership in place and whether the people in the organization are comfortable with the new behaviors, or whether she is leaving an organization that is insecure, anxious, and dependent upon her. If she has assiduously avoided a dependent relationship throughout the process and made sure that the people in the organization were prepared for the time when they would be without her assistance, her leaving should not create a trauma within the system.

Most consultants view their role as adviser, problem solver, strategist, facilitator, or change agent. Rarely do consultants speak about themselves as teachers, yet this is one of their most important roles and one that adds tremendous value to the service they provide. Value-creating consultants see their role as an educational guide and view consulting as a learning experience. What they know, and what they pick up during the process of consulting in the organization, they share with their clients, whom they view as partners in the endeavor. The people of the organization are far more informed, knowledgeable, and competent when the value-creating consultant leaves than they were when she arrived.

Capability Building: Making Them as Good as You

One midsize Boston-based management consulting firm has built its entire marketplace strategy on this principle. While you won't find glitzy marketing campaigns and a large business development function at this very successful firm, you will find a seasoned group of expert consultants who have bet their earnings, not on their own success, but the success of their clients. "We freely share our technology with our clients and other consultants, knowing full well that we may in fact be spawning our own competition who will reenter the market at cheaper consulting rates. But whatever loss to this new competition we might experience in the short term is mitigated by knowing that building self-sufficient clients who are successful at achieving their strategies will result in long-term relationships with those clients, and stronger referrals from them," explained one of the firm's partners. Having had the opportunity to observe this firm in action on several engagements, it was clear to us that their clients were absorbing new knowledge like dry sponges, and loving every minute of it. And it was equally obvious that as the clients gained self-sufficiency, the consultants were able to utilize more sophisticated and high-impact methods and tools, which, in turn, accelerated the rate of implementation and the time it took for the organization to realize a return on its investment. Needless to say, while the managers working on the engagement team were receiving accolades from their bosses in the organization, the consulting firm was being asked for three new proposals for additional work. They didn't have to "sell" the business—the referrals from the employees on the team were proof enough.

While it may seem ludicrous to try and "spawn your own competition" from a business point of view, it is actually a very effective strategy for increasing, not decreasing, your firm's long-term viability. Think about it. What better way to keep from getting complacent and relying on yesterday's success than to keep pushing the envelope of others' capabilities in order to force yourself to stay on the cutting edge. While it can be seductive to work in client organizations where the knowledge base is stuck back in the

1960s, the ego boost that comes from looking utterly brilliant no matter what you do is short-lived. When the unchallenging engagement is over, you realize that the rest of the world has gone on without you, and you're now far behind the learning curve instead of ahead of it.

Here are some important activities through which you can approach building your client's capability:

Assess learning needs. The first step in building capability is to identify those areas that, if fortified, could yield a significant improvement in personal and organizational performance. The consultant begins by getting a clear understanding of the organization's strategic intent and then identifying those capabilities that will be required to achieve that intent. He then assesses his client's abilities, skills, and knowledge base in relation to the strategy, discusses the deficiencies with the client, and prioritizes the list of capabilities to be built, indicating which are the most essential to start working on.

Set learning objectives. Using the prioritized list of capabilities to be built, the consultant works with his client to establish objectives for how the engagement at hand can serve as a vehicle through which he can increase personal capability in a given area. Together, the consultant and client set concrete objectives for using the engagement to build these capabilities.

Identify "stretch" opportunities. Large-scale initiatives can serve as great opportunities for clients to learn. They create an on-the-job event to simultaneously acquire and apply new skills and knowledge. The consultant should seek to identify those parts of the initiative that may serve as stretch opportunities—tasks or activities that might significantly accelerate a "quantum leap" of increased knowledge and skill. For example, if one of the identified capabilities is "managing complexity," the consultant might use the initiative to carve out multiple discrete projects for the client to manage simultaneously. In this context, he would work with his client to plan how the client should keep all the balls in the air at once, identifying those collective aspects of the projects that create the complexity the client must manage. The consultant must be careful not to set the client up for failure. Instead, he should carve out only as much work as he feels confident his client can accomplish successfully.

Pause for teachable moments. In the course of the initiative, there will be occasions when successful actions taken or mistakes made can provide the opportunity for learning, but these occasions might not always be obvious. It is the job of the consultant to watch for those critical moments, then to "stop action" and point out the potential for the emergence of new insight and capability. Additionally, there may be critical crossroads at which the application of a new skill or insight could produce great progress, but the client prefers to rely on the tried-and-true approach, going with what is familiar and comfortable. Here, too, is an opportunity for the consultant to "stop action" long enough to point out the client's reluctance to try something novel and to push the client to consider ideas and approaches that, while counterintuitive, could be enormously beneficial to the initiative and to the client's professional growth.

Create time for reflection. Large, complex initiatives can sometimes produce levels of intensity that seem to propel the work forward on cruise control. While such forward motion can create great momentum, it can also rush clients past the need to pause long enough to ask, "What have we learned so far?" For those with strong biases for action, pausing to reflect does not come easily. If the consultant also speeds past opportunities to reflect, he will limit his client's ability to learn to do so. A consultant should schedule time with his clients exclusively for the purpose of forcing reflection, to ask questions such as, "What made this work well?" or "Why are we still struggling with this?" or "If we had to do this over, what would we do differently or the same?" Out of such discussions comes true learning and the stage is set for acquiring new capability.

Provide collateral materials. Having set specific objectives to build certain capabilities, clients can benefit from additional resources such as articles, books, tools, seminars, videos, networking with experts outside the organization, visiting with some of your other clients who may have the capability being pursued, and so forth. A consultant can add tremendous value to his client by offering such resources, as they are needed. This is also an opportunity to be strategic in leveraging your or your firm's intellectual capital. Rather than indiscriminate distribution of knowledge—that erodes value—you can create significant value by applying intellectual property in targeted opportunities—which creates value.

Your clients will appreciate your taking the time to support them in this way, living up to your commitment to their development above and beyond the call.

Monitor progress. It is essential to watch for evidence suggesting the sought-after capability is appearing. Positive reinforcement is important to ensure that the client can repeat demonstrations of new behavior. Conversely, if progress isn't being made as expected, it is important to discuss why. It may be because the objectives were overly ambitious, that sufficient resources or support haven't been provided, or that the client just isn't trying hard enough. Without identifying and addressing obstacles to progress, acquiring new capabilities will be nearly impossible. This is especially true of senior executives whose focus is often on replicating past successes with tried-and-true skills.

Key Ingredient: The Generosity to Give

You won't be able to produce high-impact capability-building behavior without truly understanding what motivates it. It must come from a genuine desire to give of yourself to others, even when they have nothing to offer in return. It won't work if you focus exclusively on how much additional revenue you can garner by increasing the capacity of others, nor will it work if you are constantly on the lookout for the "you've taught me more than any consultant ever has" compliments. Much the way you give special gifts to important people in your life, you must view the chance to help others learn and grow in the same way. It is a delicate process. While people are learning, they feel vulnerable. Their egos are fragile. Merely fulfilling the "knowledge transfer" component of your contract (an increasingly standard clause in consulting agreements) will not result in your clients believing that you gave generously of yourself. You must build their confidence and increase their appetite to continuously learn. You must reinforce their ability and, when appropriate, look for opportunities to let them stretch in roles you might otherwise play. Figure 3-4 summarizes the capability builder role.

Something to Think About . . .

How have you helped your clients to acquire capability?

Are you comfortable in the teaching role as an important part of your consulting responsibilities?

Have you ever deliberately withheld sharing knowledge or skills with your client? Why were you reluctant to do so?

Value-Creating Role Three: Being the Truth Teller

*Allow me to point out that the emperor
really has no clothes.*

"You shall know the truth, and the truth shall set you free."

—Jesus of Nazareth

Typically consultants are called in when the organization is in crisis, which clearly is not an optimum time to do one's best work. People in crisis are more anxious, more fearful, less tolerant, less capable of seeing alternatives and solving problems, and more defensive. It is extraordinarily difficult in such a debilitated environment to engage people in a genuine exploration of possibilities when people are steeped in "CYA" thinking.

Rare are the consultants who view such chaotic times as an opportunity to question what their clients have done, challenging them to push back on the resistors and naysayers and to enact the broad changes that could make them industry leaders. It is always easier to follow the line of least resistance by allowing clients to remain within their comfort zone, especially when your personal revenue stream depends on a client's relative state of comfort. Cli-

Figure 3-4. The capability builder: "You're going to learn this time, so next time you don't need me."

Characteristics	How the Consultant Enacts the Role	How the Client System Sustains the Role	How Performance Is Enhanced
• Learning is an integral part of the relationship. • Consultant and client are both comfortable admitting, "I don't know." • Deliberate emphasis is placed on identifying and closing organizational capability gaps. • Inquiry and curiosity are visible traits during the engagement.	• Is generous with intellectual capital. • Sets specific learning objectives with the client. • Pushes the client to stretch beyond familiar and comfortable approaches. • Establishes ongoing feedback loops to monitor learning progress. • Draws attention to organizational strengths and client progress to build confidence.	• Willing to acknowledge organizational shortcomings. • Pauses and reflects to compile learning at critical milestones. • Holds consultant accountable for knowledge transfer. • Ensures staff is absorbing and applying newly acquired skill and knowledge. • Willing to risk trying new methods and approaches.	• Innovation and speed are increased. • Ability to acquire and apply new knowledge is strengthened. • Organizational confidence is fortified. • Organization becomes more adaptable to change. • Employees' sense of well-being increases as they grow and develop. • Top-talent is more easily retained.

Consequence: Sought-after results achieved.

ents typically don't listen very long to messages that run counter to all they believe to be true. As such, many consultants find it easier to enable their clients to remain in their distress, perpetuating only the illusion of change.

In our research, consultants consistently told us that the most difficult task they faced was delivering bad news to their clients, or confronting unproductive behavior or practices within the organization. Many had war stories of failed attempts to do so, which resulted in estranging their client relationship and, in some cases, ending it. We heard of numerous clever strategies devised to circumvent unpleasant messages, bury them deep in reports, rationalize their existence, downplay their potential damage, and in extreme cases, set up employees in the client organization as the kamikaze messenger.

True, getting people to be open and to work on difficult and sensitive issues can be an uphill battle. It will be especially onerous if the consultant allows himself to worry that upsetting the client is likely to result in his termination. But here's the deal—straight and to the point: If you can't deliver tough messages in a straightforward, unfiltered, uncouched, and nonjudgmental manner, change careers. Consulting is the wrong job for you. You will only continue to experience anxiety every time bad news rears its ugly head and, worse, prevent your clients from realizing opportunities to achieve needed fundamental change.

Truth Telling: Building on Honesty From Start to Finish

The decision as to the degree of honesty a consultant will demonstrate must be made on day one. It happens at the very point that management lays out what it perceives to be the problem and, frequently, what it perceives to be the solution. Right then the truth teller raises questions and points out holes in the reasoning. He doesn't equivocate, nor does he concur just to get the job. He believes there are things that he will be asked to do that shouldn't be done and those which, no matter how good he is, can't be done, and he expresses those beliefs.

As a rule of thumb, to establish an honest relationship at the outset, we always tell prospective clients about how we work:

Our work frequently requires us to uncover and therefore deliver what might initially appear to be bad news. We're not going to withhold it or downplay the problems. It's common for clients, when they hear such news, to get defensive and to dismiss our conclusions. We're willing to go toe-to-toe with you, let you vent, push back when you absolutely disagree, even yell at us. What we aren't willing to do is to agree to work with clients who are unwilling to accept the facts as they are, acknowledge their own contribution to the problem, and model for their organization a genuine desire to change. Sometimes the bad news will be about you. You may not like hearing it. Right now you might be tempted to say, "I absolutely want to hear everything, so don't hold back, I can take it." Clients tell us that all the time. Then, when we deliver the hard message, they explode. You might be the exception, but just the same, we really want you to think about that part of our relationship. Be sure you're really willing to be open, listen, and reflect on what you learn.

Two other consultants' entry experiences illustrate truth telling at the start of the engagement:

I met with the president of the company who talked for twenty minutes about the changing composition of the company's workforce and the company's commitment to promoting diversity. Then he asked me to develop a diversity program and to "run the organization through it." I was concerned about how he phrased it and started asking about what form the "commitment" took—you know, resources. Was it going to become part of the managers' performance appraisal to promote minorities, were there positions available for minorities to move into, that kind of thing. The guy hadn't even thought about it and here he was talking commitment! I told him to think about the issues I was raising and to talk with his senior people about how serious they really were before I took the job.

The company RFP (request for proposal) called for a program to encourage greater entrepreneurship, so I called
to get more information on what the company was about,
how they defined entrepreneurship, etc. Turned out, they
were a regulated industry so whole areas really couldn't
be entrepreneurial. In addition, their parent company
was highly traditional and critical of their fiscal irrespon-
sibilities. There were so many unresolved issues that entrepreneurship seemed like the last thing their culture
would be able to handle at this time. I talked to them
about it and when I saw that they were going to go their
way no matter what, I didn't even submit a proposal.

We were impressed with the consultants who told us these
stories and hope more consultants will push for corporate accountability before signing on. Value-creating consultants turn down
projects when they know they are doomed to failure. When their
gut tells them it's wrong, they turn down the engagement. They
trust their feelings. While many consultants fear that saying no will
cost them income, truth-telling consultants believe that integrity
will gain them credibility and, in the long run, more (not less) business.

Once hired and on the job, it takes constant vigil not to get
caught up in colluding with the system. It is not pleasant to be in
the position of biting the hand that feeds you, but if your findings
lead you to disagree with senior management—if your feedback
needs to be negative, if what you have to say is not what management wants to hear—then maintaining personal and professional
integrity dictates that you voice it anyway. Truth tellers believe that
they have an obligation to be honest and open, to surface conflict,
even to deliberately elicit defensive or hostile reactions. They see it
as their professional responsibility to demand that the individuals
with whom they are working acknowledge the fact that the emperor really has no clothes, that everyone knows this, and nobody
wants to talk about it. They believe that allowing the group to hide
issues makes them merely another partner in the organization's
collusive system, rather than a true partner in the organization's
ultimate success.

Admittedly, it's a difficult line to walk. The consultant needs to be close enough to senior management to gain its trust, get good information, and have access at critical times, yet the consultant can't be so close that she loses sight of her role as an outsider. When a consultant is on a long-term assignment with one company, has an office on-site, and meets with senior managers daily, it's easy to lose the objective, independent perspective she was hired for. It's easy to become a de facto member of the management team and to get sucked into office politics. But the truth-telling consultant realizes how critical it is to remain independent of the system. Michael Beers, a professor at the Harvard Business School, writes in *Across the Board* (June 1994), "Most management programs are developed by top management for everyone else. They don' t really ask, 'What's the root of the problem and how are we as top management part of the problem?'" The consultant needs to be the one to raise this question, but if she begins to identify herself with management, she is no longer in a position to do so.

Peter Block, among others, argues in his book *Flawless Consulting*, for consultants to be "authentic," to state what they see. He acknowledges, however, that this tact may not win them any friends, particularly in traditional companies where people are expected to engage in silence and denial rather than to indulge in self-expression. Even when senior managers say they want to face the issues, the signals they give off say otherwise. When consultants sense this—and most consultants are sensitive to covert messages—they are likely to sidestep any responsibility for speaking out. The farce begins, time and money are spent, but tough issues go unaddressed.

Unfortunately, organizations don't always prize truth-telling consultants for their honesty, nor do they see them as an opportunity to learn something about themselves and their company. One of the roles the consultants play, therefore, is to help senior managers learn to appreciate their chance to receive straight, unfiltered feedback. They help them to see that all of us are fallible and that any one of us can get so close to a situation that we no longer see it clearly. They remind clients that their value to them is being an outsider whose perspective is unbiased, apolitical, and as expert as their talents permit.

Nonetheless, cultivating a receptive client-relationship for truth telling is possible. Here are some things you can do to promote truth telling in your client relationships:

• *Confront personal avoidance of rejection and conflict.* Start with yourself. Each of us, to some degree, may have discomfort with the idea of "truth telling" because of the possible defensiveness or conflict it may incite. If your uneasiness prevents you from addressing important issues with your client, your ability to be a truth teller for your client will be limited. You must get to the bottom of your own avoidance to make sure that, in the heat of the moment, you can manage it, preventing it from making you recoil from circumstances that require truth-telling behavior.

• *Pick and choose your battles wisely.* Sometimes opportunities for truth telling are a mixed blessing. While they certainly present the chance to help your client grow, learn, and correct behaviors that might otherwise go unaddressed, they also, to some degree, can be a reflection of your own issues. Consultants who feel the need to confront every unproductive behavior their clients display may be motivated to do so more out of the need to experience their own power than to be helpful to their clients. Part of truth telling is learning to monitor our own motives for doing so. While we want to be sure we do not collude in organizational situations that need to be dealt with directly, for a variety of reasons, they may not be ready to be confronted. Be sure the client is ready to deal with the issue once it is raised and that the real benefit for doing so is obvious.

• *Rehearse the messages.* Good intentions count very little when telling the truth. Even the best motives can lead consultants to botch the delivery of the message. The presence of discomfort, defensiveness, and emotion can skew both the delivery of the feedback and the filters through which it is heard. The wise consultant will prepare ahead of time for the conversation by writing out and rehearsing the message, trying different language and phrasing, anticipating reactions, and ensuring that he is prepared for a variety of responses. The goal is not to dehumanize the experience with a canned message, rather to minimize the opportunity for the conversation to derail owing to misunderstanding and poor communication.

• *Extend the benefit of the doubt.* Recognize that truth-telling messages, even delivered well, have the potential to cause bad feelings. There's little that can be done to avoid this, but don't compound it by also making your client feel stupid. When clients make mistakes or behave in unproductive ways, on some level they probably know they have done so. Delivering truth-telling messages that extend this benefit of the doubt are likely to be much better received than messages wrapped in tones of "What were you thinking—do you have any idea. . . ?" Clients also need to know you believe they are capable of correcting mistakes and changing unproductive behavior. Delivering your recommendations with such benefit of the doubt can serve to encourage them to take productive action.

• *Model openness by asking for feedback.* Setting the example for your client can be a powerful way to cultivate receptivity to truth telling. Needless to say, you can also benefit from hearing your clients' viewpoints of your effectiveness as a consultant. Establish deliberate checkpoints at which you ask how well your contributions are adding value and where there are opportunities for you to make adjustments. By opening yourself up to such messages, receiving them nondefensively, and acting upon them, you are modeling for your clients what you are asking of them.

Key Ingredient: The Courage to Be Authentic

There are probably numerous reasons why truth telling and authenticity are difficult for so many consultants. Conflict aversion, fear of rejection, the stress of dealing with your own emotions as well as a client's emotions, the risk of personal credibility, and so on. What seemed to enable those consultants we observed do this exceptionally well was their captivating genuineness. One person we interviewed who'd been the client of such a consultant explained it this way:

> I just trust what John tells me. I never worry that he's got some hidden agenda or that he's withholding his point of view. He's real. It's obvious that he cares about his work and is out to help me succeed. . . . When he's here, you can tell he's being himself. He talks about his own

strengths and weaknesses as well as mine. So when he has to deliver the hard messages, I can take it, knowing that he's not coming from a place of superiority. He's just down-to-earth, caring, and very, very direct. While he has a soft touch, there's never any misunderstanding about what the issue is. . . . I don't feel as if I'm being clinically analyzed, I just feel like a good friend is telling me something a lot of people probably have thought about telling me, but never have.

It requires a great deal of courage to walk into a high-pressure situation and just "be yourself." But a high degree of authenticity can be a consultant's greatest asset. Abandoning a contrived air of sophistication, over-reliance on impressive credentials, the use of clinical-sounding jargon, and other forms of consulting veneers can go a long way to improving client relationships. The problem is that these Teflon coatings are usually crutches that help consultants face tough challenges. Without them, facing off in difficult client circumstances could well be terrifying. Paradoxically, nothing disarms contentious situations more effectively than the power of a simple, direct, caring approach free of the trappings of pretentious and pious-sounding rhetoric.

Figure 3-5 summarizes the truth-telling approach.

Something to Think About . . .

What fears underlie your reluctance to always tell your client the truth about your behavior?
Have you ever tested these assumptions?
How might you prepare your client for a relationship in which both of you are comfortable saying what you feel?

Before we look deeper at those character traits and motivation that lead to these roles in Chapter 4, we recommend you use the tool in Figure 3-6 to assess your current practices with respect to each of the three destructive and value-creating roles of consultants.

Figure 3-5. The truth teller: "Allow me to point out that the emperor really has no clothes."

Characteristics	How the Consultant Enacts the Role	How the Client System Sustains the Role	How Performance Is Enhanced
• High levels of candor and openness exist. • Decision-making criteria are based strictly on performance outcomes vs. political outcomes. • Both client and consultant are willing to be vulnerable. • Comradery is evident. • Conflict is openly managed and resolved. • Feedback about unproductive behavior is freely exchanged and acted upon.	• Contracts with client to establish the norm of feedback exchange. • Gives honest, direct feedback. • Self-discloses and models humility. • Acknowledges personal shortcomings. • Asks "tough questions" to guide client to increased understanding of unproductive behavior. • Maintains an accepting, nonjudgmental posture (separates person from behavior).	• Manages personal and organizational defensiveness when receiving hard messages. • Asks, "How did I contribute to this?" • Opens self up to scrutiny vs. seeking validation. • Confides in consultant when personal shortcomings are tough to accept. • Acknowledges when over-reliance on organization's towering strengths has become a liability.	• Ability to solve problems more quickly and thoroughly is increased. • Real root causes are surfaced and dealt with. • Organizational relationships are enhanced as unresolved conflicts are addressed. • Organizational focus is sharpened as competing priorities are clarified and agreed on. • Organizational self-reflection enables problems and opportunities to be identified and acted upon quickly.

Consequence: Sought-after results achieved.

Figure 3-6. Making the connection: How well do you perform the value-creating roles?

Use the following two assessment tools to determine the degree to which your behavior is more like the bad habit consulting roles or the value-creating consulting roles. For the self-assessment, answer the questions by considering what you *actually* do, not what you should do. If you begin to see a conspicuous absence of 1s and 2s in your responses, you might think about whether you are being as objective as you could be. We'd all like to believe that we're free of any of these behaviors, but the fact is, we're not. Be brutally honest with yourself. Both you and your clients will benefit significantly.

For the client assessment, choose clients to provide feedback with whom you have had both positive and difficult relationships to ensure balanced data.

Self-Assessment

Instructions: Answer each question with one of the following ratings:

1 = Strongly disagree   2 = Disagree   3 = Mixed feelings
4 = Agree   5 = Strongly agree

_____ 1. There is an equal distribution of work and accountability between my clients and myself during my consulting projects.

_____ 2. I believe I am obligated to transfer to my clients any expertise I have that they do not as we work together.

_____ 3. I give open, direct, nonjudgmental feedback to my clients regardless of whether it might cost me future assignments.

_____ 4. I provide more questions than answers for my clients during problem-solving activities.

_____ 5. I never withhold or delay information, ideas, or knowledge from a client as a way to prolong a project or gain another assignment.

_____ 6. When members of my client group attempt to gossip to me about other members of the group or organization, I encourage them to confront each other and not to use me as an ally in their conflict.

_____ 7. I actively avoid taking on a leadership role in my clients' organizations, preferring to function as a peer to those with whom I work.

_____ 8. I work hard to get my client groups as much exposure to senior management as I have.

_____ 9. I do not, for any reason, conceal information or agendas that I discover to be barriers to the organization's success.

_____ 10. I confront my clients when, consciously or unconsciously, they attempt to transfer the majority of work and accountability for a project to me.

_____ 11. I go out of my way not to work beyond the capability of my client groups to ensure they feel confident in their contributions.

_____ 12. I do not vent my personal frustrations or anger about the organization, its leadership, or my clients to anyone in the client organization.

_____ 13. When I market my services, I do not make lofty promises or guarantees about results over which I have no control.

_____ 14. I challenge my clients to seek opportunities to apply what they've learned from me to other problems in the organization without my help.

_____ 15. I reject assignments in which the client organization attempts to have me endorse its self-serving political agenda.

_____ 16. I encourage my clients not to give me the deferential treatment accorded to a guru.

_____ 17. I give feedback to my client groups that inflates neither the positive to make them like me more, nor the negative to make them feel they need me more.

_____ 18. If I believe my clients' organization will not be successful in what they are attempting, I openly tell them so.

_____ 19. I explicitly request that decision making and problem solving be collaborative between my client group and myself whenever possible.

_____ 20. I make opportunities to stop and teach my clients new knowledge and skills.

_____ 21. When clients approach me with predetermined problems and solutions, I challenge them to be open to alternative possibilities.

_____ 22. I publicly share the credit with my client group for our achievements.

_____ 23. I do not tell "war stories" of past successes to create the perception of being overwhelmingly more experienced or competent than my client group.

_____ 24. When clients ask me to ignore or hide sensitive or potentially disruptive information that I have discovered, I challenge their reasons to do so.

_____ 25. I work to learn as much from my clients as I attempt to teach them.

(continues)

Figure 3-6. *(continued)*

_____ 26. I contract with my clients for a specific date when my involvement in the project will end.

_____ 27. I help my client groups recognize and confront their contributions to the problems they are trying to solve.

_____ 28. I turn down assignments for which I know I am not qualified or cannot give adequate time and commitment.

_____ 29. I spend time and effort with my clients, preparing them to completely take the reigns of the project after I leave.

_____ 30. I prepare my client groups to openly accept and address any negative feedback that may emerge during the project.

Scoring Your Assessment

Transfer your scores from the survey to the grid below. Total each column and plot your scores on the horizontal barometers at the bottom of the page. Plot your scores from the Client Assessment on these barometers as well, and compare any gaps you discover.

Messiah or Partner	Building Dependency or Capability	Collusion or TruthTelling
1. _____	2. _____	3. _____
4. _____	5. _____	6. _____
7. _____	8. _____	9. _____
10. _____	11. _____	12. _____
13. _____	14. _____	15. _____
16. _____	17. _____	18. _____
19. _____	20. _____	21. _____
22. _____	23. _____	24. _____
25. _____	26. _____	27. _____
28. _____	29. _____	30. _____
_____	_____	_____
Total	Total	Total

Plot your total score from column one on this barometer:

10	20	30	40	50
Strong Messiah Tendencies			Strong Partnership Tendencies	

Plot your total score from column two on this barometer:

10	20	30	40	50
Build Unhealthy Dependency			Build Client Group Capability	

Plot your total score from column three on this barometer

10	20	30	40	50
Collude With Client Organization			Tell Truth With Client Organization	

Client Assessment

To ensure that we are providing the best possible consulting services for our clients, we are asking for candid feedback about your experience working with our firm. The best time to conduct this assessment is approximately halfway through the project so that we can respond to your concerns and make midcourse corrections. Please be brutally honest in your responses, and add any additional comments or suggestions at the end. Thank you in advance for taking the time to give us information that will allow us to serve you, and all our clients, better. Please return the completed survey to (provide client information).

Instructions: Answer each question with one of the following ratings:

1 = Strongly disagree   2 = Disagree   3 = Mixed feelings
4 = Agree   5 = Strongly agree

_____ 1. There has been an equal distribution of work and accountability between the consultant and us throughout the project.

_____ 2. The consultant works hard to transfer expertise to us and our organization during the course of our work together.

_____ 3. We receive open, direct, nonjudgmental feedback during the project.

_____ 4. The consultant provides more questions than answers to challenge our thinking.

_____ 5. We never sense the consultant is reluctant to share information, ideas, or knowledge in order to prolong the project or parlay it into more work.

_____ 6. The consultant challenges us to confront each other about our interpersonal issues and discourages us from attempting to use him/her as any ally in our conflicts.

_____ 7. The consultant actively avoids taking on an inappropriate leadership role in our project, but rather interacts as a peer with those in our organization.

(continues)

Figure 3-6. *(continued)*

_____ 8. The consultant works hard to get us equal exposure to senior management.

_____ 9. The consultant takes risks in exposing controversial information or political agendas that may be long-term barriers for our organization.

_____ 10. The consultant confronts us when the workload and accountability between the consultant and us is inappropriately unbalanced.

_____ 11. The consultant does not work beyond the level of our capability, ensuring that we feel confident in our contributions.

_____ 12. The consultant does not vent personal frustrations or anger about our organization, our leadership, or us to anyone in our organization.

_____ 13. The consultant does not make lofty promises or guarantees about results over which the consultant has no control.

_____ 14. The consultant challenges us to seek opportunities to apply what we've learned from him/her to other problems in the organization without help.

_____ 15. We believe this consultant would reject assignments in which the client organization attempted to have him/her endorse a self-serving political agenda.

_____ 16. The consultant encourages us not to give him/her the deferential treatment accorded to a "guru."

_____ 17. The consultant never seems to give feedback that inflates the positive to make us like him/her more, or inflates the negative to make us feel like we need him/her more.

_____ 18. We believe the consultant would tell us if we thought we could not be successful in what we are attempting.

_____ 19. The consultant openly requests that decision making and problem solving be collaborative whenever possible.

_____ 20. The consultant makes opportunities to stop and teach us new knowledge and skills.

_____ 21. The consultant challenges our predetermined problems and solutions, and encourages us to be open to alternative possibilities.

_____ 22. The consultant publicly shares the credit with us for any successes we achieve.

_____ 23. The consultant does not tell "war stories" of past successes, to create the perception of being overwhelmingly more experienced or competent than we are.

_____ 24. We believe this consultant, if asked to ignore or hide sensitive or potentially disruptive information, would challenge the client's reasons to do so.

_____ 25. The consultant appears to learn from us even while attempting to teach us.

_____ 26. The consultant contracted with us for a specific date when his/her involvement in the project will end.

_____ 27. The consultant helps us to recognize and confront our contributions to the problems we are trying to solve.

_____ 28. We believe this consultant would turn down assignments if the consultant were not qualified or could not give adequate time and commitment.

_____ 29. The consultant spends time and effort with us preparing us to completely take the reins of the project after the consultant leaves.

_____ 30. The consultant prepares us to openly accept and address any negative feedback that might emerge during the project.

Scoring Your Assessment

Please transfer your scores from the survey to the grid below, and total each column.

Column One	Column Two	Column Three
1. _____	2. _____	3. _____
4. _____	5. _____	6. _____
7. _____	8. _____	9. _____
10. _____	11. _____	12. _____
13. _____	14. _____	15. _____
16. _____	17. _____	18. _____
19. _____	20. _____	21. _____
22. _____	23. _____	24. _____
25. _____	26. _____	27. _____
28 _____	29. _____	30. _____
Total	Total	Total

Please add any additional comments or suggestions you may have:

_____

_____

4

Creating Lasting Value: The Power of Irreverence

> "Irreverence is the champion of liberty and its only sure defense."
>
> —Mark Twain

> "All great truths begin as blasphemies."
>
> —George Bernard Shaw

In Part One, we described the three destructive roles consultants can enact—namely, the messiah, dependency builder, and colluder. We described the negative motives underlying consultants' work in terms of their being mercenaries or missionaries, and identified the roots of these motives in the negative character traits of fear, judgment, deceit, arrogance, and greed. In Chapter 3, we described three value-creating roles consultants can enact: partner, capability builder, and truth teller. Now we describe the positive motivation underlying these roles, a motive we refer to as irreverence, which has it roots in the character traits of self-reflection, gutsiness, and tough love. We believe these three character traits give rise to the positive motive of irreverence (see Figure 3-1 in Chapter 3), which, in turn, gives rise to the three roles of the value-creating consultant. Let's see how. Figures 4-1 through 4-6 are designed as tools to help you evaluate your and your organization's capacity for self-reflection, gutsiness, and tough love.

Organizational Untouchables and Undiscussables

In virtually every organization, there are things that people in that organization hold sacred. It may be:

- Loyalty to a product that has lost market share as new products have emerged
- A pet strategy that a team developed
- A program or policy that has outlived its usefulness
- A structural arrangement that creates barriers to flexibility
- A piece of history that serves as precedent in innumerable discussions

These sacred objects are so revered that they cannot be touched. Any suggestion of changing them is looked upon with horror and the person making the suggestion is viewed as a traitor and disloyal to the persons or units involved. These untouchables can attract the devotion of organizations for years, depleting resources and energy with reckless abandon. Despite the fact that most people realize the waste associated with the "untouchable," the system's deep adulation prevents healthy change from occurring. Hallway conversations, exchanged knowing glances between employees in meetings, water cooler whispering, and other collusive communication, are frequently the result of built-up frustrations owing to the untouchable. But such collusion actually serves to give greater power to the untouchable as it represents energy that could otherwise be invested in meaningful work. It certainly doesn't help to bring about change. It is usually some major organizational event (often catastrophic), and a change in leadership, that enable the exposure of untouchables and a change in the organization's focus.

Something to Think About . . .

> What sacred objects do you hold in your own personal and professional life that may be inhibiting important progress?
> How willing would you be to relinquish them?

Analogous to untouchables are undiscussables. These are behaviors that we observe and issues that arise that need to be made
explicit, discussed, and worked upon, yet they, too, are treated as
inviolate. Through subtle messages received on the very first day at
work, employees learn that they are expected to look the other way
when these behaviors occur or issues arise, to pretend they don't
see them, and never, under any circumstances, to surface them or
mention them aloud in public. Everyone knows, for example, that
Joe does little or no work, but when he's placed on a team, no
one complains; they just exchange knowing glances. Somewhere,
somehow team members "learned" that Joe is an old buddy of the
CFO, so if he doesn't pull his weight, no one calls him on it.

Unlike untouchables, which tend to focus on policies, structures, technologies, or other nonhuman aspects of the organization, undiscussables tend to be about people and involve a
reluctance to provide feedback to those people about their behaviors. One situation we witnessed illustrates undiscussables. Helen
Smith (an actual GM whose name has been changed here) was invited to run the entire North American operation and distribution
for a large, global pharmaceutical company. The organization faced
many challenges when she was brought on board: quality issues,
regulatory infractions, and eroding profits, to name a few. Efferves-
cent, witty, and exceptionally bright, Helen came on like gangbus-
ters, immediately digging into what she viewed as necessary
changes. Unfortunately, her style was resented by her direct reports, who perceived her as a bull in a china shop and feared her
harsh and abrasive manner. She, in turn, was frustrated with her
staff's seeming inability to rise to the occasion and handle the
changes she was attempting. All she could see was resistance. The
upshot was a standoff with each side obsessed over the other's
behavior but unwilling or unable to talk about it with one another.
There was plenty of conversation in the hallways and communication over e-mails, but never directly between the parties involved,
all because the issue of confronting personalities and behavior
comes under the heading of undiscussables.

Untouchables and Undiscussables as Antibodies

What is unfortunate in this example is that Helen had much to offer
as a leader. She had a vision, the courage to change, profound

insights into the company's issues, and the support needed to pull off a large-scale change. Similarly, her direct reports had a lot to offer as well. They were an experienced, talented group with a strong customer base on which to build. Unable to directly confront one another productively to discuss and resolve the issues, both sides' energies got diverted into a broad range of nonproductive and, in fact, dysfunctional behaviors. The underlying issues in the rift between Helen and her group became a revered object, a factor that cost the company and, ultimately, the shareholder dearly.

In some cases, treating sacred cows as untouchable or allowing undiscussables to exist can be innocuous. In other cases, as with Helen's group, they can serve as antibodies that divert people's energies away from work that needs to be done and changes that need to be made. When the untouchables and undiscussables produce dysfunctional behavior, the organization suffers. Helen's group, for example, became self-absorbed, stockpiling anger, reveling in cynicism, pointing the finger of blame, producing little except for low morale. Helen became more dogmatic and rigid and less respectful of her staff members. They became each other's enemies, and thus everyone's attention turned from an external battle to compete in a difficult market to an internal battle between a leader and her organization.

There are many psychodynamic forces operating in the reverence given to untouchables and undiscussables. At some level, the people involved are engaged in protecting ego. All of us have vulnerabilities, and when we feel them being attacked, we fight back in self-protection. One mechanism that allows us to cope is denial. If we don't see the problem or talk about it, if we deny the realities, it allows us not to have to deal with it. That, in itself, allays anxieties. At another level, people enjoy having a scapegoat because that deflects attention from themselves and their responsibilities in the situation. Typically it is the leader who serves as scapegoat, since he or she is so clearly visible. It was easier and safer for the group to focus on Helen and her unpleasant management style, for example, than to have to confront their own abilities to do what was required in a large-scale change.

Modes of behavior become habits over time; we grow comfortable with them and have difficulty unlearning them in order to replace them with potentially more productive behaviors. In some corporate cultures, people learn to use complaining, whining, and criticizing in lieu of active work. Ironically, it takes almost as much mental and physical energy (maybe more) to avoid work as it does to engage in it. Habits take time and conscious effort to alter, largely because we engage in them mindlessly. Change involves becoming conscious of the habit, unlearning it, and replacing it with a new habit.

The Antidote: Irreverence

In our experience, untouchables do not become accessible and undiscussables do not get confronted without external intervention. The cultural pulls and political sanctions against it are simply too strong. We know of one excellent internal consultant who attempted to forge an inroad into her company's undiscussables by raising questions that would get a discussion going. She was pulled aside by her manager who told her, "Those are good questions, but you don't want to ask them here." She returned to the meeting mentally alternating between moving forward despite the warning and keeping her job by heeding the warning. She opted for the latter, but made the decision then and there to begin to circulate her résumé. This was not the type of company she wanted to work for.

An external consultant may be in the best position to confront untouchables and undiscussables, as well as the managers who protect them. In fact, we would argue that that's the external consultant's primary role. Someone must recognize that dysfunctional behavior is causing a unit to hemorrhage, call attention to the source of the dysfunction, and keep the pressure on for the unit to deal with the problem. This is not a comfortable role for most people, since they can expect the members of the unit to push back, often in nasty and hurtful ways. After all, those members are fighting to preserve the coping mechanisms that allow them to stay in a state of denial. They will attack anyone who tries to force them to remove the blinders. Getting these individuals to answer questions—or, better yet, to begin to raise questions—about their untouchables and undiscussables is extraordinarily difficult, but it is a necessary first step to removing one of the largest impediments to success any organization can confront. Where the organization reveres certain people and objects at the expense of performance and progress, an external consultant must be irreverent. Irreverence is the art of helping clients to:

- Recognize dysfunctional circumstances and understand their role in creating and sustaining them.
- Acknowledge their and their organization's misdirected reverence and its source.
- Identify the ideas, strategies, and solutions to which their misdirected reverence has blinded them.
- Commit to abandon their misdirected reverence and to reinvest the energy in pursuit of these new ideas, strategies, and solutions.

The consultant's efforts to move people in this direction may not only be unappreciated, they will often be attacked and rejected as well. While there will be those who breathe a sigh of relief at finally airing the smelly laundry, others will still look for a scapegoat. That role may move off the shoulders of the organizational leader and onto the consultant.

Given that many consultants are motivated by the need to be omniscient (missionary) or well-rewarded (mercenary), irreverence is ill suited to meet their needs. Not only will they fear the loss of repeat business if the client and members of the client organization become agitated, they will view the entire concept of pushing back on the organization as too risky. After all, to ask people to touch the untouchable or to discuss the undiscussable is to open Pandora's box. Not all consultants are sufficiently self-assured to trust that they will be able to contain what emerges. Therefore, they will not likely be motivated by irreverence. It takes an extraordinary consultant to do so. Pandora's box must be opened because it contains all of the bacteria that infect the organization. For the infection to cease spreading and to be cured, it is necessary to uncover and eradicate its source. When the body's natural immune system can't produce the serum to counteract the destructive antibodies, one must be imported to do so. Enter the consultant's irreverence.

Value-creating consultants are irreverent consultants. They are motivated by the desire to remove the barriers the organization puts in the way of productive change and to help the people in that organization to function in a more open, honest, and meaningful manner. They recognize how untouchables and undiscussables are a major deterrent to progress and are willing to take on the onerous task of jolting the organization out of its position of denial and numbness. The essence of the irreverent consultant is the fierce integrity and the "edge" with which she pushes back on the organization's leaders and staff to abandon their familiar comfort level in exchange for a period of time that is high in ambiguity and discomfort.

We believe that external consultants are ultimately hired to help the client do what can be terrifying—namely, to confront the sacred cows of the organization and to surface, make explicit, and discuss the undiscussables. The consultant pays a price for this, but she fully understands that any efforts taken without a commitment to confront hidden dimensions of thought and behavior infesting the organization will derail the bigger change agenda. A unit has only a finite amount of mental and physical energy. That which goes into preserving untouchables and undiscussables is unavailable for needed change. Thus, successful change demands that the consultant ruthlessly inquire into and help dismantle those flawed patterns of thinking and acting that blind the organization.

Before We Get Into It: What Irreverence Is Not

In trying on the mantle of irreverence, it is easy to become a bull in a china shop, thereby alienating the very people you need to buy into a potentially threatening and ego-damaging encounter. Therefore, we have some words of caution as you attempt to become more irreverent in your consulting practice:

• *Irreverence is not a license to be obnoxious.* Trying to challenge the thoughts and actions of our clients requires a delicate balance between being direct and being sensitive. Taking the cowboy, "in your face" approach can be off-putting and will only serve to shut clients down rather than opening them to alternative ways of thinking and acting.

• *Irreverence is not self-righteousness.* It can be easy to confuse irreverence with a pious, holier-than-thou aura that can actually debilitate clients with feelings of inadequacy. Irreverence should help level the playing field, not elevate you above your clients.

• *Irreverence is never disrespectful or judgmental.* You can never influence change from a place where someone has been made wrong. Irreverence should raise the confidence levels of clients, not raise their defenses. Irreverence should draw clients' attention toward their own actions, not the condemning actions of the consultant. A callous, critical approach will attract your clients' anger and resentment, not their willingness to engage.

Ways to Approach Irreverence

The expression "It isn't what you say, it's how you say it" is one of those timeless clichés you just can't argue with. It becomes especially important for consultants, with one slight modification: "It isn't what you say, but how, when, and why you say it."

Roaming around an organization indiscriminately tossing out your observations about undiscussables and untouchables to clients isn't exactly a recipe for productive and vital relationships. How, when, and why you offer a client your insights, especially tough messages, must be well thought through and prepared. Here are some rules of thumb we have found useful when preparing to provide clients with tough messages:

• *Contract for the privilege.* Don't assume your clients actually want or expect you to provide your irreverent insights and observations to them. Make sure that you agree at the start of the engagement that your honest assessment of undiscussable and untouchable problems and situations is something they would find useful. Give examples of what types of data you might provide, in the style in which you might provide it, so your clients can make an informed choice about whether they see any value.

• *Be nonjudgmental.* No matter how confident your clients may appear, they are still human. They feel insecure about how others perceive them and their organizations, and your approval is important to them in some form. Separate your personal disappointments and judgments from the message so they understand you are not withdrawing your faith in their organization's ability to succeed. However, being nonjudgmental doesn't necessarily mean being unemotional. It can be helpful to allow your clients to understand your feelings. Just be sure that the emotions don't carry an "edge" that inadvertently has a blaming or punishing tone.

• *Ensure the message is in the client's best interest.* If you can't identify the benefit your client will derive from the conversation, don't have it. If the message is intended to benefit your client's colleague, boss, team, or someone else who hopes your client will make needed changes, you are simply acting as an intermediary for others. This is a severely collusive role that must be avoided. Best interest doesn't mean that the client needs to like the message, but it does mean that the client can somehow benefit from hearing it. Not all insights are created equal. In fact, if we tried to act on every single piece of advice we all received, we'd spend all of our waking hours in therapy.

• *Remember that timing is everything.* Most communication rules stress the importance of timeliness. While it is true that putting off important messages too long can dilute their impact, it is also important not to rush them. Following your client back to his office right after a tense meeting in which an undiscussable issue arose but was ignored and confronting it on the spot isn't always productive, either. Sometimes a little distance from tough circumstances helps to restore openness and a balanced perspective.

In our search for irreverent consultants whose irreverence created value for their clients, we identified three consistent and critical characteristics:

• Self-reflection
• Gutsiness
• Tough love

Let's look at each of these characteristics one at a time.

Self-Reflection

"He who neglects discipline despises himself,
But he who listens to reproof acquires understanding;

> Pride goes before destruction, and a haughty spirit before stumbling . . .
> and before honor comes humility."
>
> —King Solomon

A thirty-seven-year-old senior consultant at a large consulting company sat across from us horrified. He had just been fired from the position he had held for eight years. He managed an engagement team of twelve junior consultants and four support professionals. All he could say was, "I thought they loved me." We asked him why he thought that. He said, "I've always completed my projects on budget, met or exceeded my client's expectations, and I've made a ton of money!"

"How do the consultants on your team feel about you?" we asked.

"I suppose they feel the same way. They have no reason not to!"

"You seem so certain of that. Have you ever asked them how they feel about you as their leader?"

"Well, no, but I know they'd tell me if anything was wrong."

Famous last words. When we looked at this manager's past performance appraisals and spoke to his team, we found certain words and phrases recurring: "abrasive, arrogant, self-centered, and verbose," "needs to improve people skills," "doesn't let me do my job," and "talented guy, but not when it comes to his team." We asked him if he agreed with these perceptions. He responded, "Sure, I know I have a little bit of a temper, and sometimes I drive a little hard for results, but that's no reason to fire someone."

"Did you understand what your boss meant on your last three performance appraisals about your weak people skills?"

"I thought I did. But apparently not."

It cost the organization more than $450,000 to fill this consultant's position, when you include retainers and search commissions, lost productivity, and lost billable revenue. Within eighteen months of the position being filled, however, the team saw a 27 percent increase in revenue because it was having to eat far less costs in redoing good work the previous consultant had deemed unacceptable.

Something to Think About . . .

How do you suppose the senior consultant became so self-assured?
What assumptions might have caused him to
ignore the feedback he'd received?

In his provocative book, *The Consultant's Calling,* Geoffrey Bellman writes, "For us as consultants, it is especially important to under-stand who we are and what we bring to others, though this is not a bad idea for anyone wanting to live with intention. . . . This means staying in touch with the primary tools of our trade: ourselves. . . . We should be able to look our strengths as well as our weaknesses in the eye. . . . Our livelihoods thrive on accurate readings of our clients' perceptions of us." For many of us, the idea of learning more about ourselves, and about the way others see us, can be frighteningly intimidating. It threatens the reliability of the conclu-sions we have comfortably drawn about how others see us, about how our intentions and behaviors match, and about how our "minor quirks" don't really matter in the bigger scheme of things. In the absence of real data, however, those conclusions are rarely reliable. And unless you are in the habit of regularly asking those around you to calibrate your conclusions with their honest percep-tions, you may be heading for disaster.

Changing the Illusion at the Core

If we had to pick one of the three characteristics as the cornerstone for irreverence, it would be self-reflection. Trying to effect change in people and organizations without first learning to effect change within ourselves is simply ludicrous. It is here, facing the light and dark sides of ourselves, that we learn to convert our fear to cour-age, our anger to acceptance, our greed to service, our arrogance to confidence, and our deceit to integrity. It will unquestionably be painful as it illuminates our dark sides. But it is in struggling with these unproductive and unhealthy traits that can lead us to become stronger people—and stronger consultants.

In their book *Work and the Human Spirit,* John Scherer and

Larry Shook recount testimonies of executives during their Executive Development Intensive, a five-day, one-on-one program for leaders and their spouses. Listen to Hank, a leader in his organization, disclose what he learned about himself as he reconciled the feedback of others with his self-perception. He had been told he was "aloof" and "stuck up," even "arrogant."

> Now that you mention it, I can see that I am always making sure that I don't make a mistake, even about little things, like the way I dress. I think before I speak. I want to put people at ease around me. I guess I'm keeping myself under control so I won't give anyone anything they could fault me for. That's it. I'm being careful not to give people a reason for judging me or ridiculing me. I can see that one cost is that I come across as arrogant. That's amazing to me, but I'm beginning to see how they could get that idea . . . It may be that in my mind I have to be better than everyone else just to have a right to be around. Another thing is that I feel like I have to be "on" all the time. I can't let down, even for a second, or else I might make a slip and say or do something that's not correct.

Hank is not at all unique in the dilemma he faces of reconciling what others see and what he believes about himself. All of us invest energy in maintaining the appearance or illusion of something. Through self-reflection, we can confront these illusions and their origins. We can transform them into the powerful capacity of bringing about lasting change within ourselves and for the organizations we serve.

Something to Think About . . .

> Which of Hank's feelings can you relate to? What are the ramifications of the gap between how others perceived him and what was actually behind his behavior?

Calibrating One's Effectiveness

Consultants who are able to creatively and skillfully surface those undiscussable issues draining energy from the organization make a habit of asking for feedback about their performance and about their impact on others, as well as about suggestions for strengthening their credibility and influence. Value-creating consultants firmly believe that complete candor is vital to effective performance and powerful results, acknowledging that with all the painstaking work it takes to increase quality, delight clients, grow financially, and maintain marketplace leadership, there simply isn't time for broken interactions between consultants and clients. They have to be secure and exemplary in their interpersonal ability. They must build trust by admitting and learning from mistakes. They must quickly self-correct when they have started down a path that hurts, confuses, or rejects others despite producing results. And they must be equally comfortable saying "I'm sorry" and "I'm capable." Self-reflection is the only path to building this capacity, and it has two significant ramifications for being irreverent:

1. It models for the client the requisite behavior needed to unearth those embedded issues attracting the organization's reverence.
2. It helps resist the natural impulses to reject the truth of the situation by building in an acceptance of personal fallibility.

One consultant we spoke with explained his self-reflection this way:

> It's not that I love getting feedback. Believe me, sometimes it hurts. But I'm more afraid of not getting feedback. I know I'm not perfect, and not every person in my client's organization is going to go cross-eyed at the wonder of me. I have come to expect that despite my best efforts, I'm going to irritate somebody. In fact, if everybody thought I was wonderful all the time, I'm probably not doing my job. I've learned to separate the irritation I cause in order to push progress from the residue of hurt feelings and relationships. I can control the latter. But I

have to ask for the feedback—people don't usually volunteer it. Sometimes it's the fact that I ask at all that corrects misunderstandings and helps relationships. And when the time comes for me to serve up what they've long avoided, I will have earned the credibility to do so because I will have opened myself to their scrutiny.

"Who Am I?"

Every day we face opportunities to reflect. It may mean choosing from many available solutions for a complex problem. It may mean deciding whether to reorganize, whether to accept a new assignment, what client to take on next, whether to get married, to buy or rent, to give someone another chance or shake hands and part company, to invest or divest, and on and on. Each crossroad tests the boundaries of our convictions and the fortitude of our beliefs, hopefully making the fiber of our character more resilient and us more intimately familiar with ourselves. But if we speed through these intersections without stopping to reflect and learn, we will continue to destroy opportunities to make a difference for ourselves and for others.

That human beings learn from experience is a myth. We learn from the *analysis* of the experience. Simply having an experience does nothing. That's why so many intelligent people continue to repeat unintelligent experiences. It's the reflection on the experience—especially the painful ones—that produces real learning. If you intend to be successful helping your clients achieve sustainable results, you will never be able to engender their trust or build their commitment to change if you repeatedly dodge chances to get to know yourself better. James Kouzes and Barry Posner in their book *Credibility* write, "The place to begin the enhancement of credibility is with an exploration of the inner territory. Who are you? What do you believe in? What do you stand for?" Begin your own self-reflection by seeking answers to these questions. You and those around you will be glad you did.

Lessons of Experience: Looking Back to Look Ahead

Not only is it important to reflect deeply on who we are as people, but it is equally important to reflect on our work—whether or not what we are doing is producing the results we agreed to produce. Unlike many professionals, consultants don't have complex machines, tools, and technologies to rely on. For the most part, we are the offering. Sure, our advice is often supported by tools and technology, but we are front and center as the source of advice and insight. As such, guessing at whether or not the desired outcomes are being achieved is a high-risk approach. If a doctor prescribes the wrong medicine, there is a relatively quick feedback loop in the patient's reaction that informs the doctor if his effort was unsuccessful. He can then choose a different course of action. In consulting, there is more lag time between the counsel we dispense, the solution we propose, the coaching we provide, and the effect such counsel, solutions, or coaching has on the circumstance at hand. It is essential to closely monitor how effective our suggestions are while they are being implemented, not just after the fact. While some lag time may be needed to see whether or not what has been implemented will "stick," detecting early-warning signals can help keep efforts on track or minimize the disruption of necessary course corrections. These early-warning signs include strong levels of resistance, indifference, numerous false starts, premature successes, or too many questions from your clients indicating "we don't get it."

Acquiring knowledge by monitoring how effective our work has been is half the challenge. The other half is *applying* the knowledge to subsequent initiatives. It is common for us as consultants to be the ones most impressed with the wisdom and insight our suggestions hold. Confident in the merits of our ideas, it is easy to be seduced into dismissing any signals of failure as the client's issues, or the inability of the organization to implement, stay focused, or remain committed. Taking what we learn from our successes and mistakes, and then using that knowledge to improve our efforts on behalf of our clients, builds the credibility required to be irreverent. If our clients see only our ability to point out their flaws, it makes it difficult for them to trust our conclusions. If, on the other hand, they see us taking our own medicine, they are more likely to be open to making changes in their thoughts and practices.

The foundational element that makes self-reflection work is humility—an acceptance of our own fallibility, a natural desire to learn about and correct our shortcomings. This leads to an inwardly directed scrutiny that helps to ensure we are having the intended personal and organizational impact. Moreover, this constant examination of our behavior and work strengthens our capacity to detect patterns and trends in our clients and their organizations. Continuous self-scrutiny helps build the "insight muscle" required to recognize an organization's misdirected reverence. Without self-reflection, we are unable to understand whether we are having a positive affect, we will lack credibility when pointing out our clients' opportunities for change, and our ability to demonstrate insight about organizational patterns of behavior will be weakened.

The Shift to Self-Reflection

At a small Washington D.C.–based consulting firm, a negative client satisfaction response prompted the managing partner to adopt a significant method of ensuring the firm was continuously aware of how it was experienced by clients and prospects. The monthly event, called "Second Tuesday," was a gathering of both clients and consultants to discuss how the previous month had gone on their respective engagements. Lunch was served and best practices were shared around building great relationships. When glitches were identified, they could be rectified immediately. Clients believed these consultants genuinely wanted to learn how they could provide better service and respected the process by offering both positive and negative examples, without being opportunistic and using the consultant's mistakes to their advantage. In fact, in some cases clients would join in, asking, "Is there anything we could do differently to help you do your job?" It rubs off. Instead of blaming others and excusing mistakes, both clients and consultants learned to be responsible for their own behavior.

People in organizations blame and rationalize everyday. Self-reflection creates the context for people to both welcome and promote individual and corporate self-discovery. To make the behavioral shift toward self-reflection, consultants need to be aware of new compass headings with which to navigate. Here are some examples.

Arrogance → Humility

A posture of humility suggests that you don't consider yourself or your organization "better" than any other. Humility guards against condescension toward others and allows you to freely recognize and acknowledge value outside yourself. During difficult periods of transition, when engagements are typically at their apex, people have a strong need to know they are valued. Humility enables the expression of value to others and prevents the common response of self-absorption during intense periods. Irreverence begins with a balanced perspective of who you are and who you are not.

"I already know" → "I don't know"

Consultants who are adept at self-reflection realize that life-long success is directly attributable to lifelong learning. Those who adopt a position of "I don't know" open themselves to new perspectives on the world and continuously seek out new information about who they are and the way they operate. An expression of "I don't know" engenders the trust of others, which enables collective learning to happen faster. Irreverence requires continuous learning.

Self-Doubt → Self-Confidence

Consultants who are truly self-confident demonstrate an ease in exercising what they are good at. They feel no need to exaggerate accomplishments or take undeserved credit. They shun haughty, boastful behavior while accepting praise graciously. Irreverence requires genuine self-confidence.

Impervious → Inquisitive

Self-reflective consultants do not see themselves as impervious to error. They recognize their human fallibility and, as such, place as much value on questions as they do on answers. They regularly seek out better ways of doing things and consciously attempt to learn from mistakes. An environment conducive to learning and relearning builds resilience for the commonly frantic consultant's life. Irreverence requires consultants to "inquire" into how things can be better.

Feedback Averse → Feedback Inviting

Being aware of how their behavior affects others is very important to consultants who demonstrate self-reflection. They recognize that it is impossible to know with 100 percent accuracy how well your intentions match what others experience. As such, they thrive on soliciting the perceptions of those they work with and for. Irreverence requires consistent monitoring of personal impact on others.

Gutsiness

"Be strong and courageous, and act."

—King David, to his son Solomon

Figure 4-1. Making the personal connection: self-reflection.

Use the following questions to prompt your thinking about the value of self-reflection. After spending some time in quiet reflection, you may want to start a Value-Creating Journal to record your thoughts and responses on an ongoing basis.

1. Think about the last time you received developmental feedback that made you defensive and that you ultimately dismissed. Disregarding whether or not the delivery of the feedback was effective, what was it about the information that made you defensive? Was your pride or ego overly inflated? What aspects of receiving developmental feedback are difficult for you? Why?

2. Contrast the experience in question 1 with the last time you received developmental feedback to which you displayed a humble response and changed your behavior. What about the feedback and the surrounding circumstances was sufficiently severe to elicit a humble response and a desire to change?

3. Make a list of at least three people you feel sufficiently close to and trust enough to solicit feedback from. Prepare three or four direct questions inquiring about the impact your behavior has on them and what you might do to improve or change. Schedule appointments to see these people and follow through on their comments. Document both the positive and developmental feedback you receive, looking for trends and patterns.

Figure 4-2. Making the organizational connection: self-reflection.

---

1. Think about the last time your firm received negative feedback from a client or employee that solicited a defensive response, and where the feedback was ultimately dismissed. Disregarding whether or not the delivery of the feedback was effective, what was it about the information that caused a defensive response? Was the firm's pride or ego overly inflated? Is getting external or internal feedback a routine part of the way your firm operates? Is acting upon the feedback also a routine part of operations, or is the firm just collecting the information to appear as though feedback is important?

2. Contrast the experience from question 1 with the last time your firm received negative feedback from a client or employee and displayed a humble response, effecting a change in the way something was done. What about the feedback and the surrounding circumstances were sufficiently severe to elicit a humble response and a desire to change? What impending consequences served as a wake-up call to your firm? How might you help people believe in the existence of those potential consequences every day?

3. Make a list of at least three clients and/or employee groups to solicit feedback from. Prepare three or four direct questions inquiring about the impact your firm's behavior has on them and what might be done to improve or change. Schedule appointments to see these people and follow through. Document both the positive and developmental feedback you receive and look for trends and patterns.

Let's face it. Consulting is a risky business. Sure, people may look at us and see the expensive suits, the fancy dinners, the travel, the elbow-rubbing with important people, the opportunity to be "influential," and the significant fees and think, "Whoa, cushy job." The fact is, to become a value-creating consultant takes real gutsiness. It is one thing to have the insight to recognize the counterproductive direction of an organization's reverence and the intelligence to see a way out from behind the complex issues blocking performance. It is quite another to walk into a senior executive's office and talk about your findings with blunt candor. Consultants need to know how to present a balance, when to push and when to withdraw, how to be direct and still be diplomatic, how to pinpoint accountability without judging, how to provoke action without coming across as arrogant, and how to show empathy without letting clients off the hook—none of which is the least bit easy. To put oneself in this situation takes guts.

One executive put it this way:

> I can't stand wimpy consultants. If you're going to traipse through my organization digging up all the skeletons, you damn well better not pull your punches when it comes time to offer up the goods. I pay good money to these people, and it aggravates me to no end that when they come into my office, I have to drag the bad news out of them. It's like pulling teeth. I'm a big boy, I can take it. Of course, I might get defensive. I might even get loud. But do they honestly think trying to make me feel good, or to warm me up first, is helpful? It wastes my time, and it makes me wonder why I hired them in the first place.

It's not hard to understand how some consultants might be intimidated by such a client. But cowering under the pressure of such a client's domineering style only reinforces his stereotype of "wimpy" consultants. One might argue that his behavior is disrespectful, doesn't invite the candor of others, and seems to indicate an unwillingness to listen. If that is the case, then the value-creating consultant would direct the conversation at such behavior and not try to force out the issues or temper them in order to temper him.

Being a gutsy consultant often takes the form of having to discuss undiscussables that we know may initially be difficult for the client to hear, even though the issue needs to be addressed, nonetheless. While we are committed to being "loving but direct," we are not exempt from the temptation to rationalize reasons to leave the issue buried instead of incurring the potential risk that exposing it brings. Our net conclusion is that there is rarely a good reason to withhold important information that could improve the performance of an individual or an organization, or that might prevent derailment. Gutsiness, then, becomes an act of caring.

One client of ours, a senior executive, was struggling with a productivity issue in his department. He clearly saw that he was personally contributing to the problem, but he couldn't figure out how. After weeks of observing how his department operated, we noticed that the vast majority of activity in which he was involved took place in the morning. His involvement or activity was almost never requested in the afternoon. We asked him if he was aware of this, and he said it was not a conscious work habit. We asked several of his senior staff members if they were aware of the practice and, if so, if they could shed some light on it for us. The first few people we spoke with were clearly aware, but nervously denied it. We went back and observed the senior executive in the afternoon to see if we could detect any notable difference in his behavior. With close observation, we could.

Apparently, the executive was in the habit of drinking alcohol with his lunch. When he returned from lunch, his breath and clothing contained the odor of alcohol and his already short attention span became even shorter during afternoon conversations. We went to some people we hadn't spoken with yet and asked them specifically if they chose to engage this leader in the morning as opposed to the afternoon. They confirmed that they did, but wouldn't say why. Evidently, an unspoken norm had been established throughout the department not to engage this leader after lunch. Now that it was clear that alcohol and its ensuing behavior were the issues at which people's reverence was directed, we faced a choice. With only our observations of his department's behaviors, and free of any suggestion that he might have a more significant problem, we approached him. Our decision to do so did not come without much debate and anxious consideration. We contemplated the many ways to spin the information. After considerable reflection concerning our own values and what we were trying to accomplish, we were compelled to surface the undiscussable. We knew it was the right thing to do. So we went to him, simply stating our observations and concerns about the impact of his behavior on productivity, suggesting he change his lunchtime beverage selection. At first he was defensive, but he still listened. He told us later that what we did was more what a friend would do than a consultant. We doubt that productivity significantly improved in his department from that single intervention, but it did open the door for more productive work to follow. We believe he can now make more fully informed choices about his own behavior, and his department staff members can restructure their work to optimize both their time and their leader's time. They can direct their reverence at improving performance instead of at secretly working around their leader's behavior.

Something to Think About . . .

> What risks were involved in disclosing the feedback to the executive? In not disclosing the feedback?
> In what types of relationships do you find being gutsy most threatening?
> How do you respond when someone shares risky information or feedback with you?

Gutsiness is important not only in the way we present issues to our clients, but also in those actions we encourage our clients to take. In the face of difficult, unfamiliar challenges and public scrutiny, it is easy for leaders to resort to those strengths that have historically propelled their career. Waving the banner of change, they merely intensify those strengths as though they were taking different action. It is at this point the value-creating consultant must not only raise the leader's awareness of what he or she is doing, but also propose alternative actions that may require the leader to relinquish the tried-and-true in exchange for a bolder, riskier approach.

One consultant recounted an opportunity she had to challenge her client to explore a high-risk solution:

> The data weren't that complex. The division of the company my client was leading simply wasn't producing the bottom-line results demanded by corporate. It wasn't a bad business, just your basic packaged-goods commodity, okay-margin kind of business. My client had reengineered, invested in product line extensions, sponsored new marketing campaigns, modified the sales compensation plan, experimented with nontraditional distribution channels—all of which produced incremental improvements. But the returns did not match the other divisions of the organization, whose products and services re-

volved around newer technologies that supplied growth markets. The CEO decided he wanted to invest in high-growth industries. The problem was that, despite producing some of the original products on which the company was founded, this division was now facing stiff overseas competition and pricing pressure and served a saturated market. Nobody, least of all my client, wanted to consider anything that suggested this now-lackluster division couldn't one day shine again. My client was now the third general manager to lead this division in five years. I could see he was scared. The fact of the matter was that the CEO was determined to satisfy the board's and shareholder's appetite for growth, and this division simply didn't have the leverage opportunities to help. And although I'm sure people had thought about it, nobody openly acknowledged the reality that the division would be better off in some other organization's portfolio where it might be able to provide leverage.

My recommendation to my client was that he recommend to the CEO that a suitable buyer be identified and that the division be sold. Nothing could have been more distasteful to him, and he couldn't imagine the CEO's reaction. But he knew in his gut it was the best alternative. This company never divested anything. To them, divesting seemed like "quitting" and was the same as conceding defeat. The company had been successful turning around floundering organizations it had acquired, so this would be a tough pill to swallow. . . . It took us a couple of months to develop a well-documented proposal to the CEO and his team detailing the options and describing the obvious benefits of divesting a division that could no longer contribute to the overall strategic intent of the organization. I was proud of my client who, during the meeting, took a stand with a very resistant and contentious CEO, saying, "Look, sentimentality and tradition are nice, and I realize this division has a strong emotional pull because of the brand. But those aren't good enough reasons to keep pouring resources into it. This is probably the hardest thing I've ever had to do in my career, but let's face the facts. Someone else with more compatible businesses will probably do a better job than us at making this division viable. We can't eat our cake and have it. If growth is what we're going after, we're not going to find it here." After he finished, the silence in the room was palpable. He looked at me for reassurance, and I smiled at him. He knew he'd just helped change the future of the organization. Was the notion of selling the division a brilliant insight? No. But helping my client to accept the conclusion and getting him to champion the proposal to the CEO and the board—that's where I made my contribution.

Fear and the Risks of Risk Aversion

In Chapter 2, we briefly discussed how bad habit consultants manifested fear. Because we believe fear to be such a fundamental barrier to consulting effectiveness, we thought it was important to discuss it in terms of gutsiness and the corrosive role it plays in risk taking. Several years ago, we worked with a large manufacturing organization in an effort to change their control-oriented culture to one that promoted speed and creativity. We had collected lots of data through interviews and a survey on those behaviors the culture currently favored. At a meeting of the top seventy-five executives, we presented our findings. People were nervous about what the data might suggest and even more anxious about the response of their command-and-control leader. The summary data weren't particularly interesting, with one exception. On the dimension of integrity, there was clearly a dip in the bar graph. Before we had the chance to open a discussion about the data's ramifications, one woman raised her hand. Her intentions were quickly obvious: to discredit the data and us. She said, "In looking at the data, it's difficult for me to grasp any relevant message. You certainly can't suggest this slight difference in the integrity dimension has any meaning. Was there a t-test done on the data? Is there a normative database to which we might compare ourselves? How valid was this instrument? Was it tested for reliability? I would certainly want to see the factor analysis on the items before I was willing to concede these data have any significance."

The room was very silent. It was clearly a moment of truth for us, for the project, and for the credibility of the change process so many of the leaders in the room wanted. We paused for a moment to set aside our emotional reaction to the woman's disruptive and antagonistic behavior. After quickly weighing the options, we decided the investment in change already made was too important to risk—we needed to be direct. We paused for a moment, looked at each other, then said, "Well, to respond to your questions about the integrity of the measurement: The items all were tested and a factor analysis done on the dimensions. We carefully established validity and the alpha reliability was 0.89. With the exception of those items we put in at the company's request, the rest are from a database for which there are norms to which we could compare. We agree that the aggregate data doesn't tell as interesting a story as the data when it is broken down to a more granular level, and we should study that data. With regard to your conclusion that the integrity dimension's lower score may not have any significance, let's test that hypothesis: By a show of hands, how many of you in this room have never lied to anyone else in this room?" No one raised their hands. The silence was more palpable. The woman looked chagrined.

Our goal wasn't to publicly embarrass her. But we did need to stand up to the collusion in the room to sabotage a project whose change ramifications were important. We concluded, "There's no reason to pretend we don't know what these data are telling us, is there?"

Gutsy consultants know that courage is not the absence of fear and uncertainty, so they don't try to impose undue certainty on risky situations. Rather, they know that courage is taking action despite fear and risk, using the best information available, and being guided by deeply held principles. In the case cited in the previous paragraphs, we were very aware of the risk such a response posed, and we certainly had a lot of anxiety about it. (In fact, if we'd had time to prepare a response, we probably would have talked ourselves out of responding the way we did.) In this case, the risk paid off. A candid and open discussion about their behavior as leaders followed our intervention and set the stage for more productive work later on. The leader of the organization thanked us after the meeting for not letting them off the hook.

The Shift to Gutsiness

The Bible makes approximately thirty-eight references to God or an Angel addressing man directly. Nearly all of those interactions begin with the words "Fear not." Clearly God knew that fear was going to be an issue for mankind.

Consultants that operate out of fear deprive their clients of the opportunity to uncover hidden abilities and imaginative solutions that, with courage, would otherwise be discovered. Gusty consultants adopt a passion for the adventure in each assignment and stir up that spirit in their clients. When this happens, clients become liberated to act with courage despite their fear, rather than become paralyzed by their fear. Here are some compass headings that you might use to uncover the gutsiness within you, your firm, and your clients.

Fear → Tenacity

Gutsy consultants fully accept what they are uncertain or insecure about. They embrace the potential of failure and act despite it. They are tenacious in pursuit of their intended purpose or goal and manifest a significant degree of endurance along the way. They struggle to overcome the regressive forces pulling them back to what is familiar and comfortable. Irreverence requires unbridled determination.

Indifference → Conviction

Courage comes from that Latin root meaning "heart." In Western culture, the heart is the seat of the emotions and beliefs, thus the expressions "Put your heart into it" and "You broke my heart." Gutsy consultants have resolute convictions in their heart and mind about what they are trying to accomplish. They speak passionately about their mission and are never wishy-washy about it. Passion and conviction are the fuel of irreverence.

Rigidity → Adaptability

Because we no longer live in certain times, gutsy consultants recognize that the swift pace of change renders the half-life of any idea or method very brief, so they avoid a "one size fits all" approach to anything. They remain flexible and are able to adapt their thinking and relationships to accommodate an ever-changing environment. Irreverence requires agility to adapt to a perpetual state of transition.

Conflict Avoiding → Conflict Inviting

To many people the notion of conflict is bad. It's a destructive experience that is hurtful and unproductive. But to the gutsy, conflict is just the opposite. Skilled at resolving conflict in a productive and relationship-enhancing way, these consultants seek out conflict knowing that within the resolution may lie a breakthrough—a new perspective or innovative idea not yet discovered. Healthy conflict resolution builds trust-based relationships, which, in turn, cause innovation to happen faster. Irreverence demands a thorough explorations of opposing points of view.

Timidity → Boldness

The actions of gutsy consultants are rarely tentative. While they calculate their risks intelligently, they are seldom shy about the decisions they make or the style they use to implement their decisions. Bold action supported by intelligent judgment inspires them by providing the energy they need to face the challenges of change. Knowing that timid behavior can breed apprehension, gutsy consultants combine intrepid, visionary language and clear, decisive action. Irreverence spurs audacious action.

Figure 4-3. Making the personal connection: gutsiness.

Use the following questions to prompt your thinking about the value of gutsiness. After spending some time in quiet reflection, write down your thoughts and responses in your Value-Creating Journal.

1. Think about the last time you responded to a threatening situation with fear, refraining from taking action. What about the situation caused you fear? What specifically were you afraid of? Loss of status? Loss of respect? Being wrong? Punishment from a leader or other authority? How did you feel about yourself after not acting courageously? Now, look for a pattern that may explain this type of risk-averse response in your life. Can you distinguish any trends among the kinds of risky situations you find frightening and those you don't?

2. Contrast the experience uncovered in question 1 to a time when you acted "gutsy" regardless of the presence of fear. What about the situation was compelling enough to motivate you to act? What were you thinking and feeling in the moments right before you decided to act? How did you feel about yourself and your courage afterward? What can you do to increase your confidence to act courageously, despite any fear, more consistently in your life?

3. Make a list of all the situations or people you fear most. Next to each one, write down what specifically it is that you fear about them. Identify any themes or patterns that appear. Can you see how you may have learned these fears earlier in your life? Select the one fear you feel relatively sure you could conquer with concerted effort. Make a plan to construct opportunities in which you can openly confront this fearful circumstance or person. Involve a close friend, colleague, or significant other to provide encouragement and support. Once you feel confident you've conquered this fear (be patient, it will take some time), move on to another.

Figure 4-4. Making the organizational connection: gutsiness.

1. Think about the last time your firm or your practice responded to a threatening situation with fear, refraining from taking action. What about the situation caused fear? What was the perceived threat? Competition? Public criticism? How did the organization's leaders seem to feel after not acting courageously? Is there a pattern of this type of risk-averse response in the organization's history? Can you distinguish any trends among the kinds of risky situations the organization finds threatening?

2. Contrast the experience uncovered in question 1 to a time when your firm or practice acted courageously, regardless of the presence of fear. What about the situation was compelling enough to motivate action? What can be done to increase your organization's ability to act courageously despite fear?

3. Make a list of all the things your firm or practice seems to fear most. Next to each one, write down specifically what threat is perceived in that situation. Identify any themes or patterns that appear. Can you see how the firm's culture, structure, leaders, and systems are reinforcing these fears? What changes need to take place to allow gutsiness to flourish in your organization?

Tough Love

> "Whoever loves discipline loves knowledge,
> but he who hates reproof is stupid . . .
> Do not reproof a scoffer, lest he hate you,
> Reprove a wise man, and he will love you."
>
> —King Solomon

What would you do?

Imagine working with a client for nearly two years on a major overhaul of a billion-dollar division of an organization. Recall the late-night team meetings . . . the dozens of times you were stranded in airports because of canceled flights . . . the lengthy presentations to recalcitrant audiences . . . the tedious excavation of insights from piles and piles of pilot-test data . . . the fierce debating of options over early breakfasts and late dinners . . . the covert efforts of organizational rebels to sabotage the initiative . . . the waiting on hold while accounts payable tracked down your ninety-day past-due invoice. Now recall the early signs of success—the division's first profitable quarter in years, newly acquired customers who defected from competitors, and the overall mood of the organization changing from defeat to upbeat.

Then, a new crossroads appears—your client company faces a major decision: to merge or not to merge. All the data suggest the turnaround is still fragile. The systems are not fully in place. Some countries are lagging behind the implementation of the new organization. Although things are progressing nicely, by no means is the division out of the woods. All of the members of your client's executive team are shouting, "Don't do it!" The thought of the horrid disruption a merger would bring now has them terrified. You implore your client to pass on the opportunity, citing bad timing and numerous incompatibility issues with the target organization as reasonable deal breakers. Too late. Deal fever has struck hard.

It is now eight months after the deal. You stayed on to help integrate the two organizations, but everyone's worst nightmare played out—worse than they'd feared. Earnings are in a free fall. Newly acquired customers are defecting in droves, with some returning to the competitors from whom they'd come. Despite early warnings, corporate is livid. The two organizations agree on how to divorce as quietly as possible, and all that is left to do now is find an appropriate scapegoat. You know where the guns are aimed. In fact, if you were holding one of the guns, you might consider shooting your client yourself for years of emotional and intellectual blood and sweat destroyed in a burst of greed and ambition. Some newspaper articles even suggested your firm encouraged the deal, while others mentioned you by name with insinuations about "trusted advisors" unable to stop the deal. Totally dejected, looking as down-trodden as any human could, your client comes to you and says, "I don't know why, but they've agreed to give me six months to try and patch this thing back up. I told them I knew how badly I screwed up, that I realized if I had just stayed the course this place would be humming right now. I've let a lot of people down—especially my team. I don't know if they'll trust me with another chance, but I do believe I can get the place back on its feet again. Will you help?"

Situations like this one bring out the best and worst in us. There is no obvious or right answer. On the one hand, doesn't everyone deserve a second chance? Shouldn't the client be allowed the opportunity to redeem himself? After all, he'd turned the place around once. On the other hand, if he was so easily sidetracked from his mission once, what's to say he has really learned his lesson? How do you know that the next capricious whim won't sweep him away like before?

As his consultant, I might reflect on my options. If I say yes, is it because I just feel sorry for him? Is it because I can take advantage of his weak position and clean up on fees? Do I believe he can pull it off again? Will I be letting him off too easily? How will he really learn from this mistake if I roll over and agree to help bail him out? Should I play hard-to-get? Or, if I say no, am I being overly harsh and unforgiving? Am I concerned about being associated with a maniacal client—not once, but twice? Will I risk my reputation? Am I so angry about what he's done that a second chance is simply out of the question? Can I trust him? Am I feeling guilty for not pushing him harder when I had the chance? If I were choosing between a very challenging, interesting assignment with a premier organization or going back to his organization for a second shot, what would I choose?"

All very tough questions for any consultant.

Something to Think About . . .

> What criteria would you use to make the decision whether or not to help your client?
> Whatever you decide, what can you do to be helpful to the client in the way you present your response?

Forgiveness and Accountability: The Essence of a Consultant's Tough Love

The situation described in the previous paragraphs raises the questions, "How forgiving should I be?" and "How stringently does a client need to be held accountable?" The reality is that these forces are neither opposite nor mutually exclusive. In fact, we believe they go hand in hand. One without the other frequently leads to hurtful results. Forgiveness without accountability may relieve clients from the emotional burden of their mistakes, but does nothing to ensure they learn from the mistakes. Extending forgiveness does not mean tolerating substandard performance. If someone repeatedly makes the same errors, misses deadlines, produces shoddy work, no matter how sorry that person is, forgiving her for her inabilities doesn't mean continuing to accept them. Forgiveness should liberate people from past transgressions in the hopes of building their confidence and fortifying the relationship. It should not liberate them from their obligation to perform their duties acceptably.

Conversely, accountability without forgiveness often serves to induce fear and guilt, not only debilitating the needed confidence to change, but making one feel blameworthy and incapable of success. Fear and guilt lead to second guessing, stalled progress, and increased failure. Either attribute—forgiveness and accountability—without the other, then, can lead clients to repeat the same mistake.

Consultants play an important role in helping their clients move through difficult intersections. Forgiveness and accountability are frequently translated by the organization into guilt and blame and enacted in passive-aggressive ways. While professing to forgive the manager in the previous story by allowing him a second shot at a turnaround, those in charge may simultaneously withhold support and slip in oblique reminders of his failure, rubbing his nose in the tragedy through innuendo. The more sadistic spectators may even enjoy the chance to watch him go down in flames a second time. Repugnant though this may sound, it is the harsh reality of organizational life. These dual love-hate messages drain energy from the individual, virtually setting him up for failure as his own self-doubts eat away at his capabilities. When clients lose resilience, having nowhere to turn to regain their footing after such trauma, consultants can be especially instrumental in helping restore focus, confidence, and sound thinking.

Instead of colluding with the organization to inflict the toxins of guilt and blame, consultants can help clients discover the liberating and rejuvenating rewards of true forgiveness and accountability. It is in this combination of forgiveness and accountability that consultants demonstrate "tough love." Penetrating the usual boundaries of professional relationships protected by pretentious veneers and "nice knowin' ya" exit options, consultants risk the personal investment of truly caring for their clients' well-being in both good and bad times. By extending forgiveness, consultants help their clients acknowledge their mistakes, make amends with those who've been affected by them, and shed the burden of needless self-deprecation. By acting as a source of accountability, consultants help their clients both to extract valuable learning from their mistakes and to make meaningful commitments to apply the learning to future problems.

Being an agent of tough love for clients requires consultants to push the conventional boundaries of the client-consultant relationship. It means breaking down your clients' defenses, gaining their complete trust and, ultimately, access to their heart and mind. The latter is critical to influencing change because new behavior emanates from emotions, not intellect. Thus, simply providing ideas for clients is rarely sufficient to provoke change, but challenging their "heart set" as well as their mind-set can.

Binocular Vision Is the Key to Tough Love

The essence of tough love is being able to simultaneously hold in view the actions and behaviors of a client that are unproductive, even destructive, while at the same time seeing the value of the client's positive attributes, talents, and motives. It means being able to genuinely discuss the client's positive and negative qualities with equal levels of significance. In the case cited earlier, we have a client whose ambition and drive successfully helped turn around a failing organization. His insights, leadership, and untiring efforts brought the organization to the brink of a potentially extraordinary future. That same ambition and drive led him to make a disastrous decision—against the advice of many—to engage in a merger that returned the organization to a state of decline. What would a tough love response look like to this client's request for help? We think a response from a consultant displaying tough love might go something like this:

> To be honest, I'm apprehensive about engaging with your organization again. I certainly don't doubt that your talents—which I realize are extensive—could turn this place around a second time. But you acknowledged yourself that you are starting this time with a lot less credibility and fewer willing supporters than the first time. That doesn't make my job any easier, either. What concerns me is the unconstrained certainty with which you plowed ahead, despite how many of us pleaded with you to rethink your assumptions. I don't know what it was that blinded you to the clearly insurmountable obstacles we all saw—a burning surge of ambition, or just plain willfulness—but if it happened once, what's to say it couldn't happen again? I appreciate the obvious sense of remorse

you're feeling, and I'm sure this experience has been painful enough to produce some lessons learned, but I have to be honest. My confidence in our relationship has been shaken. I'm sure your hindsight has enabled you to see all the consequences the rest of us faced, so I'll spare you the list. And I'm sure you've suffered a lot of pain in silence the rest of us can't see. It's not that I want to withdraw my support—I consider you a valued colleague and friend. Whether we work together again or not, that won't change. I'm certainly not going to hold this over your head—we all need to let it go and move on. But what happened was pretty public. My name, and my firm's name, was often printed in the same paragraphs as yours. This hasn't exactly enhanced our reputation as consultants. I need you to give me some time to think about what engaging again might look like. Let's talk again in a week.

We recognize that some readers may find the suggestion of speaking to a client this way a little grating. One might think the consultant is being overly harsh or arrogant, presuming his help is all that necessary to begin with. One might also think that any good client worth his salt would never be so deferent to a consultant or tolerate such a response. Maybe so. But our point is this: The relationship between a consultant and client should be close and resilient enough that the option exists to have conversations such as this one—whether the issue resides with the client or the consultant.

Tough love is difficult enough to practice in our relationships with friends, spouses, and children, much less our clients. But if you think about the wonderful outcomes tough love has brought about in your own life, it isn't hard to imagine how great the benefits to our clients could be.

For No Reason at All

Encouraging our clients to display tough love in the face of their own difficult circumstances can be another way to demonstrate this form of irreverence. During an executive coaching session, a client lamented his anguish over the neglect and abuse he suffered from his boss.

Client: You have no idea what I've had to put up with these past years. He takes advantage of me, steals my ideas and gets the credit, doesn't give me any access to the organization's leaders, makes sarcastic remarks about my appearance in front of my staff, and has absolutely no commitment to helping me advance my career.

Consultant: How long have you been this angry?

Client: Since the day he started as my boss six years ago.

Consultant: And does he know how frustrated you are by his behavior?

Client: Who knows? He's basically not interested. I spend half my day consumed in fantasies about getting back at him. I know it's ridiculous, but I can't help it.

Consultant: Why don't you confront him?

Client: What good would that do? He's not going to change.

Consultant: Maybe not. But you might at least feel less burdened knowing you've conveyed your frustrations to him directly. Once you've done that, you can more easily accept the fact that he's probably not going to change, forgive him for all he's done to you, and move on with your life.

Client: What! Forgive him? Why on earth would I do that? He sure as hell isn't sorry and would never ask for forgiveness if he was sorry.

Consultant: What does him not being sorry and not asking for forgiveness have to do with you forgiving him? You're the only one who's suffering here. He seems to be doing just fine. And it appears that much of your stress is a result of your anger toward him, more so than his actions toward you. It's your career. Why don't you take responsibility for it, let go, and move on? But you should at least give him the chance to respond by telling him what's on your mind.

Client: Are you saying to forgive . . . just because . . . just to forgive?

Consultant: Exactly.

Client: I actually never thought of that before.

And that's precisely what he did. He confronted his boss, liberated himself from enslavement to his anger, and moved on. And his career blossomed. His boss was eventually fired and our client got promoted. Medgar Evers so eloquently said, "When you hate, the only one who suffers is you. Because most of the people you hate don't know it, and the rest don't care."

The Shift to Tough Love

The story is often retold, in a variety of versions, of a young computer engineer at IBM who, after making a million-dollar mistake, held his head low as he entered the office of the company's founder, Thomas J. Watson, Sr., resignation letter in hand. Seeing what the paper contained, Watson shoved the letter back at the young man and said, "I'm not accepting that! I just spent a million dollars on your training. You stick around and make it pay off."

That's a perfect illustration of tough love. Imagine the engineer's renewed confidence and commitment. Those are the defining moments in an organization's life that make or break the possibility of breakthrough and sustainable change. These compass headings may help lead you and your clients to defining moments of your own.

Incriminating Others → Solving Problems

Consultants focused on change know that resolving an issue is far more productive than finding a scapegoat. You can never have change when the primary focus is making people wrong. Problem solving results in the building of many options, whereas blaming only results in people guarding their positions. Irreverence is focused on making something right and not on making someone wrong.

Enabling → Challenging

For a variety of reasons, consultants too often minimize the consequences of their client's negative behavior and actions, especially if the client is visibly struggling with those behaviors and actions. Consultants showing tough love have the ability to separate the person from the behavior, demonstrating virtually unconditional regard for the person but uncompromising scrutiny of the behavior. Irreverence keeps people's self-respect intact while confronting their unproductive behavior and actions.

Vengeance → Reconciliation

Consultants help clients focus their energies onto the initiative at hand, and away from the temptation to invest it unproductively in getting even when an offense occurs. Instead, they find a way to strengthen partnerships through mutual commitment to resolution. Irreverence requires forfeiture of the "right to retaliate."

Guilt Infliction → Coaching

Consultants use tough love to help clients learn from their mistakes, regardless of how much their mistakes hurt. They avoid paralyzing people with feelings of inadequacy just to maintain the illusion of superior righteousness. Irreverence demands an unconditional acceptance that people's imperfections may be more obvious during times of change.

Entitlement → Responsibility

Instead of harboring resentment when life doesn't match their expectations, irreverent consultants take full ownership of the circumstances they encounter, regardless of how the circumstances originated. They are able to adjust their expectations, and rather than always feeling entitled to have things go their way, they take responsibility for the way things go. Irreverence abolishes the flawed assumption that life should be the way we see and want it.

"Yeah, but . . ." → "I'm sorry"

Defending one's position or actions paradoxically perpetuates self-imposed guilt. The need to be right comes with the cost of harboring the guilt that naturally occurs when we do something that has a negative effect outside our intentions. Both clients and consultants showing tough love are quick to say, "I'm sorry." Seeking the forgiveness and acceptance of others liberates us to forgive and accept ourselves. Irreverence requires a constant exchange of grace.

Figure 4-5. Making the personal connection: tough love.

Use the following questions to prompt your thinking about the characteristic of tough love. After spending some time in quiet reflection, write down your thoughts and responses in your Value-Creating Journal.

1. Think about the relationships in your life in which you find it difficult to forgive or in which you are currently harboring unforgiveness. Does the other person know you are angry? Have you withheld trust as a result? What would the other person have to do to restore your total faith and trust in the relationship and for you to forgive? Could you forgive people regardless of their level of (or lack of) remorse?

2. Generally, when someone does something that hurts or disappoints you, are you someone who forgives and forgets, forgives but doesn't forget, or doesn't forgive? Are you someone who is uncomfortable confronting others when they have hurt you? What limitations or conditions do you put on forgiveness, or on holding others accountable when they do or say something hurtful? Do these choices affect the level of gratification and intimacy you are able to achieve in your relationships? If you are not satisfied with how gratified by or how intimate you can become in your relationships, what adjustments can you make regarding your expectations of others, your tolerance of shortcomings, and your ability to let go when others disappoint or hurt you?

3. Think about a time when you were confronted by someone who felt hurt or disappointed by something you did. After seeking the person's forgiveness, you felt totally absolved, restoring and even strengthening the relationship. What did you learn? What impact did receiving forgiveness have on your commitment to the relationship and on your commitment to making sure you tried extra hard to avoid the same mistake again?

4. Think about a similar situation, except that after asking for forgiveness, you did not feel absolved or that the relationship was restored. Instead, you felt the person withholding trust and somewhat withdrawn from the relationship. How did it make you feel about the relationship and about yourself? If you felt the relationship was valuable enough to pursue, what could you do to let the person know that you feel estranged and that you would like to find a way to put the unpleasantness behind you?

5. Look back at each entry in your Value-Creating Journal. What overarching themes do you see emerging about yourself? What have you learned about yourself? How would you characterize your strengths and development needs in the context of these three characteristics of irreverence? Prioritize a list for each one, and ensure that your action plans are integrated and aligned. Now, implement them!

Figure 4-6. Making the organizational connection: tough love.

1. Identify as many unresolved conflicts as you can between individuals or departments within your firm or a client's firm. What is the history of each conflict? Have you observed a steady erosion of trust between those involved? What attempts (if any) have been made to reconcile and move beyond the issues? Have the appropriate people been told of the impact of their actions? How many people have been affected by each conflict? What has been the impact on overall performance by the perpetuation of this conflict? How many missed opportunities for improvement or innovation would you say there have been as a result of these conflicts?

2. Identify as many effective partnerships as possible between key individuals or departments within your firm or a client's firm. How have they managed to negotiate their differences? How have they been able to build enough trust to not question each other's motives, compete, or hold grudges for the times they disappoint each other? What roles have accountability and forgiveness played in the relationship?

3. What could be done to introduce tough love into the ongoing feuds you identified in question 1? How might the notion of reconciliation be received? What unforeseen consequences of guilt and blame might motivate those involved to consider reconciliation as a more productive, and far more gratifying, choice than remaining at war?

Part Three

The Partners and the Partnership

"A man, to be greatly good, must put himself in the place of another and of many others; the pains and pleasures of his species must become his own."

—Shelley

Up to this point, we have focused nearly exclusively on the consultant's contribution to the relationship with the client. Now we broaden our attention to the other half of the relationship, the client. In Chapter 5, we explore those characteristics we believe comprise, if you will, a "client of choice," focusing on those behaviors that make for a good client and that contribute to a productive partnership. As with good consultants, we believe good clients are made, not born. As such, part of the consultant's job in the relationship is not only to manage her own behavior, but, in some measure, to help shape those client behaviors that will make the client a productive member of the partnership. We have observed five characteristics in those clients tasked by the organization to lead a large, complex initiative that either enabled their success or, when underdeveloped or overextended, disabled it. They are a results orientation, intellectual curiosity, optimism, self-confidence, and ambition.

In Chapter 6, we look at the intersection of the client-consultant relationship, at the attributes that apply to both members of the partnership. These attributes are equality, advocacy, respect, trustworthiness, and hope. They form the glue that helps bond a value-creating consultant with a client of choice. They are not mere by-products of either the client's or the consultant's functioning. Rather, they are additional requirements that can ensure the partnership is sustainable and productive. If each member of the partnership does a superb job in his or her respective roles, it still doesn't ensure that the relationship will produce optimal value. Both partners must do a superb job both in their respective roles *and in the relationship* before optimal value can be achieved. As such, we felt it was important to explicitly look at those behaviors that are required of both members of the partnership in addition to their distinctive roles.

Part Three concludes with Chapter 7, where we look at those professionals inside the organization on whom external consultants must often depend. For the purposes of this book, we will call them "internal consultants," those staff professionals whose specialized expertise contributes to the client's overall aspirations. We will also discuss the often tenuous relationship between internal and external consultants, which, if managed poorly, can result in an unproductive, competitive, and hostile dynamic, derailed initiatives, and ruined engagements.

Profile of the Client of Choice

"Like an earring of gold and an ornament of fine gold is a wise reprover to a listening ear."

—King Solomon

Clients are a funny breed. They come in all shapes and sizes. Some are fun to work with, some insufferable. Some are flexible, some are rigid and moody. Some have a thick skin, others are especially temperamental and fragile. Some are smart and some, well, aren't. Whatever idiosyncrasies characterize our clients, we must never lose sight of two very important facts: First, we are obligated to our clients to deliver the help they rely on us for, and second, they put the food on our tables. Having a nice business card, fancy letterhead, a shingle outside your door that says "Consultant," a premier address, a published book or an Ivy League credential does not make one a consultant. Having paying, satisfied clients does.

Nonetheless, because we realize that not all clients are created equal, we thought it would be helpful to build a profile of those characteristics we have observed in clients in the successful engagements we studied, as well as those characteristics that consultants told us they wanted in their clients. The virtues of integrity and trustworthiness were blanket requirements and will be addressed in Chapter 6, because they must be exhibited by both partners. The consultant's wish list was lengthy and included such traits as a can-do attitude, flexibility, reliability, consistency, commitment, daring, open-mindedness, hard-working, participative, visionary, positive, confident, friendly, respectful, supported by others, politically savvy, intelligent, articulate, self-aware, adventurous, and so on. As we combined these traits with our observations of organizational leaders successfully leading complex initiatives with the support of consultants, we distilled the list down to five characteristics that seemed most consistent across both the consultants' wish list and our observations. They are:

- Results orientation
- Intellectual curiosity
- Optimism
- Self-confidence
- Ambition

This list is by no means exhaustive; rather it is a good starter set of characteristics you should look for in clients with whom you will likely enjoy a successful engagement. When any of these requirements are overextended or underdeveloped, the initiative and the relationship almost always suffer. We examined how the right amount, too much, or too little of each characteristic effects both the partnership with the consultant as well as the initiative at hand.

People who rise to positions of leadership usually do so, in large part, because of some strong personal attributes that set them apart from others who may be of equal technical competence. When faced with new challenges, a client's natural instincts are to rely heavily on her strengths (those unique capabilities that have earmarked past successes) while at the same time doing as much as possible to camouflage weaknesses (those personal limitations that have historically been thorns in the client's side). Frequently, these limitations are either underdeveloped capabilities that have gone unattended at the expense of playing up strengths, or they are strengths that have expanded into overdrive, thus exceeding their usefulness and becoming a liability. In the consultant-client partnership, they can be both constructive and destructive elements, and they can make or break the success of the outcomes being pursued. Let's see how.

Results Orientation: Get the Job Done Right and Fast

In its healthy state, results orientation drives clients to achieve the highest possible levels of performance. It provides constant focus on anticipated outcomes and motivates a sense of closure on decisions. Clearly, then, it is a critical attribute when pursuing any form of change.

One of the greatest challenges clients face when pursuing large-scale improvement in performance is the fact that while they are intently focused on the initiative, the rest of the organization, by necessity, must conduct business as usual. People in the organization on whom clients must depend to successfully implement the initiative are steeped in their own priorities and may also not be that particularly interested in change. Getting and keeping the attention of these key constituents can be exhausting for clients. A healthy level of results orientation will help them maintain the needed level of determination and perseverance in the face of such fragmented attention spans, multiple priorities, and organizational resistance. For the consultant, a client with the right amount of results orientation can sustain a brisk pace without lengthy interruptions or unnecessary distractions. Few things are more frustrating for consultants than the infamous phone calls received from clients the night before an important meeting, with the client suddenly announcing, "We need to cancel tomorrow's meeting—the people in manufacturing aren't convinced we need to move forward yet. I don't want to push them too hard. Let me work on them—I'll call you next week."

When overplayed, results orientation becomes an intolerance of ambiguity and a hunger for immediate gratification. This causes clients to make hasty decisions and rush past the need to wait, on occasion, for optimal solutions to fully emerge. During periods of complex change, uncertainty is a reality and pushing for closure too quickly can result in suboptimal decisions and incomplete solutions that only address symptoms. It also imbalances the consultant relationship in that it forces the consultant to take a distant back seat in important decisions. It can also promote collusion between the consultant and the client's staff who, burned out from a relentless pace and workload, are begging for mercy but are unable to garner their leader's patience and leniency. They turn to the consultant whom they hope can carry the message forward on their behalf. The consultant is now on the brink of stepping into some of the traps described in Part One, adopting bad habits such as collusion that may feel productive for the moment, but that will damage the initiative and relationship in the long run.

In one information technology firm, we watched a senior leader's impatience and drive for closure lead to excessive financial waste. The company was faced with numerous antiquated platforms that required upgrades or replacements to compete successfully in its current markets. Because it had ignored the need for so long, any viable solution introduced great complexity. No sooner did the organization head down one path, reorganizing the staff and allocating monies, when the leader's need for immediate gratification took over, his impatience becoming abusive as he abandoned one effort and started over with another. This continued for three years with little progress made toward bringing the technology up to current market standards. Eventually, his staff stopped taking him seriously, the consultants exchanged "knowing glances" with the staff when they recognized that an initiative-shift was imminent. The vicious cycle plunged into continuous turmoil. It is essential for clients who possess a strong results orientation to balance it with extra patience, to develop an increased comfort with ambiguity, and to plan meaningful pauses in their progress to ensure that they are not merely putting Band-Aids on situations requiring major surgery.

On the other hand, when clients lack a sufficient degree of results orientation, a different set of unfortunate consequences ensue. First, initiatives drag on indefinitely, often to a permanent state of incompletion. Unimportant distractions push back deadlines and those accountable for the initiative come to conclude their leader is not serious. As a consequence, they must feign progress and commitment to get by. If the client fails to demonstrate a results orientation early on, then the initiative will likely lose credibility within the organization and, subsequently, the needed support from important constituents. One consultant described her client to us:

> This guy can't seem to get anything done. No matter how small we cut up the milestones, he just doesn't seem to feel any sense of urgency about getting this thing finished. It's clear the rest of the organization has long stopped waiting for this project to end and has found other ways to solve the problems this guy was supposed to solve. Whenever he has to do a progress update at the

executive staff meeting, I watch others roll their eyes. I don't know what else to do to light a fire under him. And my biggest fear is that when someone finally holds a gun to his head, he'll point the finger at me as though I've dropped the ball.

In addition to the obvious ways a lack of results orientation can derail the initiative, it also has toxic effects on the consultant relationship. You can see that the consultant in the previous example is already feeling greater ownership for the project than her client. This is a dangerous place for the consultant to be, because it may foster an unhealthy dependency and continue to further numb the client's already desensitized sense of urgency. In addition, the consultant's fear of being blamed for the failure may move her to become defensive, making her concerned with her own image at the expense of her client's needs. Again, these are trends the consultant must resolutely guard against.

Something to Think About . . .

> How have you typically dealt with a client's results orientation? What might you do differently?

Intellectual Curiosity: See the Possibilities

The ability to imagine how things might be different than they are is at the core of the truly visionary client. The willingness to test tried-and-true methods in the hope of discovering ever-greater ways to satisfy customers, produce new products, and capture new markets is the heartbeat of real innovation and courageous risk taking. This attribute can be summed up as intellectual curiosity, the capacity to think about the current reality in several new versions. It is here that a picture forms in the mind of the client as she embarks on the path of change. This can be an invigorating characteristic to have in a client. First, it lends a sense of adventure to the initiative, and it opens up possibilities to push beyond the boundaries of convention. It also provides a greater opportunity for the initiative to deliver optimal outcomes rather than "more of the same, only different." It also helps the consultant maintain her focus on providing the knowledge and insight necessary to translate the vision into concrete actions to be taken with the client.

Unfortunately, what often happens to a client who has a strong bent toward intellectual curiosity is that she becomes overly enamored with the process of experimentation and gets caught up in change simply for the sake of change, with no clear purpose. Multiple initiatives get launched in the organization and curiosity becomes a near obsession, resulting in an indiscriminate unraveling of processes and systems that were actually fine to begin with. Corporate America is littered with painful stories of organizations that began meaningful work applying technologies such as reengineering, TQM, and Six-Sigma. They got swept up in the ideals and potential such technologies represented and launched indiscriminate applications of them all over the organization, often losing sight of the original intent. Never was the old adage more true, "If you give someone a hammer, then everywhere they look they see nails."

The intellectually curious client, gifted in imagining many possible alternatives to what currently exists, must ground herself, putting boundaries around the changes she embarks on and establishing a team to keep the changes on track toward a clearly defined goal. The danger to the consultant relationship is that, if the consultant has any mercenary tendencies at all, they will surely flare up at the opportunity to take on every possible project the client can drum up. Taking a dramatic departure from the initial aspirations of the initiative, the consultant is now engrossed in keeping all the balls in the air rather than achieving the results defined at the outset. Extreme mercenaries will recognize their client's itch to experiment, smell the blood, and eagerly propose lofty, expansive projects that allege to have far-reaching impact. When exorbitant resources have been wasted, the relationship is almost guaranteed to turn hostile and bitter.

In one small consumer-electronics manufacturing company, the COO was charged with ambitious growth objectives. Chomping at the bit to get rolling, he hired a large consulting firm to help size up all the potential market opportunities that could be pursued and to identify each of the organizational adjustments that would be required to successfully go after these opportunities. When the research was done, the consulting firm served up eleven options the organization could choose from to pursue growth. Some were discrete and included new products and customers; some could work in tandem with others and included product extensions and broadening existing customer bases. Each of the eleven options was accompanied by a series of large initiatives that would install the needed technology, systems, structures, and staff to make the option viable, along with the suggested time frames to implement each one. To the consulting firm's credit, it recommended that the client choose just one or two of the options and the corresponding initiatives to start with and, once results were tangible, revisit the remaining options. The COO agreed. Within weeks after starting, he was asking the consulting firm about the other options, wanting to "begin thinking about" when to start them. Before long, he had expanded the scope of the work to include what amounted to eight of the eleven options and nearly all of the accompanying initiatives. The consulting firm, tired of cautioning him to keep the boundaries of the work tighter, concluded that since failure was inevitable anyway, it may as well enjoy the revenue stream while it could. The organization quickly reached a state of future shock, the point at which change came too fast to productively assimilate. The board of directors intervened because too many capital expenditures were being requested simultaneously, and eventually the scope of the work was significantly scaled back and given to a new leader to oversee. The consulting firm was kept on, giving the "we tried to stop him" speech to the new leader.

In cases where intellectual curiosity is limited, clients tend to drum up only minor modifications to existing issues and, at best, variations on a theme of one or two well-bounded ideas. This can make the consultant's job very difficult. In the absence of an inspiring picture to paint for the organization, the consultant often winds up in the position of creating a vision for the client. Unable to truly embrace the vision, the client must continuously be propped up to sound credible and compelling. What usually comes out of such a client's mouth is a diffuse picture of a vaguely nice-sounding future. Ultimately, the minor modifications originally suggested by the client are what actually get done. Intellectually uncurious clients are also commonly inflexible in their view of the world and their approach to work. They are comfortable with established routine and uncomfortable with the notion of deviating from it. Consultants, in their zeal to push the envelope, come across as dogmatic and pushy to such clients. Eventually, the client becomes unable to tolerate the prodding of the consultant and the relationship ends in mutual frustration.

Something to Think About . . .

How have you typically dealt with your client's intellectual curiosity? What might you do differently?

Optimism: The Future Is Bright

Maintaining a hopeful, positive perspective during risky change efforts is essential. It is important for clients to believe that life will be better despite the turmoil and stress of change in order to help instill that belief in others. Surely, amid an uncertain future, no one would enthusiastically follow a leader who painted a picture of dismal gloom expressed through cynicism and pessimism. Clients who arc optimistic about the potential outcomes of the initiatives on which they embark spread a contagious energy throughout the organization that builds commitment and determination among the workforce. It also helps the consultant to know that in the face of difficult and distressing data, the client won't cave in from despair. Clients who have learned to identify possibilities in problems make a consultant's job much easier when it comes to steering through seemingly perilous circumstances.

However, playing optimism to an extreme actually results in the client losing credibility because she is seen as "too much of a cheerleader" and naive about the obstacles that might impede progress. Extremely optimistic people tend to believe the best of others' intentions, so the notion of people resisting change on purpose is inconceivable to them. They can't imagine others not wanting to participate. Because of a "glass half full" attitude, they often minimize or dismiss the potential of barriers to change. Even when given legitimate problems, these clients turn to the "do whatever it takes" response, depleting resources and frustrating people who simply want their concerns heard. Blind naivete actually winds up infecting the workforce with doubt and cynicism because people conclude this leader is out of touch with reality. The very conditions this attribute seeks to eliminate—despair and cynicism—may come about if optimism is carried to an extreme. At best, the client stirs up hype that appears to be genuine commitment, but is actually only superficial energy and bandwagonism. The consultant may then be put into the position of being the prophet of doom, continuously pointing out the potential fatal traps into which the client is headed. Falling on deaf ears, these gloomy forecasts get the consultant pigeonholed as an impediment to, rather than an enabler of, progress.

A woman spearheading the implementation of a new performance management process in an advertising agency fell victim to her own naive optimism. She was so passionate about the need for such a process that she was oblivious to the rest of the organization's indifference to and mockery of her work. Her excitement seemed to escalate as those around her grew more unreceptive. However, she would do such things as tell people in the art department how enthusiastic others in the organization were about the process, obtusely assuming they wouldn't validate the claim. She interpreted people's tolerance of her twenty-minute staff meeting presentations as enthusiasm. Not realizing the implications of introducing such a process in a creative organization averse to structured approaches to anything, she forged ahead, confident she could win them over. While she may have converted a few people in the organization into believers, the project ultimately died under its own weight. The consultants working alongside her tried to get her attention, asking her to consider a different interpretation to the responses she was seeing. Not only were they unsuccessful, they too were seen as out of touch and were unable to gain support for additional work they'd hoped to do in other parts of the organization. Overly optimistic clients must build in reality checks throughout their initiatives. They must go out of their way to confront resistance and identify roadblocks. They must temper their "pep talk" instincts with realistic discussion of the challenges, mistakes, and risks associated with the initiative. This helps ensure clearer judgment in their decision making and helps maintain their credibility with those who are affected by and, ultimately, must live with the work.

In situations where the client is the grim reaper, exhaling a death cloud over a potential new initiative, the serious attention of others is unattainable. The client's ability to effect change will be limited by excessive pessimism. Consultants will either not welcome the work, or will choose not to continue the relationship once the client's toxic disposition is seen for what it is. This happened to a member of one client's staff. She was notorious for always having the doomsday point of view on any issue. It got to the point where even potentially useful insights were dismissed by her colleagues, having been labeled with "the Eeyore factor." Nonetheless, consultants who find themselves working with such clients should either quickly confront the behavior and its effect on the work or find a way to gracefully exit the relationship.

Something to Think About . . .

How have you typically dealt with your client's optimism? What might you do differently?

Self-Confidence: I Can Do This

Having a belief in one's self, one's ideas, and one's decisions is vital when attempting to launch a new initiative. Clients must believe they have the ability to influence their organization in a positive way. Anyone who has ever occupied a leadership role knows it can be a lonely one. Self-doubt and second-guessing only compound such feelings of loneliness. Large, complex initiatives often require difficult decisions that can be unpopular when implemented, inviting the scorn of others and the isolation that comes to clients who make tough calls. Confident clients are able to withstand the feelings of alienation and rejection that accompany such decisions. Without confidence, these clients would cave in to the pressures from others to leave things as they are or to shape the change in a way that is convenient or advantageous to them. Clients with a healthy level of confidence are able to gauge more accurately if they are pushing their organization too hard or not enough. They know when to stand up for their convictions in the face of resistance, and they are confident enough to admit when their judgment has been misguided. For consultants to such clients, it means being able to provide just the right levels of nudging and pausing that the client needs. It also means the consultant doesn't have to worry that the client is going to crumble at the first sign of trouble, so the consultant can be direct and straightforward about issues that need discussion.

Unfortunately, if a client's confidence grows beyond what is appropriate, she winds up believing she can influence people or circumstances she in fact cannot. She begins to believe she is impervious to errors in judgment. She gets further and further away from a healthy sense of caution, concluding that if success has mounted thus far, how could she ever fail? The danger here is that as the client conveys this sense of being impervious, people will tire of trying to convince her otherwise, leaving her to her own demise. Her attempts to influence people and circumstances wind up offending and alienating those essential to success.

A division president of a smaller business unit in a wholesale food manufacturing company was promoted to run the company's largest business unit. Known for his cowboy leadership style and acknowledged for his great success in growing the small manufacturing unit, he was confidently viewed by top executives as someone who would be equally successful in this service arm of the company. He was equally confident. However, this business was dramatically different from the one he'd come from, providing services versus manufactured products, and generating three times the revenue with a workforce twice the size. Discounting these major differences, he began to embark on the same growth strategy he'd employed in his previous assignment, ignoring the foreboding of the senior executives who reported to him. Despite their caution and disregarding the fact that they ran the operating units of the business, he proceeded to restructure the company to resemble that of his former business unit, still sure that the transplanted business model would yield similar results despite significant marketplace differences. The more his senior staff members pushed back, the more he excluded them from decisions. Early indications are that, at best, the strategy will produce small to moderate growth in one area while having little or no impact on the majority of the business unit. He has gone through three sets of consultants, each of whom has tried to point out the potential pitfalls of his approach. Consultants to such clients risk being put into the position of rubber stamping a strategy so the client can say to resistors, "Even the experts agree."

Confident clients must guard against overconfidence by continually including others in their decisions and listening closely to messages of caution or warning. These clients should also regularly test their assumptions about their effectiveness and the progress of the initiative with a variety of people, especially those who seem most cautious. They must strike a balance between neither second-guessing themselves nor ignoring potential flaws in their thinking or shortcomings in their ability to influence.

When clients suffer from low levels of self-confidence, the initiative and the consultant relationship are surely at risk. In one financial services firm, a promising young woman, very bright and viewed as having high potential, was tormented by a lack of self-confidence. She second-guessed her decisions, constantly worrying what others thought of her. She questioned whether the organization would recant on her proposed career path if it found out she was so insecure. She was given a project to lead as a stretch assignment to help develop her leadership ability. Sadly, her incessant doubt led to her worst fear—others doubting her ability. Unable to implement any of her brilliant plans, the project was passed on to another manager. Despite numerous attempts to reassure her, her teammates and the consultants working with her were unable to build her confidence level. Consultants who recognize their clients' limited self-confidence would do well to have candid discussions with them about the potential liability such a limitation poses. They should discuss options for addressing the issue, delaying the project until the client is confident enough to handle it or passing the leadership role onto someone better suited for the job.

Something to Think About . . .

How have you typically dealt with your client's self-confidence? What might you do differently?

Ambition: The Drive to Succeed

Successful clients have a sense of drive. They are self-propelled toward goals and are not easily swayed from their task. Given the enormous difficulty surrounding any change effort, ambition is an important attribute when faced with what appear to be insurmountable obstacles. Clients who need a great deal of external stimuli to motivate them to overcome challenging circumstances do not typically succeed when leading major initiatives. Effective clients can draw their energy from within and maintain their drive despite the lack of external encouragement. A healthy dose of ambition fuels a client's tenacity to "take the hill" when approaching difficult initiatives or circumstances that might otherwise be intimidating. The client is able to maintain simultaneous views of the personal as well as the organizational benefits the initiative will reap. It is important that the client have some clearly established incentives to replenish her ambition—rewards she will personally gain as well as rewards others will gain. This enables the consultant to help the client stay focused on the initiative should distractions begin to draw her attention away.

Ambition becomes precarious when the client's attention is captivated by the potential personal rather than organizational benefits of a successful initiative. Judgment becomes severely impaired and the client takes on an almost Don Quixote attitude of pompous heroism. She develops a sense of entitlement, looking for the rewards to her career as a result of her work. Once the ego has tasted the delight of increased power and recognition, its appetite for more can become insatiable. The client becomes overly directive and curt, being experienced as abrasive. She becomes less interested in the change initiative itself and pursues ways to broadcast its impact, depicting herself as the pivotal nucleus of success. She may even take credit for the work of others. The consultant then becomes nothing more than another source of leverage for the client's selfish gain, kept in the background, merely to feed the client the lines to make her look brilliant. Any suggestion from the consultant that the initiative is failing, support is fading, or delays are possible are met with hostility and threats. The consultant is therefore forced to spare no expense or resource to meet the client's demands or risk severe vengeance at the notion of ending the relationship. Consultants who recognize the potential for extreme ambition in their clients should be wary of the possible pitfalls the relationship may experience.

In a *BusinessWeek* (April 1991) cover story, "CEO Disease," John Byrne and William Symonds tell tales of horror of five CEOs whose gargantuan ambition led to the demise of their careers and, in some cases, to the destruction of the organization. They write:

> Many chief executives come to believe they are much more than [mortal]. The perquisites and deferences create a protective cocoon . . . "they view the company as their own," says former Westinghouse CEO Douglas Danforth. . . . Some people's personalities change completely. If you're not careful, you can be seduced. It is almost axiomatic that those who rise or raid their way to the top of large corporations are intensely driven. That's not bad in itself. But trouble can arise when this drive is fueled by what Harvard Business School professor Abraham Zaleznik calls, "unhealthy narcissism . . . they are striving to satisfy inner, ego-related needs." Harry Levinson, a corporate psychologist says, "They think they have the right to be condescending and contemptuous to people who serve them . . . they think they are entitled to privilege and the royal treatment."

One consultant lamented about an experience he had with an overly ambitious client:

> I've never seen so much ego in one person. This guy was out for the top spot and nothing was going to stop him. It didn't matter who he had to hurt, eliminate, or what he

had to do. If it made him successful, or made him look successful, he'd do it. In fact, he would out and out ask us, "What's this going to do for my career?" when referring to aspects of our proposal. And if we even hinted that something he wanted done wasn't possible, he'd lob a veiled threat at us, "Well, maybe I should invite another firm to bid." Cutthroat, this man was appropriately feared in the organization, and anyone politically savvy enough to win him over could punch their career ticket for life. We could have milked that revenue stream for years if we didn't care about what it would do to our reputation. But after a while, working with him became almost prostitutional, and we could no longer tolerate being asked to compromise the integrity of our work and our principles. I heard he's now one step away from the chairman's office. I wonder how he'll take him out.

Ambitious leaders must force themselves to learn to manage success in bite-size chunks. They must become very aware of how their ego is absorbing increased recognition and influence, and watch out for the subtle, gradual increase in the desire for more. They must go out of their way to include others in recognition and even exclude themselves in order to spotlight the hard work of those less likely to get organization-wide acknowledgment and appreciation.

Clients who have a minimal degree of ambition tend to be easily discouraged by difficult obstacles that surface during the initiative. They may also be motivated by factors other than the tangible or intangible rewards the initiative may bring. For instance, a client who is not driven to advance his career may not be all that motivated to succeed leading an initiative whose success may give rise to a promotion. Insufficient ambition may lead to a client adopting a "just get it finished" attitude toward a complex initiative. The path of least resistance will be very attractive to such a client as well. The consultant is then forced to act in a quality control manner, trying to prevent short-term thinking from rendering the results unsustainable. When the consultant starts to care more about the quality of the results than the client, the relationship is imbalanced, and the client inappropriately relies on the consultant for motivation and incentive.

Something to Think About . . .

How have you typically dealt with your client's ambition? What might you do differently?

Gratification and Regratification: Helping Clients Turn Liabilities Into Assets

If writing this book has taught us anything, it has taught us that the old cliché, "You can't teach an old dog new tricks" is, in many ways, dumb. While it is certainly true that well-grooved habits developed over time are hard to break, it is by no means impossible and definitely worth trying! Each of the client attributes—results orientation, intellectual curiosity, optimism, self-confidence, and ambition—as well as its overextended or underdeveloped state, are behaviors serving some purpose in the life of its owner. If it weren't serving some purpose, meeting some need, a person wouldn't employ it. For example, overextending results orientation to satisfy a need for immediate gratification and ease an intolerance of ambiguity helps a client feel more in control. Excessive experimentation allows a client to feel productive and to experience a significant surge of accomplishment, regardless of the results. A naive dismissal of resistance and obstacles, or unrestrained optimism, allows a client to avoid rejection and maintain a blissful perspective of the world. Extreme self-confidence that creates a robust sense of imperviousness keeps a client from facing personal limitations that might be too overwhelming to confront. And aggressive, heroic ambition can potentially accelerate the advancement of a career and increase personal wealth.

What's important to recognize is that each of these needs is legitimate and, for the most part, we all have them. It's perfectly reasonable to want to feel more in control and productive, not to feel rejected or inadequate, and to desire career advancement. What is not reasonable is to adopt a set of behaviors that will not only fail to meet this need, but at the same time, potentially hurt others, not to mention one's self. The challenge is to pause long enough to separate the need from the behavior chosen (consciously or unconsciously) to meet the need. The crucial question then becomes, "Is this behavior the only way to meet this need or could I learn to meet it in a different way that eliminates the negative consequences this behavior produces?"

Finding the answer to this question is what we refer to as regratification. It is the process of learning to be gratified by a different behavior to meet the same need. How many times have you heard new fathers admit that they learned to love playing with their children at night instead of working late? Their need for significance, previously found in the productivity of work, is now found in fatherhood. And once they figure out that playing with a toddler doesn't have to have a "measurable outcome," it actually becomes fun! In the extreme forms, people who were once chemically dependent have learned to find their identities in healthy, productive activities so that the once-addictive behaviors lost their charm. Clients who have gratified their need for power by clenching it with tight reins can now gratify that same need by giving power freely to others, recognizing that power is an expandable pie—the more you give, the more you get (see Figure 5-1 for an example of regratification). So, for example, the client who desires to minimize ambiguity, have immediate gratification, and feel more in control through excessive results orientation may learn to meet this need by ensuring that he has quicker access to information, establishing more milestones within the initiative, and spending more time with key people in the initiative to get more frequent updates on progress. (Of course, it is essential he do so without driving his key people nuts.) The overly naive client will actually see optimism spread in the organization by holding balanced discussions about all that is going well, including obstacles that may be getting in the way. Accentuating the positive aspects of the initiative will have greater credibility when honestly discussed in light of remaining challenges. Keeping the boundaries of the initiative well controlled will actually help the highly curious client feel more productive because results actually get accomplished rather than spawning a legion of initiatives that may feel productive but accomplish very little. Again, the issue is to separate the need from the behavior,

Figure 5-1. Example of gratification and regratification: the need for control.

	The Need →	The Behaviors →	The Needs Met →	The Unintended → Consequences	The Outcome
Gratification	Control	• Over-scrutinizing/monitoring • Micro-managing • Excessively controlling decision making and resources • Withholding or filtering information	• Sense of personal power remains intact • Circumstances *seem* under one's own control	• Make others feel less capable; stunt their growth • Own flawed assumptions become blinders • Others withdraw support, feeling resentment, distrusted, and intruded upon • Performance declines	Loss of Control
Regratification	Control	• Delegating authority with mutually-agreed upon milestones and checkpoints • Using MIS and other reliable means to get performance updates • Sharing decisions about resource allocation	• Sense of personal power remains intact • Circumstances are *actually* under control—flawed assumptions are surfaced and addressed	• Others become more capable • Others volunteer greater levels of support, feeling trusted and respected • Performance exceeds expected levels	Maintain shared control

and then to identify more productive behaviors that can still meet the need while having a positive effect on others, and on the initiative.

In the case where the client has an insufficient degree of the characteristic, the process is slightly different. Building capability is a different challenge from moderating existing capability. A client who lacks results orientation may simply enjoy a very methodical and slower-paced approach to work, or in fact may severely procrastinate. The intellectually uncurious client may never have experienced her latent creative side and simply need the nudge to do so, or she may in fact be very narrow-minded and rigid. The degree to which the client lacks a certain capability will determine the actions to be taken.

Whether having too much or too little, the wise consultant of choice will work alongside her client to figure out how best to adjust the current level of capability to meet the needs of the initiative. The process of regratification begins by helping a client create a place in her mind where two things happen:

- The client recognizes that while a particular behavior may be meeting a specific need, it also may be causing undesirable consequences for others and for the initiative.
- The client must believe that it is possible to learn a whole new behavior, trusting that her need for gratification will still be met, even if not via a tried-and-true familiar behavior.

Figure 5-2 outlines the right balance of characteristics to look for in a client of choice. At the end of this chapter, we include a tool to help you analyze your clients' current capability levels with respect to each of the five "client of choice" characteristics. It is meant as a tool to help you form some initial thoughts on what might be done to adjust those characteristics of your clients that need to come down a notch or need a nudge to come out more.

Choose Wisely

As we mentioned earlier, not all clients are created equal. Even with the best of intentions, consultants can be seduced into unproduc-

(text continues on page 160)

Figure 5-2. Profile of a client of choice.

Client Characteristic	Right Amount		Too Much		Too Little	
	Helps Client-Consultant Relationship	Helps Initiative	Burdens Client-Consultant Relationship	Risks to Initiative	Burdens Client-Consultant Relationship	Risks to Initiative
Results Orientation	• Facilitates closure on decisions. • Minimizes unnecessary distractions.	• Sustains pace and productivity. • Desired outcomes remain priority. • Secures attention of key constituents.	• Promotes collusion between consultant and client staff. • Distances consultant from important decisions.	• Suboptimal solutions adopted. • Organizational burnout occurs.	• Creates dependency. • Puts consultant on the defensive to avoid blame.	• Work drags on indefinitely. • Legitimacy of project loses credibility.
Intellectual Curiosity	• Allows consultant to stay focused on translating vision into recommended actions.	• Creates sense of adventure. • Yields most innovative solutions.	• Promotes mercenary behavior. • Shifts consultant's focus from results to juggling many projects.	• Unnecessary and expansive broadening of scope occurs. • Resources are wasted.	• Must prop up client to appear visionary. • Mutual frustration from excessive debate over degree of needed change.	• Minor, incremental change achieved. • Organization becomes jaded, feeling it is running in place.

Optimism	• Consultant can help navigate directly through difficulties.	• Energizes organization. • Sustains persistence and commitment.	• Consultant is seen as prophet of doom. • Client's loss of credibility makes consultant guilty by association.	• Cynicism impairs momentum as the client is seen as "out of touch." • Bandwagonism replaces commitment.	• "Eeyore factor" makes relationship unappealing to consultant.	• Short-lived organizational commitment. • Negativity spreads.
Self-Confidence	• Consultant can be direct and straightforward with tough issues. • Consultant has more accurate sense of when to push or pause.	• Better able to gauge appropriate pace and timing of implementation. • More effective in resistance management.	• Consultant is used as "rubber stamp" to validate client's decisions.	• Errors in judgment and flawed assumptions lead to bad decisions. • Arrogance alienates key constituents.	• Lack of confidence consumes focus of work and energies. • Both partners suffer loss of credibility.	• Disruption of progress as leadership is transferred to others. • Organization loses confidence in the viability of solutions.
Ambition	• Consultant has a "hook" to keep client focused.	• Maintains tenacity when things get tough. • Momentum sustained as "carrots" to client and organization are seen.	• Consultant becomes pawn in client's pursuit of personal gain. • Hostility emerges.	• Client's self-serving behavior attracts organizational resentment and withdrawn support.	• Consultant becomes source of quality control.	• Path of least resistance leads to short-term solutions. • Organization support is hard to sustain.

tive bad habits because of the ineffective behavior of poorly chosen clients. Don't get lured into believing that the signals you get in the first days of contact with the client, which indicate the presence of some of these overextended or underdeveloped characteristics, will just "go away" or "work themselves out" as the relationship progresses. They won't. Don't get seduced by potentially large revenue opportunities that lead you to minimize the potential destructive influences such behaviors can have. A relationship with such a client may wind up costing you more than you profit from the engagement. Choose wisely. Longer-term relationships with effective clients will be far more beneficial than bouncing from one bad client to another.

Before we turn our attention to those characteristics that must appear at the center of the client-consultant relationship, those elements that build a genuine partnership between the two, we recommend that you assess your clients using the tool provided in Figure 5-3. It offers a chance to better understand your clients' capabilities with respect to each of the attributes discussed in this chapter.

Figure 5-3. Making the connection: assessing your client's capabilities.

Use the following scales to determine where your client is in respect to each of the five client-of-choice characteristics. For instances where your client has too much or too little, use the "Plan for Adjustment" section to determine how you can best encourage and assist your client with his or her development.

If your relationship with the client is particularly strong, you may want to have him or her use this tool separately as a self-assessment, and then compare your responses as a way to begin the conversation, or you can complete it together.

1. RESULTS ORIENTATION

Too Little	Right Amount	Too Much
• Decisions and progress drag on indefinitely • Easily distracted by unimportant issues • Frequently changes priorities	• Reaches closure on decisions • Remains focused on desired outcomes • Helps key constituents maintain attention and commitment	• Intolerance of ambiguity • Hasty decision making • Advocates suboptimal solutions • Causes burnout for others

Plan for Adjustment

1. What need do you suspect your client may be trying to meet with this behavior?

2. How can you help your client recognize the unintended consequences of this behavior?

3. What recommendations can you make to help your client develop new behavior to meet this need?

Recommended Development Activities:

(continues)

Figure 5-3. *(continued)*

---

2. INTELLECTUAL CURIOSITY

Too Little	Right Amount	Too Much

Too Little	Right Amount	Too Much
• Inflexible thinking • Uninspiring leadership • Rigid approach to work; comfortable with established routine	• Generates imaginative and novel ideas • Open to possibilities and challenging the status quo • Leads others to push the boundaries of convention • Able to spot patterns and trends inside and outside the organization	• Initiates change for change's sake • Launches rampant and indiscriminate change efforts • Diffuse focus • Wastes resources

Plan for Adjustment

1. What need do you suspect your client may be trying to meet with this behavior?

2. How can you help your client recognize the unintended consequences of this behavior?

3. What recommendations can you make to help your client develop new behavior to meet this need?

Recommended Development Activities:

3. OPTIMISM

Too Little	Right Amount	Too Much
• "Eeyore factor"–sees negative aspects of every issue; glass is always "half empty" • Deenergizes others with excessive criticism and negativity	• Stays hopeful and positive in the face of adverse circumstances • Energizes others with a "glass half full" attitude • Can separate the good from the bad and see both objectively	• Naivete about resistance and obstacles to change • Out of touch with others' needs and frustrations; can't hear "voice of reality" • Dismisses/ignores concerns • Superficial cheerleading seen as manipulative

Plan for Adjustment

1. What need do you suspect your client may be trying to meet with this behavior?

2. How can you help your client recognize the unintended consequences of this behavior?

3. What recommendations can you make to help your client develop new behavior to meet this need?

Recommended Development Activities:

(continues)

Figure 5-3. *(continued)*

4. SELF-CONFIDENCE

Too Little	Right Amount	Too Much

Too Little	Right Amount	Too Much
• Second-guessing decisions • Self-doubt attracts the doubt of others • Excessive concern over others' opinions and judgments • Overpersonalizes criticism and resistance	• Sense of self-assurance in own ideas and decisions • Belief in own ability to influence positive change • Can make unpopular decisions without recoiling • Asks for feedback; tests own assumptions	• Intractable when others disagree • Behaves as though infallible • Gets brazen and reckless when influencing others

Plan for Adjustment

1. What need do you suspect your client may be trying to meet with this behavior?

2. How can you help your client recognize the unintended consequences of this behavior?

3. What recommendations can you make to help your client develop new behavior to meet this need?

Recommended Development Activities:

5. AMBITION

Too Little	Right Amount	Too Much

Too Little	Right Amount	Too Much
• Easily discouraged by challenging obstacles • Comfortable with easiest solutions; takes path of least resistance • Sense of urgency not apparent	• Healthy level of inner drive • Perseveres in the face of tough circumstances • Tenacious • Can maintain dual focus on personal and organizational rewards	• Self-serving; overly opportunistic when managing career • Takes credit for others' work • Becomes overly directive and curt, sometimes vindictive, when others deviate from instructions or jeopardize rewards

Plan for Adjustment

1. What need do you suspect your client may be trying to meet with this behavior?

2. How can you help your client recognize the unintended consequences of this behavior?

3. What recommendations can you make to help your client develop new behavior to meet this need?

Recommended Development Activities:

⑥

Developing a Down to EARTH Partnership

"There is neither East nor West, Border, nor Breed, nor Birth, When two strong men stand face to face, though they come From the ends of the earth."

—Rudyard Kipling

The success of an engagement relies heavily on the relationship that develops between the client and consultant, a relationship we believe is most effective when it takes the form of a genuine partnership. It is in the context of the client-consultant interactions that the true value of an engagement comes into being. But achieving a genuine partnership is easier said than done. It begins to develop during the first encounter and, like a good marriage, continues to be worked on over time.

A genuine partnership has five primary traits: equality, advocacy, respect, trust, and hope. It is neither an accident nor a contrivance that these traits form the acronym for EARTH. Rather, it is a reflection of the characteristics that drive a successful partnership and an indication that these characteristics are genuine and down-to-earth, not pie-in-the-sky platitudes. In this chapter we look at each of the five characteristics from the perspective of the client and the consultant.

Equality

Equality begins with an equal commitment to the process, by both consultant and client, from problem definition through achievement of objectives. Too often consultants find themselves forging ahead full-steam only to discover that their client has veered off into a new interest or endeavor. When the consultant is demonstrating greater investment in the outcome than the client, he needs to step back and reassess the situation for himself and with the client.

Equality means the conversations and debates are engaged in by coequals. Each has the right and responsibility to present an opinion and debate differences. While the client has the right to make a final decision unilaterally, having the ultimate responsibility within the company, that decision should be based on maximum input and influence from the consultant.

The relationship is bound to go awry when either the consultant or the client pulls rank. It is not unusual for a consultant, once hired, to have her comments and suggestions ignored and to wonder why she was brought in. It is possible, in this circumstance, that the client was merely looking for a rubber stamp, a victim to blame, or a person to bring credibility to a project. Unbeknownst to the consultant, there was never an intention to genuinely partner in the initiative. This very situation happened to us when we were invited in to a financial company and engaged in an introductory conversation about our preferred mode of operating—namely, partnering. We briefly defined what we meant and were delighted when the client smiled and said that was exactly what he was looking for. We were extremely surprised, then, to learn that meetings on the initiative had been held (of which we were unaware), memos and letters had gone out, and people in the company were talking to us about things they assumed we knew but didn't. At some point, we brought these events to the attention of our client. "Oh," he said, "I really didn't think you needed to be there. We were doing just fine." We indicated that we were delighted things were going well, but we felt, in a partnership, that we should at least discuss where we did or did not belong. The response back to us was, "I'll call you when I need you." It became increasingly apparent that this client maintained a "pop up" view of partnering. Roughly, it translated to this: "I do my thing while the going's good and I call you in whenever I need external credibility or support for what it is I want to do." After we explained that that was not our understanding, nor did we work that way, we mutually parted ways.

Consultants also pull rank when they take the attitude, "I

know more than you, that's why you brought me in, now listen to me!" This can be particularly true of consultants with a messiah complex who can totally overwhelm a client. It is easy to recognize an overbearing consultant when you hear an excess of comments such as "What you need to do . . ." or "You've got to . . ." Consultants with earned doctorates or other impressive credentials can also be intimidating. They need to be particularly careful about maintaining balance in the relationship.

Equality implies symmetry, an even balance in the participation of consultant and client. While one of the pair might play more of a role than the other in a particular phase (e.g., the consultant during the planning, the client during implementation), there is always a consistent give and take among coequals.

Something to Think About . . .

Reflect on your most recent engagement and the relationship between you and the client. How did you evaluate equality?
If you sensed inequality, how did it manifest itself? How did you deal with it?

Advocacy

Every organization and every change initiative has resisters and naysayers pushing back on the client's desire to move forward, resenting the intrusion of a consultant. These negative forces are strong, so the consultant and client need to be advocates for one another, championing one another's ideas and buoying one another's spirits. Each needs to be a public voice for the other, supporting each other's ideas and efforts once decided upon, sometimes upward in the organization with senior executives, sometimes downward with employees, and sometimes outward to customers, suppliers, vendors or investors. The consultant should be an outspoken supporter of the client, on the lookout for opportunities to actively praise her work, bolster her credibility, enhance her reputation throughout the organization, and, when necessary, defend her position and intercede on her behalf. We were present at an off-site meeting of a division of a manufacturing firm that was struggling to sustain its recent efforts at quality management while introducing much-needed process changes. There was a lot going on, and the division manager was juggling several balls at once, trying to make changes in a union environment, keep morale up, and meet promised deadlines all at the same time. At the meeting, the manager's boss began to publicly berate him for failing to submit some paperwork that was due the day before. As quickly as we could, we took the boss aside and provided him with a perspective on what the manager was attempting, how much he had already accomplished, despite the complexities of his task, and how badly he needed and deserved his boss's support, particularly in front of his direct reports. After the break, the boss returned to the room and praised the group on its progress to date, noting especially the leadership of the manager in making it all come together. Outside of the meeting, he apologized to the manager for his poor timing and judgment, and again reiterated his appreciation of all the manager had done.

Sometimes being an advocate for the client means the consultant deflects attention and credit away from himself and places them on the client. Sometimes it means the consultant chooses to sit it out when his client has the chance to look good in front of important people. It doesn't mean adopting a posture of extreme deference or false humility. True partnership means not being consumed with opportunities to gratify one's own ego at the expense of opportunities to make the client look good. Once "on board," the consultant becomes partisan, endorsing the client's comments, applauding her efforts, and recommending her plans be followed. Disagreements are debated in private. Publicly, there is agreement and unity.

Similarly, having brought in the consultant, the client should protect her by endorsing her right to be there, express her opinions, debate the ideas of others, raise questions, and challenge assumptions. We have known clients who, when things turned bleak in their organization, threw the consultant to the wolves as a peace offering. We have also known consultants who have protected themselves and their careers in an organization by hanging the client out to dry, denigrating his capabilities and pointing the finger at him for failing to manage the project well.

In genuine partnerships, there is a commitment to actively support one another. Dissatisfaction along the way on the part of either the consultant or the client is openly discussed and handled professionally. If the problem cannot be resolved, there is agreement to sever the relationship. It is not dealt with through mutual sabotage.

Something to Think About . . .

> Reflect on your most recent engagement and the relationship between you and the client. Were you an advocate for your client? How did the client respond?
> What else might you have done to advocate for your client?

Respect

There is no partnership without respect. Respect underlies our ability to view one another as equals and to relate to one another nonjudgmentally. The lack of respect creates disequilibrium, which immediately negates the primary element of partnership—namely, equality. As such, it is a linchpin in the client-consultant relationship.

Respect must be earned over time. It is not given immediately or readily, but rather is based on the accumulation of evidence that convinces one partner that the other partner is worthy of respect. This suggests that the early days of the partnership arc tentative, watchful, even cautious on both sides. Although the consultant probably enters the organization with a positive reputation achieved elsewhere, she still needs to earn the respect of this particular client and this particular organization. In other words, consultants must continually "earn their stripes."

Each of us has our own standard by which we calibrate our readiness to respect another person and our own lens for the elements that must be present to award respect. Some of us focus on competence and respect partners for their intelligence or expertise. Others of us look for affiliation and appreciate personal loyalty. Still others respect hard work and pitching in wherever one is needed. Whatever the focus, each of us compiles a unique set of characteristics that must be in place before we accord respect to others. It is important that we be in touch with our lens and how it impacts our perceptions of others.

During an engagement at a university, there was an individual who was extremely thoughtful about his work, reflecting on what had transpired that day and laboriously planning what he wanted to attempt the next day. His interactions with others were low-key and his conversations somewhat academic and conceptual. He was the quintessential ivory-tower professor. It seemed as though he was moving at a snail's pace to effect change and that he didn't have the forceful energy needed to move a traditional, political organization forward. It came as a shock to find, several months down the road, that the conversations at faculty meetings had changed: People were more civil to one another, personal agendas appeared to be diminishing in favor of a common good, and changes were being approved as territorial considerations lessened. Suddenly aware that his style was working, our respect for him was boundless. Learning that many roads can lead to Rome has helped us to accelerate the process of awarding respect. It was a key moment for us to be caught in our own egocentric belief that our way was the best way, if not the only way. Respect comes in many guises.

Lack of respect for an individual can be one of the greatest unspoken barriers to collaboration in the workplace. One of our interviewees shared the fact that she never considered herself a good team player and actively disliked working in teams. "Every time I was on a team I became demoralized and angry. I felt people used me, that I carried more than my share of work and contributed more than my share of information, knowledge, or data to the project. I was always ticked off with my teammates and swore, if I could, I'd never go onto another team voluntarily. Then I got a chance to work with some really super people. They were smart, hard-working . . . my kind of people. I came to realize I'm a good team player, but I need to respect the people on the team." What lies behind much of the unproductive behavior in organizations can be explained by the lack of respect underlying people's interactions, but since people can't comfortably acknowledge this lack of respect, it becomes another elephant on the table, yet another undiscussable. Here's an example:

> Steve's client, Bill, was a nice enough guy, but in Steve's estimation he really wasn't capable of effecting the complex changes that needed to be made to turn his division around. He didn't respect either Bill's technical competence or his ability to get what was needed from the people in the unit. On the other hand, Bill's top aide, Mike, seemed to have everything needed to make the changes work.
>
> Rather than express his perceptions directly to Bill, Steve persuaded the kindly gentleman that his time could be better spent running the business and leaving the change to Mike. He stroked Bill's ego with tons of flattery regarding his excellent leadership of the division, then turned to Mike as his collaborator. The result was disastrous. People in the division liked Bill and perceived that Mike was making a power play to wrest control of the division away from Bill. So they resisted, blocked, and sabotaged all of Mike's efforts. The change effort went nowhere.
>
> We had occasion to talk with Steve about the engagement a year later and found him still dismayed at the failure. "I don't get it. It was a great idea for a change that was absolutely necessary and they had a terrific guy to lead it. I don't understand why they gave him such a hard time." We asked him if he had a chance to redo the engagement, would he do anything differently. All of his comments addressed specific aspects of the changes

(timing, resources, and strategy). Not once did he speak of his initial step of pushing Bill aside and putting Mike in his place. Finally, we asked Steve directly how he felt about that decision. He said, "I just didn't respect the guy. I still don't believe he had what was needed to do the job. He's a nice guy, but that doesn't cut it for me." No matter how long we debriefed the event, Steve never saw how his lack of respect for Bill's capabilities lay at the core of all that came after. In many organizations, people like Steve make decisions and act in ways to circumvent the people for whom they have no respect, therein sowing the seeds of their next problem. Even if Steve was correct in his evaluation of Bill's abilities, had he coached and supported Bill through the change, he might have succeeded. He could not have done worse.

To demonstrate respect, the consultant and client must be cognizant of each other's value system so that respect can be accorded as each likes to receive it. If, for example, I want to be respected for my intellect and wisdom, but my partner observes, comments upon, and praises my interactions with people, a skill I personally don't value strongly, I may not feel respected. I may hear his comments but not "interpret" them as respect. Similarly, if my lens focuses solely on my partner's intellect when she prides herself on her people skills, I may unintentionally fail to convey my respect for her in ways she can feel good about herself and her work.

Respect can be conveyed by dealing truthfully with one another, paying attention to each other's ideas, and actively listening to one another's thoughts and concerns. Respect is transmitted by verbal and nonverbal behavior . . . how individuals speak to one another, the kinds of questions and input they ask of each other, their tone of voice, their facial expression. All too often we've seen disrespect displayed when people silently roll their eyes when someone says something with which they disagree. Whether consultant and client agree with one another or not, each is deserving of the other's respect. Without respect, neither will have confidence in the other, nor will they trust one another.

Something to Think About . . .

Reflect on your most recent engagement and
the relationship between you and the client.
How did you accord respect to your partner?
How carefully did you assess what your client
would want to be respected for?
How did respecting or not respecting your client
impact your work?

Trust

Stephen Covey says, "Trust is the glue in life." It is arguably the
most desired value in an organization and the most difficult to
achieve. Attaining it has become even more problematic in today's
workplace. Cost-cutting strategies at many companies produced
waves of downsizing, which precipitated a major distrust of management. This was followed by a decade of mergers and acquisitions where companies, particularly those that were publicly
traded, were legally prevented from making information public
until final approvals were obtained from government or regulatory
agencies. The result was that workers obtained information
through the rumor mill. The impact has been devastating to workers who no longer believe anything they hear from anyone. It is in
this environment that the consultant and client must establish trust
in one another. It is not easy. It takes time for the individuals involved to get to know one another, observe each other's behaviors,
and become convinced that their partner will always behave in
ways that preserve the relationship.

Developing trust depends largely on our belief that we will
hear the whole, unvarnished truth from our partner, whether that
truth is good, bad, or indifferent. This is especially important in a
consulting relationship because it means the client can truly believe the consultant when he receives praise and not discount it as
mere flattery, knowing that it is genuine because he has also been
the recipient of hard hitting criticism. A client once said to us, "I
appreciate that compliment because I know you mean it. You guys

call it as you see it so I always know where I stand . . . even when it hurts!"

Developing trust also depends on our belief that our partner will behave in predictable ways, being consistent in word and deed. It's not only a case of "say what you mean," but also "mean what you say," even if it's unpleasant or unpopular. All of us "test" one another by watching for congruence or incongruence between what we say and what we do. Nothing kills trust faster than when our partners see behaviors that are inconsistent with what we espouse. There are too many examples of this in organizations, and workers at all levels have become distrustful. We hold people accountable on objective measures, then reward performance on subjective criteria. We downsize workers to cut costs, then award senior executives extravagant bonuses. There is good reason behind the fact that the most overused expression in management circles throughout the last two decades has been "walk the talk." Not to do so destroys credibility, which destroys trust.

Both consultant and client must see the other as credible, respect each other's integrity, and believe the other to be open and fair. These are high expectations and not easy to achieve. That is what makes trust so risky. If I trust you, it means I open myself up to sharing the innermost parts of myself with you. It means I allow you to see and know my fallibilities. Such self-disclosure makes me extraordinarily vulnerable. If I have been mistaken in my judgment of you, I can be terribly hurt. No matter how strong an ego the individual may have, everyone can feel the pain of misplaced trust.

The alternative is not acceptable, however. An effective consultant-client relationship requires unassailable trust. Once broken, it can never be repaired and the engagement will self-abort. Thus, being politically correct, having categories of undiscussable topics, monitoring what we say and do for fear of offending, dissembling, being duplicitous, maintaining the guise of trust while not trusting at all . . . all of this is debilitating, exhausting, and nonproductive in terms of establishing an effective partnership. Energies applied to protecting the self are drawn away from a focus on the business matters at hand. Simple candor, consistent behavior, and personal integrity are a lot simpler, less taxing, and more effective. Both parties to the relationship should monitor their own and their partner's behaviors: Are disagreements aired or do they suddenly disappear from the table? Is there a comfort level with critiquing one another's ideas? Are new issues raised in a timely, forthright manner?

Authenticity is an important part of establishing trust in a relationship. If either the consultant or client senses inauthenticity, it should be raised immediately and confronted head-on. While the candor and authenticity required to establish trust may create discomfort in some individuals, it is so critical to an effective partnership that the discomfort must be overcome no matter how difficult. As consultants, we will promise to be worthy of a client's trust. We will demonstrate integrity, reliability, and honesty . . . but we expect the same in return. Edward R. Morrow once wrote, "To be persuasive, we must be believable; to be believable, we must be credible; to be credible, we must be truthful."

Something to Think About . . .

Reflect on your most recent engagement and the relationship between you and the client. If you were standing in your client's shoes, would you trust you?
What in your behavior should your client see as trustworthy?
If you acted inauthentically, what was the effect?
How do you feel when you sense a client is being inauthentic with you?

Hope

Events in America, from Watergate to Whitewater, the fall of the Russian and Japanese markets, and worldwide racial and ethnic wars, all have created a degree of cynicism in the political and economic arenas that has not been seen in decades. Downsizing, insider-trading scandals, inequities in salaries between executives and workers, and fads that have gone nowhere have brought the cynicism into the American workplace. Workers' energies are funneled into unhealthy negativism; they view the organization in terms of failed third-quarter earnings, lost markets, and critiques of product packaging or brand naming. Suddenly "the land of opportunity" is facing a moral crisis that is leaving workers demoralized, suspicious, and loyal only to themselves. Their glass is perennially half empty. Hope of something better appears to have disappeared as people brace themselves for worse to come. Suddenly, people have lost confidence that the future holds something better for them.

Not only must consultants and clients struggle against the general cynicism pervasive in today's companies, they must also fight the wave of cynicism aimed at their own profession and the work they do. The many books and articles appearing in the past several years that bashed consultants have made their job more difficult. In this stressful environment, consultants and clients must serve as a support system for one another, bolstering one another's spirits when they flag, inspiring confidence in one another, and providing optimism about their efforts and their probability for success. Their relationship should be built on a strong belief in the future and in their ability to effect a productive outcome for the organization. There are numerous reasons to lose heart over the course of a change initiative: a sponsor moving on to another initiative and withdrawing support, losing necessary resources owing to corporate cost-cutting, inept managers incapable of implementing an intervention, political sabotage from unexpected quarters. The list could go on. In an effective partnership, each party supports the other during "down" times by providing alternative ways to navigate through the problem and helping to turn the situation around.

A couple of years ago we were working with the HR department of a financial services organization. The department had prepared a performance appraisal and career development program that was to go online in the morning. The ballyhoo surrounding the program meant everyone would anxiously turn on their computers when they arrived at work to see what the new system looked like. The only problem was that at midnight, the system was still not up and running correctly. The HR manager with responsibility for the project was beside herself with worry. She mentally envisioned her bonus and job going down the drain. Throughout that long night, we worked alongside her, encouraging her to keep up her spirits, helping out where we could and generally offering moral support to the troops. They knew we had no insider information to guarantee the project would be a success, but they nevertheless appreciated our being there and offering our support. By morning, the system was perfect and the HR manager, tremendously relieved, thanked us "for being there." Sometimes that's all it takes!

One way to raise the level of hope is to change one's lens, to begin to see the glass as half full, to look to solve problems rather than complain about them, to focus on the opportunities in the situation rather than the drawbacks, to see what can be gained rather than what might be lost. Along with changing one's lens, it helps to change one's language, to talk about opportunities rather than problems, to describe challenges rather than what makes you overwhelmed. This is not to suggest that the consultant or client should suddenly see the world through rose-colored glasses, but rather to suggest they should help one another to stay positive and optimistic, looking past the obstacles in a situation to the possibilities it presents. Michelangelo wrote, "The great danger for most of us is not that our aim is too high and we miss it, but that it is too low and we reach it." Too many people in organizations see only the difficulties and the reasons why things can't be done. They should take heed of Henry Ford's comment: "Whether you believe you will succeed or fail, you are right." He clearly understood that our outlook has a lot to do with how we create our world and how we deal with events in our lives. How we view the organization and how we interpret situations are within our control. We can decide how to react; it's our choice.

There are days every one of us has probably thought about giving up and throwing in the towel. What helps on those days are the friends who take us out of ourselves, who get us to physically or emotionally leave the situation until we are ready to take a new perspective and view the situation in a new light. It helps if the friend has the ability to provide alternative suggestions, but that isn't even always necessary. Sometimes just having a good listener and supportive ally is sufficient. That is a critical role consultants and clients must play for one another.

Something to Think About . . .

Reflect on your most recent engagement and the relationship between you and the client. How do you support your client with hope that the glass is half full?

How do you ensure that your own enthusiasm doesn't lead you to misread signals from the organization, resistance—that is, to misread resistance?

The EARTH Model

When a partnership is built on the traits represented by the EARTH model, the relationship is more likely to flow smoothly and to result in the desired sustainable outcomes. It is characterized by both partners' willingness to disagree and to challenge one another, an interaction not typical in most client-consultant relationships. More typical is having both parties acquiesce to one another's opinions, maintaining an artificial politeness or the opposite—staunchly defending their own position out of a need to prove themselves right.

In the effective partnerships we have observed, clients and consultants did not hesitate to challenge each other's assumptions or to push back on one another when either believed something in the relationship felt amiss. Much like the bantering of two long-term colleagues, neither consultant nor client appeared threatened by such behavior. To the contrary, they seemed more uncomfortable allowing something off-kilter in the relationship to remain unaddressed. Here is an example of the kind of dialogue you would expect to hear in a healthy partnership:

Client: Jack, I wasn't really comfortable with the way that meeting went. We ought to talk about it.

Consultant: I agree, Judy. It didn't feel good to me, either. Tell me what didn't work for you.

Client: Well, for one thing, we've always shared the spotlight in the past. Even though we never explicitly said so, I just thought it was understood that we were a team and had equal airtime. In that meeting, it kind of looked to me as if you were grandstanding because the head of the European division was in the room. You interrupted me a couple of times, and it just seemed so unlike all the other presentations we've done. What was the deal?

Consultant: I'm sorry that's how I came across. I certainly wasn't trying to hog the stage to overshadow you. But I won't try to deny the fact that I was very aware of his being in the room. Last week, in Phoenix, you talked so much about how you want to move this process into Europe, I guess I got a little overzealous. Sorry about that. Maybe we should have checked in with each other before the meeting to get on the same page. When did you find out he was going to be there?

Client: The day before yesterday. I meant to leave you a voice mail to give you the heads up, but yesterday was so crazy, I just forgot. I assume that what you're getting at is that it would have been helpful to you to know ahead of time? I'll own that one—I should have made sure you knew.

Consultant: You did seem a little on edge this morning when I got here. Were you nervous about him being here?

Client: Hell, yes. You know how much is riding on this.

Consultant: I don't know if anyone else picked up on it, but you did seem a little tense in the meeting. I don't know if you realize it, but at one point you gave him the numbers for South America when he asked for Asia . . .

Client: That's why you chimed in with the Asia stuff?

Consultant: Yeah. I was trying to be subtle about it, but I guess I did it more abruptly than I ought to have, but I just didn't want it to come back to bite us later. I got the feeling he's the kind of guy who'd check. Anyway, I'm sorry if you felt upstaged. What else do you think I could have done?

Client: Well, maybe you could have suggested a break, pulled me off to the side and let me know, and given me the chance to correct myself rather than doing it in front of everyone.

Consultant: You're right, I just didn't think of it at the time.

Client: And I'm sorry you felt blindsided by not knowing he was coming. Thanks for covering for me, in any case. At the end of the day, I think we walked away in a positive light. I just didn't want to leave any residue between us.

It is apparent that this client and consultant are capable of having an open discussion of an incident that made each of them uncomfortable and to do so in a way that was neither blaming nor defending. There was an acknowledgment of a problem and a genuine desire on the part of both the client and consultant to identify and resolve exactly what that problem was. For the client, Judy, to confront Jack with the sense that he was "grandstanding" and for Jack to acknowledge that he was, in fact, "overzealous" took courage for both parties. This ability to identify the underlying dynamic in the situation and then explore alternative ways in which it might have been handled epitomizes what a partnership is all about:

Equality:	It is apparent that these two individuals share an equal commitment to the success of the global endeavor.
Advocacy:	Jack realizes a need for greater advocacy with regard to Judy, particularly in public.
Respect:	The two avoid a blaming, attack mode—giving each other the benefit of the doubt.
Trust:	Each is willing to acknowledge his or her respective contributions to the situation.
Hope:	Both are hopeful that their mutual efforts will yield significant success despite the stakes at hand.

Using EARTH With the Client's Staff

In today's workplace, where workers see their job security eroded by technology downsizing, mergers and acquisitions, and outsourcing, consultants, with their seemingly insouciant lifestyle and reportedly huge fees, are greatly resented. Frequently all that staff members see are teams of consultants invading their workspace, bringing in yet another "fad du jour," and creating more work for them as they demand information and call for additional meetings. Already overburdened in a workplace in which the motto is "do more with less," staff members can feel used and abused by consultants.

To turn their perspective around, consultants need to apply the characteristics of the EARTH model to their relationship with the client's staff as well as to the client. Without the staff's support or commitment to the project, success will be unattainable, despite the fact that the one-on-one relationship between the consultant and the client is model-perfect. The client's staff must always be treated in a manner that conveys the message, "We are all in this together."

To get the staff on board, each member must be treated as an equal contributor to the project's success. To this end, the consultant must help individuals on staff see where they fit and what roles they can play. When they feel shut out by an exclusionary relationship between their boss and the consultant, they experience a sense of threat. At best, this worrisome state can divert energies away from the project; at worst, it can produce dysfunctional behavior. Staff members need to be engaged in supporting the initiative, not in competing with the consultant for their boss's time and attention. Enjoin the staff in the initiative, help them to see their importance and value to its success, and you will be surprised at the energy and enthusiasm they bring to the effort.

Advocate for their right to participate. Take the time to identify each person's strengths and ways to contribute to the project. Let your clients know how smart and capable you feel they are. In return, they will become your staunchest supporters.

Remember that everyone needs respect. If staff members are treated as second-class citizens or slave labor rather than as capable partners and important contributors in a collaborative effort, they will not support the initiative and, worse, may actively seek to sabotage it.

Let's try to imagine the consultant's job from the staff's perspective: Consultants enter the workplace, often in large numbers. They infiltrate the space making demands of already-busy people in order to meet their own needs. They attempt to implement something on behalf of the staff who, in most cases, have had no say in the discussions, and who have had their concerns ignored. Then the consultant leaves, having collected a large fee for having accomplished little or nothing, with no consequence or accountability. If this were your perspective, would you open your arms to consultants and readily place your trust in them? We know we wouldn't!

Unfortunately, most workers' experiences with consultants have left them leery as to the value of these "predators." Their cynicism will be hard to overcome, but consultants must work to do just that. As with respect, a project will have little chance of success unless the staff trusts the consultants sufficiently to join them in the effort. Respect and trust can be developed and sustained by open, honest, two-way communication. Staff members must believe that the consultant will come directly to them with any issues he may have about them or the work they are doing. They need to know he will not discuss individuals and situations with the client (their boss) behind their back. Too often consultants learn information about staff members indirectly, which they then feed back to their client. If people sense that the consultant is colluding with their boss against them, you can bet they will do everything in their power to see to it that the consultant and the initiative do not succeed. Consultants must also realize that staff members have insights and ideas they could never have, and must heed warnings of problems from the staff. People are more willing to extend trust when they feel heard and understood.

When the consultant and the client's staff do not work well together, it can spell disaster all around, as we once observed in a large utility company. A senior internal consultant desperately wanted to lead a project that got assigned to an external consultant. The project involved redesigning the entire customer service function, a project that carried high visibility and the opportunity for career development and learning. Instead of seeking a partnership role supporting the external consultant, she spent many hours spitefully searching for ways to sabotage his success. She spread rumors of his incompetence, maligned his credibility with the initiative's target population, ultimately building factions of detractors that would withhold their support. Along with a number of unfortunate organizational obstacles, her efforts proved successful and the initiative derailed. Her boastful "I told you so" won no one's favor, and she wound up with less organizational equity than she started with. Her boss, after realizing her contribution to the initiative's failure, dramatically withdrew his support from her function and used public forums to shame her with comments such as, "Projects like this new initiative really need professional, trust-worthy, reliable folks. We'll just have to check the other divisions to see if they can loan us someone to help." Shortly after, she left the organization. No one won. Both the client and the external con-sultant had a failed initiative and a blemish on their record, and the internal consultant felt compelled to leave an organization she liked. While the internal consultant may have played the greater role in the fiasco, the client and external consultant were at fault as well. They did nothing to ensure the support of people internal to the organization, going about the change process as though they alone could make it happen. A big mistake.

Hope is a vital motivator in the change equation. If the staff members are to contribute to the effort, they must be optimistic regarding its chance for success. Build in minigoals that allow them to experience that success and to enjoy the satisfaction of having contributed to it. Keep the tone of the endeavor upbeat and, while being honest in providing feedback and rigorous in demanding ac-countability, avoid criticism and blame. To the degree that people find meaning and fun in their work, they will support the initiative and work tirelessly to ensure its success.

Parallel Play vs. True Partnership

Some consultants and clients view their relationship as a partner-ship when, in fact, what they are engaging in is parallel play. If you carefully observe very young children playing together, you will notice that they rarely come together. Rather, they occupy adjacent space while engaging in their own activity. Often they talk to them-selves as they play and, when they converse with an adult, talk about friends the adult may not know—but whom the young child assumes they know—since their world is the only world that exists. This is because, developmentally, very young children are still highly egocentric, with little awareness of themselves in relation to others. This changes over time as youngsters learn to see them-selves less as the center of the universe and more in relation to others.

This same developmental phenomenon occurs with the client-consultant relationship. A genuine partnership means the client and consultant interact meaningfully with one another, converse and act in relation to one another, when dealing with the task at hand. When we see consultants or clients off doing their own thing, claiming to be working in partnership but, in fact, working in isolation, we hypothesize that they are either in the early days of developing the relationship and feeling their way with one another, or they are professing to be working together when, in fact, their egocentrism is creating a parallel-play situation. Obviously, the relationship cannot be as fulfilling or develop to be as effective in the latter situation. A genuine partnership is a matter of maturity and selflessness; the opposite of immaturity and egocentrism. There is no place for bloated egos in a profession whose primary function is to act in the service of others.

This does not imply the client-consultant relationship should be unhealthily symbiotic or codependent. There are always different roles to play and distinct boundaries to be maintained. These should be made explicit at the outset and maintained throughout the initiative. Both client and consultant should feel free to discuss the overstepping of roles or boundaries with one another should either believe that is occurring. As with most things in life, avoid the extremes. The client, the consultant, and client's staff need to balance their separate roles along with the requisite relationships among the three entities.

In sum, a large-scale change effort is a monumental undertaking. Consultants cannot succeed alone, no matter how large or capable the size of their team, because change is an endeavor built on relationships. They enhance their probability of success, however, if they establish a genuine partnership with their client and the client's staff. This can be most readily achieved by following the values expressed in the EARTH model.

Genuine partnerships are most effectively established when pursued right from the beginning of the relationship. Use Figure 6-1 as a tool to help guide the conversation between you and your client as you begin an engagement together. Be as precise as possible. Choose an agreeable way to document your conversation, monitor progress, and hold one another accountable.

Figure 6-1. Making the connection: the down to EARTH contract.

Use the following outline to facilitate a discussion with your client on how you will form a mutually beneficial and gratifying partnership for an impending engagement. This conversation is most valuable at the start of an engagement, but can also be useful to make midcourse adjustments if tension or disagreements begin to emerge too frequently. We recommend documenting the results of the conversation so each of you can refer to the agreed-upon approaches as needed.

1. **EQUALITY**   Having a mutually agreed-upon understanding of each others' roles, approach to conflict and decisions, and contributions to the initiative.

CONSULTANT	CLIENT
Personal view of own and client's role	Personal view of own and consultant's role

Agreed-Upon View of Each Other's Role

Preferred approach to decision making and conflict management	Preferred approach to decision making and conflict management

Agreed-Upon Approach to Decision Making
and Conflict Management

Contributions ⟸⟹ Mutually Agreed Upon ⟸⟹ Contributions

(Time, Abilities, Tasks, Deliverables)	(Time, Abilities, Tasks, Deliverables)

2. ADVOCACY Providing mutual support; championing each other's ideas and promoting each other's contributions, credibility, and reputation.

CONSULTANT	CLIENT
Personal expectations regarding advocacy from client	Personal expectations regarding advocacy from consultant

Mutually agreed-upon approaches to and opportunities for advocacy

Consultant for Client	Client for Consultant

3. RESPECT & TRUSTWORTHINESS Demonstrating mutual appreciation for each other's abilities and viewpoints, behaving predictably over time through consistency between words and actions, keeping commitments, takes responsibility for own actions and mistakes.

CONSULTANT	CLIENT
Personal view of respect & trustworthiness	Personal view of respect & trustworthiness
How I display to others	How I display to others

(continues)

Figure 6-1. *(continued)*

How I expect it from others	How I expect it from others

Mutually agreed-upon opportunities for and
evidence of respect & trustworthiness

Consultant to Client	Client to Consultant

4. HOPE   Providing encouragement and a positive perspective in the face of adverse challenges; drawing attention to the possibilities difficult circumstances present while realistically contending with obstacles; agreeing to support those who have become discouraged.

CONSULTANT	CLIENT
Situations that tend to cause discouragement	Situations that tend to cause discouragement
Personal sources of hope	Personal sources of hope

Anticipated obstacles in this engagement that may lead to discouragement	Anticipated obstacles in this engagement that may lead to discouragement

Mutually agreed-upon ways to encourage each other

Consultant to Client	Client to Consultant

7

Making Peace in Enemy Territory: Working With the Internal Consultant

"It is not best that we should all think alike; it is difference of opinion that makes horse races."

—Mark Twain

External consultants, anxious to begin the exciting challenge of a new assignment and with the best of intentions, can enter the organization at full speed, insensitive to those already working on the issues. But that Lone Ranger type of behavior can instantly alienate people within the organization who are involved in the engagement, particularly the internal consultants assigned to the same project. Many organizations employ full-time internal consultants whose primary responsibility is to enhance the organization's capabilities by developing people and supporting processes and technologies. They tend to be housed among the strategic planners (analysts, strategists, researchers), the human resources function (training and education, organization development, organization effectiveness), a total quality function (process engineers, quality consultants, reengineering teams), and in a technical support function, where they provide technical services to manufacturing and operations lines, or within information systems. External consultants are frequently asked to work with one or more of these internal consultants who are expected to serve as a liaison between the external person and the organization as well as a partner serving the goals of the initiative. External consultants need all the help and support they can get from internal people and should make every effort to enjoin these internals in a collaborative effort.

In this chapter, we take a close look at the internal consultant and her relationship with the external consultant, which is similar to but different from the relationship between the external consultant and the client. Our suggestions regarding this working relationship evolved from both our interviews and observations while on assignment. We felt this relationship was critical enough to warrant specific attention given the level of frustration and struggle we heard about. We encourage our readers who are internal consultants to remain open and nondefensive in the face of criticisms and recommendations for change. We found that internal consultants, like their external counterparts, engage in both good and bad habits as they practice their profession. We can all improve. As a consultant of any kind, if you've faced the challenges of working on complex initiatives in an adversarial relationship with your internal or external counterpart, this is a chance to better understand how you may have contributed to the struggles, and how you may better optimize the relationship in the future.

Advantages and Disadvantages of Internal and External Consultants

Internal consultants, unlike the consultants we have been describing to this point, are members of the organization, which gives them both an advantage and a disadvantage (see Figure 7-1). On the plus side is that they are usually familiar with the culture and the language of the organization. They know the norms and political realities as well as how things "work" in their system. They may also be more committed to a project than an external consultant since they have to live with the consequences of their work. They know that their job may be on the line. In addition, because it is their full-time focus, they may be able to give more time to the organization and may be less expensive than hiring someone from outside since they can be used on several projects.

On the downside, internal consultants may identify with and

Figure 7-1. Advantages and disadvantages of external and internal consultants.

	External Consultant	Internal Consultant
Advantages	• Outsider: independent of politics • Objective perspective • Potentially higher risk quotient • Greater knowledge base, skills, experiences • Can refuse an assignment	• Member of the organization: knows the players and understands the culture, history, politics, and norms • Committed to project's success; has personal accountability • Full-time commitment • Less expensive
Disadvantages	• Potentially cautious and political to retain work • Close scrutiny; high accountability • Committed more to own practice	• As member of the organization, may not be "heard" or may be part of the problem • Subjective perspective • Cautious; plays internal politics • Not always cutting edge

even be part of the problem. Because they have to live with their clients, they may tend to be cautious and, despite their best efforts, to get caught up in the organizational politics. In addition, they may lack perspective, having only the organizational lens through which to view the problem, and they may not have the required special knowledge or skill. Perhaps the biggest drawback for internal consultants is the truism, "You cannot be a prophet in your own land." External consultants coming into an organization from the outside saying the same thing the internal consultant has said for years will be heard far more readily. Rightly or wrongly, outsiders are seen as "experts" and are assumed to have greater influence within the organization; after all, someone sufficiently high up in the organization with the needed authority brought them in.

The advantages external consultants have stem largely from the fact that they are, at least theoretically, independent of the organization's politics, which should support their ability to be objective about the situation or problem and the client's role in it. It allows them to see more clearly and to act more aggressively. In addition, external consultants tend to have a greater knowledge or skill base, more varied experiences, and a broader perspective than internal consultants. Perhaps the greatest difference between external and internal consultants is that the external consultant is free to refuse an assignment. On the other hand, their success or failure in that assignment is more closely scrutinized and another assignment will rarely be forthcoming if the assessment is anything less than extremely satisfactory. The most significant disadvantage associated with external consultants is the fact that their primary commitment is to their own practice and not to the organization for whom they are consulting. In most cases, the interests of the consultant and the client are synchronous, but not always.

By pairing effectively, the disadvantages of one are compensated for by the advantages of the other. Collaboration creates a win-win situation for both.

Consulting to SCALE

The perceived differences between internal and external consultants can lead them to be leery of one another at the outset as each wonders whether the other will turn out to be friend or foe. In the best case, the external and internal consultants see one another as professionals with different (not necessarily better or worse) areas of expertise they can bring to bear on the project. Their concern consistently focuses on what is best for the initiative and the organization, and they work collaboratively from the outset to achieve their end goals. In the worst-case scenario, the relationship begins adversarially. This shouldn't be unexpected if you put yourself in the internal consultant's shoes for just a moment. She has been hired to develop the organization's capability in some way and most probably views herself as the resident expert on strategy, the market and industry, change, learning, the development of people, a specific technology or methodology, or on general management. Wanting to show the organization her abilities, she looks around for what is needed and where to apply her skills. Lo and behold, what does she find? A slew of external consultants working on the very projects she identifies for herself as being in her domain. It should not surprise us if she turns around and, literally, retires to her office, giving up or, conversely, takes up arms to reclaim a piece of the action. In either case, she is not likely to instantly view the external consultant as a friend, colleague, or collaborator.

Recognizing the internal consultant's bind and understanding that she can be an invaluable source of information and assistance, the wise external consultant will make every effort to win her support and enlist her wholehearted participation throughout the initiative. There are five ways in which the external consultant can reciprocate, helping the internal consultant to do her job more effectively. They are by:

1. Increasing the internal consultant's business **S**avvy in working with line management
2. Increasing as well the consultant's **C**ompetence
3. Sharing responsibility and **A**ccountability
4. Supporting the internal consultant's **L**earning
5. **E**mpowering the internal consultant within her own organization

It may appear arrogant for the external consultant to coach and mentor an internal person on matters of savvy, competence, accountability, learning, and empowerment (SCALE); however, the reality is that there is much the external consultant can provide to internal people. These five areas emerged as themes in our research with respect to limitations of internal consultants and how such limitations impaired the relationship with the external consultant. Ironically, consulting companies often have better industry intelligence than the company itself, and its consultants are frequently better read, more knowledgeable, and more cutting edge than company employees. It is, after all, their stock-in-trade. Rather than allowing the internal consultants' limitations to be an obstacle, the wise external consultant will find ways to build up the capabilities of their internal partners. The trick here is for *both* the internal and external consultant to acknowledge that they each have something to offer the other and to collaborate in the best interests of the company and the engagement.

Gaining Business Savvy

Whereas many internal consultants believe themselves to be right at the forefront of breakthroughs for their organizations, most line managers view them differently, as did one general manager we interviewed who alluded to the organization's internal consultants as "the people from corporate who sit around and smoke pipes, blow smoke up in the air, and pontificate about the possibilities." Others spoke of them as being "out of touch with reality" and "totally ignorant of real business issues."

We had occasion to witness reactions such as this in practice. We were asked to help a large financial services company transform its traditional training department into one that practiced performance consulting. The major difference in the approaches is that the traditional approach assumes training is the solution to performance issues, and the role of the internal consultant is largely to act as "order taker" and provider of a variety of training workshops to which line managers can elect to refer employees. There is little or no contact between the line manager and the function providing training. In contrast, performance consulting encourages a variety of interventions to address performance issues and requires intense interaction between the line manager and the internal consultant, particularly regarding the line's goals and needs. In our initiative, when the first line manager was contacted to participate, he laughed aloud then said, "You can't be serious! What do they (internal consultants) know about our work? I don't want them near my people. We have too much to do and they'll just be in the way." His reaction was fairly typical of those of other line people. We rapidly learned that this engagement was not going to succeed without the internal consultants getting a major grounding in the line organization's business, accompanied by a significant change in how the line managers came to view the internal consultants.

Because internal consultants sometimes lack a strong sense

of business, in general, and the work of their line organization, specifically, they often end up working on isolated projects, narrow in scope and unrelated to any major business imperative. While the people involved truly believe they are contributing in some grand way to the organization and have a sincere belief that their work is making a difference, the line people are often completely unaware of their work. The value internal consultants tend to add is limited to being an extra pair of hands on large projects, to troubleshoot emergent crises, to facilitate a meeting, to proofread technical design documents or revised policies, to upgrade systems and install new processes, to write a report, to serve on a task force, to make a presentation to senior management, or to make the arrangements for another department's off-site meeting. All of this is certainly necessary work. But the necessity of the work relative to the cost of having these functions is unbalanced, considering that the salaries of some individual contributors in these roles exceed $100,000. Internal consultants with high salaries feel the need to justify their existence, so they must identify projects and at least give the appearance of being busy. However, when they have little understanding of how their work is linked to the business strategy or to the bottom line, the choice of project and the value it creates to the organization is frequently dubious. Criteria for determining what projects to take on often becomes political, a function of the opportunity for visibility, and in essence self-serving or function-serving "busy work."

External consultants can help change this situation by coaching internal consultants in some basic business concepts and acumen. They can help them to become knowledgeable about the organization's business, industry, trends, and competitors so that they can speak the language of those at the table and meaningfully participate in a discussion of the business, and influence the outcome. They can help them reduce or eliminate their own technical jargon. They can ensure they are aware of the trends in their industry, how they compare to their competitors, what their organization's culture is and how it works for or against the initiative at hand. They can include these internal people in business planning and the creation of strategy, pointing out how their work is linked to the organization's mission and strategic direction, seeing it as supporting their line's business plan.

In keeping with this education, external consultants can encourage the internal people to begin developing relationships within the company just as they do—visiting manufacturing plants, R&D laboratories, field business unit offices, and other client locations—in order to build credibility, trust, and rapport. They can also model how they continuously monitor and review their work to ensure it is congruent with the unit's mission, supportive of the business's priorities, and value-added activity. As the project progresses, they can point out how they track the assigned roles and responsibilities, making sure they continue to be on time and within budget on all deliverables. Providing a comprehensive business education and helping internal consultants to be more savvy about their particular line business can benefit both internal and external consultants in that they will share a common vocabulary, set of understandings, and focus.

The assistance can and should be two-way. The internal consultant has much to offer the external consultant with regard to business savvy, but in her case it is likely to be specific to the organization's culture, history. and politics. For example, the internal person can provide invaluable insights about individuals in the organization, as well as internal relationships and informal networks. She can also enlighten the external consultant about past history that might affect the project.

A case in point: One external consultant we know was invited to design and implement a senior management development program for a high tech organization's university. He was excited about the challenge, knowing it had to be a fabulous yet relevant program or senior managers wouldn't attend. He began speculating aloud about all the things that could be done when the internal consultant pulled him aside and began asking him questions: "Are you aware there is an existing management development program and that when it has been offered it's been poorly attended? Did you know it was designed by the man who hired you? No? Well, I'm telling you this because you might want to go easy in there."

"What would you suggest I do?" asked the external consultant.

"Well, given that we've lost some significant market share over the last six months to overseas competition, you ought to ask about how they are intending to respond. I know they're struggling with how to build more global capability—if you could offer some relevant insights and ideas on how to build that kind of strength, I think you'd have their attention and raise their interest level."

The internal consultant's intervention changed the external consultant's approach and very likely saved his assignment by alerting him to assumptions he was making and questions he should have been raising about history.

In a different high tech company, an internal consultant coached the external consultant in the organization's norms. Wanting the project to be successful, she recognized how important it was for the outsider to understand the culture from the outset. "We're not very good about providing feedback here. We're what I would call 'polite.' Criticizing people or their work just isn't done. I know how important you feel feedback is, but I'd caution you to be very careful in presenting it." Forewarned is forearmed. The external consultant was grateful for her advice and understood how critical it would be in shaping his interventions, avoiding what might have been a disaster.

Something to Think About . . .

Think of a recent engagement in which there were internal consultants. How savvy were they about their business?
How did you help strengthen their business awareness and knowledge?
What were the benefits to you?
How has an internal consultant helped improve your approach to an engagement?

Strengthening Competence

Internal consultants can fail to have credibility within their own organization not only because they lack business savvy, but also because they are not always viewed as competent. One reason is that many have their degrees in what are perceived as "soft" disciplines such as psychology, sociology, communications, etc., and have not been schooled in the technical fields so prized by line managers. Further, a substantial proportion of them are people who "fell" into their staff position without appropriate schooling or experience.

One might question how those internal consultants who do not appear to offer significant value to the organization continue to maintain their jobs and their relatively substantial salaries. One explanation is that they are able to demonstrate the appearance of competence. They drop names of current authors, use the latest buzzwords and tools, quote the gurus they heard at conferences and statistics they read in recent articles. They keep a steady flow of initiatives going, hold meetings and keep long hours, leaving them as stressed by the work overload as any other employee, thereby demonstrating their worth. They summarize articles for people, write job descriptions, conduct surveys and analyze the results, analyze market and industry trends, write presentations for senior leaders complete with beautiful overhead transparencies and exquisite graphics, conduct training programs, respond to requests for technical assistance, serve on cross-functional task forces as facilitators, run quality forums for managers, manage external vendors and contractors, and respond to senior management's requests for information. The question rarely asked by themselves or others is whether these efforts add value to the company. In our experience, these activities were rarely linked to a broader organizational strategy or initiative, or even to each other.

As global competition heats up, organizations will increase the pressure on employees to work harder, smarter, and faster. Internal consultants will never add value to their organization in this environment if all they can contribute is quality staff work and administrative support. They will need to help line people manage performance through a variety of technologies and develop excellent consulting skills to facilitate the management of growth. But a vicious cycle is already in place: Because internal consultants are not always viewed as competent, they are not seen as a value-added resource and are underutilized. Then, because they are rarely called upon for serious performance problems, they fail to gain sufficient experience and opportunity to learn and develop their skills. As a result, they produce mediocre results on major projects, which results in their being seen as incompetent, and the cycle is complete. It is not surprising, therefore, that when critical business problems arise, the first people line managers call in are external consultants with whom they have a long-standing relationship or who are highly recommended by colleagues. They rarely give a thought to the possibility that there might be help at hand within the organization.

External consultants skilled in solid performance-enhancing capabilities and change management can play a significant role in developing internal consultants' capabilities. To do so would not be an act of altruism. In fact, it would be self-serving in that it brings a competent collaborator on board. To this end, external consultants can begin by helping the internal consultants to better diagnose the problem, teaching them how to get at the root causes of issues. They can provide them with an array of tools and techniques for collecting and analyzing data that will allow them to build a composite view of the department's or organization's current performance and create action plans for improvement. They can share their repertoire of strategies and interventions to ensure the solutions crafted will represent a broad range of perspectives that give them multiple options. Perhaps most critical, they can establish a norm of courageous consulting by modeling how to give feedback that is direct and nonjudgmental as well as how to take risks with recommendations that stretch their abilities beyond their comfort zone. Through their own consulting style, they can demonstrate a holistic approach to intervention that emphasizes integration of programs and systems throughout the organization. By helping to improve internal consultants' competence, external consultants can help them to be more effective and to add value to their organization.

Once again, assistance is two-way. The external consultant's superior consulting skills may be diminished by unfamiliar organizational structures or systems. Internal consultants can help them navigate through or around these barriers. For example, while technologically literate, the external consultant does not necessarily know his clients' human resources information system (HRIS) or the company's intranet system, or that the company is using SAP software or specific cycle-time reducing tools, yet the internal consultant can provide invaluable information on everything from talent to sales data to project management. Not only does assistance on these systems speed up the learning curve for the external consultant when he comes on board, but having necessary data at his fingertips also enhances his credibility and people's perception of his competence.

In one company we know, the CEO and his senior team spent the better part of the previous year benchmarking systemwide technological architectures, finally deciding on one that they recently installed. After its initial shakeout, the new system performed beautifully and the senior people were extraordinarily proud of their efforts and results. Not knowing this, an external consultant we know, upon starting an assignment with the company, launched his own best-practice study. When the CEO got wind of the fact that the company was paying for something totally unnecessary, he was furious and wanted the consultant removed. The internal consultant, believing the external consultant had a lot to offer the organization, argued the man's case, agreed to help redirect his efforts, and volunteered to collaborate more closely with him to support the existing system. By helping to refocus the external consultant's efforts, the internal consultant helped him earn the respect of the organization by ensuring maximum returns on investment.

Something to Think About . . .

In your work with internal consultants, how did you perceive their competence?
How did you help build on their potential and enhance their skills?
What were the benefits to you?
How did an internal consultant increase your competence on a project?

Building Accountability

Two factors contribute to the fact that, in many organizations, internal consultants often owe little accountability to anyone. First, they are frequently a corporate expense and costs for their services are rarely charged back to the client. In a world where "you get what you pay for," units consider internal consultation a "freebie" and, therefore, worth about as much. They rarely use the service and, when they do, because they have not had to pay, tend not to complain too loudly when the results aren't satisfactory. Instead, they go "outside" the next time they need assistance. Second, internal consultants tend not to tie work elements to expected outcome. Consciously or unconsciously, it suits their purposes better to maintain some vaguely defined end-point. In the absence of specific goals, there is nothing to measure; hence, no quantifiable assessment of results and effectiveness. Unfortunately, not being accountable contributes to the perception that these service providers are neither competent nor credible.

Internal consultants, believing they have something to offer, don't understand why people in the organization don't take advantage of their services. Rather than look inward for the answer—at themselves, their skills, their processes and track record—they look outward and defend themselves by blaming other aspects of the organization. They may use any variety of things—a toxic culture, an inexperienced leader, senior management's bias against their function—to explain why they have minimal impact. They put themselves in the role of victim, making it difficult, if not impossible, to get to a point where they can see themselves as catalysts and agents of change.

Once again, the external consultant can help the internal consultants in the course of their mutual collaboration on a project. He can model as well as discuss the need to identify deliverables, make them explicit, measure them, and take responsibility for the results. He can help generate an awareness that each component of work needs to be tied to a targeted outcome such as cost savings, productivity, turnover, sales, or customer satisfaction. External consultants know, possibly better than anyone, that having a results orientation is what keeps them in business. If they don't produce, they often don't get paid or, worse, they can be sued. This adds a certain urgency to their commitment to success. Most take accountability seriously. Unfortunately, many internal consultants don't feel the same degree of responsibility and urgency. They don't believe they'll go out of business if they fail to make a difference. External consultants can help internal consultants to appreciate that, while annihilation may not be in the picture, unless they can demonstrate effectiveness, they will never be viewed as full players in any project.

Accountability is a two-way street, and as we discussed throughout Part One of this book, external consultants often view "showing up" as all they are accountable for. Steeped in their own methodologies, external consultants can sometimes lose sight of the organization's requirements. Internal consultants can be excellent "guard rails" to help external consultants stay on track. One senior executive told us:

> I got so tired of having to translate the consultant's jargon and approaches into understandable and concrete terms, I finally stopped going to the meetings and let my internal people fill me in afterward. When they began to sense I was questioning the value of these consultants, they took the consultants aside and agreed to meet with them prior to our meetings to help ensure their presentations, language, and recommendations were relevant to us. My own people know me, so they knew what I was looking for from this project. They worked with the external consultants to ensure we got the results we were after and, eventually, I started attending the meetings again. I was pleasantly surprised to realize I could get through them and learn something. It wouldn't have happened if my people hadn't straightened the consultants out.

Something to Think About . . .

In your work with internal consultants, how have you encouraged them to share in responsibility and accountability for the project?

Where have internal consultants "missed the boat" on specifying deliverables?

How did you assist them in making connections and measuring those connections?

How have internal consultants served as "guard rails" for you, alerting you to possible missteps?

Supporting Learning

Any consultants, internal or external, are only as good as the depth and breadth of their knowledge, skills, and experiences. Therefore, their value is in direct proportion to their learning. For them, it is not a matter of keeping up with, but rather, keeping ahead of the curve. This isn't easy in an information age, when the half-life of any concept, idea, fad, technology, or model can be measured in nanoseconds. Managers expect consultants to have current readings, new technologies and tools, and industry knowledge, including what different companies are planning, doing, and creating. This often-intangible array of intellect accounts for a huge proportion of their fee.

Organizations have a right to expect the same cutting-edge intellect from their internal consultants. Surprisingly, they don't. Too many organizations, while willing to purchase the knowledge and skills of an external consultant, do not foster learning in their own organization nor expect it of their internal consultants. Many of the people with whom we spoke believed that learning was something they finished when they obtained their MBA. Incredibly, some of these were people at the top level of management in their organization or managing directors in prominent consulting firms. Sometimes the organizational culture not only didn't encourage learning, it was clearly more comfortable with the status quo, rewarding individuals who employed the same models, techniques, and concepts as they had decades ago across all types of organizational problems. What they knew once is what they use now. Those individuals who sought learning outside the organization were often frustrated by the fact that, on their return to the office, they found no receptivity to their desire to try out their new learning.

Perhaps the greatest contribution external consultants can make to the internal consultants on their projects is to encourage and support their ongoing learning. They can encourage them to analyze their own competencies as objectively as possible and to design a developmental plan that will fortify their weak areas and fill in gaps. They might recommend that they become voracious readers not only in quantity, but in quality, suggesting not only business books, but also readings in science, art, history, and so forth, since creative ideas frequently come from areas less familiar to us than our own discipline. They can also suggest trade journals, industry publications, and interesting magazines in a variety of areas.

As part of the internal consultants' developmental plan, the external consultant might encourage them to attend external learning events—spend time at local university business schools or at industry-specific seminars and workshops to learn more about their own craft as well as about their organization's business. They might suggest they join professional societies and attend conferences to both strengthen and broaden their repertoire of skills, especially those requisite to current and upcoming organizational projects. They might also suggest to senior management that they bring in guest speakers to lecture on current trends and topics.

Most of all, external consultants can model a hunger for knowledge and an intellectual curiosity. They can show the joy they feel at raising questions and exploring answers. They can demonstrate the gratification that comes from applying their learning to current critical business problems.

Granted, sometimes the shoe is on the other foot, and it's the external consultant who's become stale while the internal consultant has remained current. In such cases, external consultants would do well to learn from these internal partners rather than be threatened by them or dismissive of their knowledge. One external consultant from a large management consulting firm told us about an engagement in which he was relieved to realize how much the internal consultant in the organization's strategic planning function knew about mass customization, the engagement at hand. "In fact, there was stuff she knew that I didn't know. Because we've approached it one way since we've started offering consulting services in this area, I've never thought about it another way. She was able to offer an alternative approach that enhanced the implementation in her organization, and I think made our practice area in this discipline more well-rounded." External consultants should approach a relationship with internal consultants with the starting assumption that they can learn something, not with the assumption of "stupid until proven intelligent."

Something to Think About . . .

Think of a recent engagement in which there were internal consultants. How did you demonstrate intellectual curiosity? How did you share the many opportunities available for gratifying that curiosity?

How do you keep on the cutting edge of information and technology?

When have you learned from an internal consultant? Did it change your perspective on their capability?

Empowering the Function

Many internal consulting units earn minimal respect from their organization, as evidenced by the number of projects that are run by external consultants and from which they are excluded. Internal consultants need to lay claim to what is theirs, but they are not in a position to do so until the first four characteristics of SCALE have been met: Only when they have business savvy, consulting competence, and cutting-edge learning, only when they act as if they are responsible and accountable for what is happening, will they be in a position to command respect.

Internal consultants need to empower themselves and to raise their function to a higher professional level. To do this, they need to believe that they will go out of business if they don't make a difference and turn this sense of urgency into a strong commitment to improve themselves and their function. This means no longer hiding behind administrative work or sitting at their desk waiting for the phone to ring with someone requesting their assistance. Rather, they will have to get out of their offices and work with the line managers to improve the business unit's overall performance by contributing measurable value and producing innovative solutions.

Once they are assured among themselves that they have raised the quality of their service, they need to educate the workplace about what they have to offer. They will need to communicate with the organization in every possible way—by developing a brochure, a catalog, a one-page briefing, a short videotape—to describe their services and to inform their entire constituent base about the services the function provides that they might want. They will need to spell out the types of problems they can and can't assist them with, what costs might be incurred, and how they can obtain general information about the function. They will need to network, particularly in-house, helping to build and maintain relationships with key clients up and down the hierarchy. They might arrange lunches, make casual drop-in visits, contact people via e-mail and phone calls, or send personal notes and attach an article or book summary relevant to the recent work they did with the client. If a line department is holding an all-hands staff meeting, they might ask to attend to keep current on business issues and recent trends. This would give them the opportunity to meet new people and, if appropriate, to introduce those individuals to the service the unit offers.

At first blush, it may not seem to be in the external consultant's best interest to foster the empowerment of internal consultants and their function. However, to think that is to subscribe to a zero-sum belief in change. To the contrary. There is enough change to generate more initiatives than there are consultants, either internal or external. Between strategic changes, mergers and acquisitions, operational changes, technological changes, cultural changes, innovative and yet unclear changes, there is plenty of work out there to be had by all. External consultants, once again, can only benefit from having informed, knowledgeable, and skilled collaborators when they work on engagements. They should do everything they can to develop and support the empowerment of their internal colleagues. And it certainly behooves internal consultants to take advantage of whatever the external consultant can provide to enhance their learning and professionalism. Today's trend is to outsource functions such as staff consulting units. If the function is seen as expensive and non-value-added, rest assured, its days are numbered. Internal consultants are high-priced staff workers unless they play a significant role in identifying and solving the complex challenges faced by the organization.

Similarly, it is in the internal consultants' best interest to do whatever she can to ensure the external consultant is fully deployed and has the opportunity to make the impact possible from an outsider. Rather than competing with or being threatened by him, the internal consultant should promote the external consultant's benefits and encourage the organization to listen to and deploy them.

We know an internal consultant at a financial investment organization who became totally frustrated by the fact that her organization would bring in consultants, spend an absurd amount of money on them, then proceed to ignore their recommendations. This sequence happened time and again. Finally, when senior management rejected the findings of its external consultants yet again, she blurted out, "Why did you hire them? In fact, why do you hire anyone? You never listen to anyone's recommendations. You're just wasting money, not to mention everyone's time and energies. You don't listen to us and you don't listen to them. How many opinions are you going to get? Are you just waiting for someone to say, 'You don't need to do anything; Everything's okay as it is?' I hate to say it, but I feel as if no one here wants to face the music. The problem won't go away just because we send the consulting firm away. We either deal with this now, or it deals with us later." After her outburst, the internal consultant worried that perhaps she had risked her job with her candor. To the contrary, her self-empowerment forced the executives to confront what was happening. Reluctantly, they agreed that her perceptions had a ring of truth. They brought back the last group of consultants and revisited the engagement and the recommendations. Everyone won: The internal consultant began to see positive changes and forward movement in her organization, and the external consultant got an extended engagement. Most importantly, the organization began to change. Passivity is rarely an effective approach. Empowerment at least improves the odds.

Something to Think About . . .

What suggestions would you offer internal consultants for how to promote themselves and their function?

> What are the benefits to you of helping internal
> consultants to become empowered?
> How has an internal consultant empowered
> you?

EARTH Still Applies

Although SCALE underscores the needs and issues of internal consultants, the relationship between the internal and external consultant should still be in keeping with the principles of EARTH—equality, advocacy, respect, trust, and hope. Not only are the values represented by these acronyms not mutually exclusive, they should be addressed concurrently. External consultants should treat internal consultants as equal partners, being careful to ensure the internal members of the team are not placed in the back seat by anyone on the project or given the grunt work that always accompanies large projects.

They should advocate for the internal consultants by helping them to build their sphere of influence within their own organization, pointing out to senior management their importance to the project. Remember, it is difficult for them to be a prophet in their own land, so always share the credit for the successful business results with them. When the project is completed, let them present at meetings, credit their assistance in newsletters and memos, and encourage them to share their experiences with peers and leaders in the organization

Offering respect and trust to internal consultants is critical since people in this function often do not receive them from their own associates. It is difficult, if not impossible, however, to extend respect and trust to people who do not demonstrate reasons for you to do so. Thus, it is important to carefully structure assignments for the internal consultants within the context of the broader engagement that are small and that guarantee success. Internal consultants want to do well, but they don't always have the knowledge or skills. Help them. Let them earn your respect and trust.

Internal consultants often work in a cynical and negative environment. Help them exchange this for a culture of hope and celebration. Share with them the joy in your work and collaboration and an optimistic way of looking at things. Use creative humor when things get ambiguous, tense, or uncertain. Let them see that while it's important to take work seriously, it shouldn't be taken too seriously. And always keep in mind that whether you want to believe it or not, whether the evidence suggests it or not, you do need them as much as they need you. We're not suggesting that you consult to SCALE merely out of the goodness of your heart, but to ensure that those vital benefits internal consultants can provide are brought to bear in the engagement.

By using the characteristics of SCALE and EARTH, external and internal consultants can improve not only their own professionalism, but also that of the consulting field. Such a vision of a value-added profession should stimulate all consultants everywhere to work together to share their knowledge, skills, and experiences for mutual benefit and the greater good of their mutual client.

Part Four

Conquering the Engagement From Hell

"The ultimate measure of a man is not where he stands in moments of comfort and convenience, but where he stands at times of challenge and controversy."

—Martin Luther King, Jr.

The concepts and approaches we've discussed to this point will only be helpful to the extent that you find a way to make them relevant in the context of the client organizations to which you are consulting. As an intermediary step between the concepts we have presented and a real-time engagement, we have designed a simulation that runs through Chapters 8, 9, and 10 to give you an opportunity to "consult" to a client organization applying the concepts we've discussed. We'll provide the engagement. You provide the value-creating responses. We suggest you gather a small group of your consulting colleagues, pile the table with a bunch of your favorite snacks or order lunch in, and have some fun with this. To push the buttons of any latent bad-habit instincts, we're going to make this a little tough. Don't be tempted to merely "give the right answer" just because this is a simulation. Examine your initial impulses to the presenting issues and client behavior. Use this as an opportunity to test the higher ground of value-creating behavior when your instincts—consciously or not—may be screaming for you to do otherwise. Imagine yourself acting in new and different ways—just for the heck of it.

A good friend of ours, Dan Pryor, tells a wonderful story about trying on new behavior. He has an aunt who, every Christmas, gives him an ugly, often polyester shirt that winds up on the shelf in his closet with previous years' ugly shirts from the same aunt. One time, when the rest of the closet offered no clean shirts, he was forced to choose one of the shirts from his aunt. Certain it would look repulsive, he looked in the mirror after putting it on and, to his surprise, it didn't look half bad. New behavior is often the same way. Sometimes new options, especially those that we think are against the grain of our well-grooved instincts, initially appear very unappealing. However, given a fair shot, these choices often surprise us with their fresh relevance and perspective. Hopefully, none of the options we've presented thus far are "unappealing," but they may provoke some discomfort because changing behavior often does. Work through the discomfort, examine its source, and allow yourself some introspective time to sort through your beliefs, ideals, assumptions, models and approaches, training, and aspirations with regard to being a consultant. If you began a Value-Creating Journal back in Chapter 4, we suggest you use it to jot down any thoughts, questions, or ideas that might pop up during this exercise.

Disclaimer: This scenario and all the people in it are fictitious. Any resemblance to real-life situations is purely coincidental.

Welcome to Summit Consulting

You are a senior partner with Summit Consulting, a small consulting firm located in a major midwestern city. There are approximately seventy-five consultants in your firm, along with an additional forty employees providing support functions and services. Your revenue last year was $46 million and your target revenue for this year is $53 million, representing somewhere in the neighborhood of 15 percent growth. Since Summit was founded in 1975, it has enjoyed healthy growth, with the exception of some lean years in the mid-1980s. You have been averaging double-digit growth for the past five years. The third quarter is coming to an end, and the firm is slightly behind plan, just crossing the $50 million mark.

Like many consulting firms, the war to attract and retain quality talent is a challenge. With the exception of losing one talented consultant to a competitor raid earlier this year, Summit has managed to keep and grow some very bright consultants whom you and your fellow firm leaders feel have great potential. However, the firm is taking no chances and has begun to identify key high-potential consultants for whom it is developing what it hopes will be "raid proof" retention plans. While these plans will require unplanned expenditures to beef up this year's bonus pool, the alternative risks of future losses are far greater.

Summit's clients have included a number of Fortune 500 companies headquartered in your home city and the client's respective locations and subsidiaries throughout the United States and some parts of Europe, as well as numerous Fortune 1000 organizations in a variety of industries that could never afford to pay the fees of the larger management consulting firms. Summit's specialty areas have included benchmarking and best-practice studies, market and industry competitive analysis, strategy formulation and implementation, and some recent venturing into the six-sigma process redesign craze. Because of some successful engagements in the late1980s helping clients link their total quality efforts to their business strategy, you think the firm may have a unique offering to help bridge strategy with six-sigma initiatives and avert the common dissipation of focus and results that can happen when organizations undertake such massive efforts. The managing partners of Summit have been discussing the potential of expanding the firm's offering into planning and integration support for merger and acquisition (M&A) activity. Since this is such a "hot" practice area for the consulting industry today, and some of Summit's existing clients are in the thick of acquiring or being acquired, capitalizing on the opportunity seems worth exploring. Leveraging Summit's expertise in building growth strategies could be an effective launching pad.

You have been with Summit for nearly nine years, following a four-year stint with one of the Big Five management consulting firms. You have an MBA from the University of Michigan. You are a well-respected consultant and project leader in the firm. Your engagement teams have always given you high marks with respect to client relationship management and project leadership. You are anticipating a promotion to the firm's management committee at the end of the year, but feel that bringing in one more "big" client would clinch the opportunity. You suspect there are two of you contending for the management committee spot that will become available January 1, and after nine years of loyal and successful service, you think it should be yours.

That's the context from which you will be consulting. The subsequent chapters will represent various parts of the engagement process. We have designed the simulation as follows and recommend that you approach it this way:

• At critical points along the journey, we "stop action" and let you "consult." We have provided a series of questions for you to use in forming your responses, excavating your assumptions, and deciding what actions to take with your client. The questions are only meant to prompt your thinking. Life serves up few opportunities for "right" answers, so don't approach this as a fill-in-the-blank exercise. Wrestle with the choices available and the underlying motivations directing you toward or away from them.

• When you identify the "additional information you would like," go back and reflect on the information you *didn't* ask for, because you weren't inclined to ask for it. The questions you didn't ask can reveal as much about your motives and values as those questions you felt compelled to ask.

• Use the case as an opportunity to reflect on your work, your approaches, and your assumptions. (We recognize the limitations of developing a simulated engagement with a simulated client, so in the spirit of what we're trying to accomplish, try not to get caught up in the absence of detail you wish was there or how certain things are said.)

• Finally, be sure to select one or two of the value-creating behaviors to consciously try out. Let the self-assessment results from Chapter 3 help you decide which value-creating behaviors to experiment with.

• When you have completed the simulation, go back and review your responses and choices. Ask a valued colleague for feedback on your actions and ideas, then use the input to build a development plan in which you target the skills, knowledge, and attributes you may wish to develop or fortify over the next year. Select only one or two—there's no extra credit for overly ambitious goals that are unachievable.

We wish you well and commend you in advance for acting upon the courage of your convictions. If each of us reflects on our craft, solicits feedback, and takes risks with new behavior, we can overhaul our industry—even if it's one consultant at a time.

8

Meet Your Client: Rampart Systems

> "Life is like playing a violin solo in public, and learning the instrument as one goes along."
>
> —Samuel Butler

You arrive early one morning at your office at Summit Consulting, a beautifully appointed suite of offices in a corporate park just north of the city. You have some e-mail and expense reports to catch up on and want to get an early start before the weekly senior partner staff meeting. Your assistant, Joyce, has left you a message from the night before from a Bill Cavell, calling from Rampart Systems. The message came in at 7:30 p.m. last night.

Rampart . . . where have I heard that name? you think to yourself as you ponder the vaguely familiar company name. *Didn't I read about them last week—something about a merger?* Putting the message on the cradle of your phone, you decide you'll call him in a little while, once normal business hours begin.

Joyce comes bounding into your office at about 8:20. "Did you call that guy?"

"You mean . . . Bill Cavell?"

"Yeah, he was pretty bent on talking to you. Seemed kind of upset you weren't here last night. When I told him you'd left around six, he made some joke about 'typical consultants keeping early hours.' Anyway, I told him you'd call him first thing this morning. He said he'd be in early."

"Mr. Cavell's office." A lovely voice answered the phone. "Oh yes, he's expecting your call, please hold on."

Expecting my call? you think to yourself. *Hmm. I wonder who the heck this guy is.*

"Bill Cavell."

"Hi, Bill, this is (your name) from Summit Consulting returning your call."

"Yeah, yeah. Listen, you people did some work for Atlas technology last year?"

"Yes, we did, as a matter of fact. I led that engagement—Tim Ryan was our client there."

"Yeah, I know—Tim and I play golf together. He said you guys did a great job. I'm not a big fan of consultants myself, but I think we're gonna need some help here. We just acquired a small company out in California and we're trying to figure out how to get our money's worth out of them."

"I knew I'd seen your company name somewhere. I read about your acquisition last week. You guys are a network systems company, right? Intranets, websites, e-commerce, like that?"

"That's right. And we just bought this little mom-and-pop outfit out in California that specializes in Internet marketing called Demarka. A lot of our customers have been asking for support once their web pages are up and the hardware is in, and we can't develop the marketing programs to help them leverage their investment. So we took the bet that buying the capability might be a way to expand our services. We paid a pretty high premium for them, but we're hoping it will pay off quickly. We need to figure out how to marry the capabilities, and we need to figure out how best to bundle the services. So far, we haven't been able to identify anyone out there our size who provides this kind of end-to-end capability, nor have we figured out how best to identify the market opportunities and go to market with the goods. Basically, we don't know what we don't know. And I don't feel like stepping on any land mines and flushing our $65 million down the toilet. I already have an idea about how I want to integrate the two companies, and I already know who out in California I'm gonna keep and who I have to eliminate. But my gut says, whatever I do, I don't have much time to waste if I want to get to market fast. Can you help?"

Forming the Value-Creating Response

We've already discussed how value is created right from the start of a relationship. Whether or not Bill becomes your client, think about the response options you have to his question and how you can best begin the relationship. Think about the following:

> What was your first instinct when Bill asked, "Can you help?"
> What tentative conclusions have you already formed about Bill, based on his opening comments? What concerns or questions do his comments raise for you—specifically, about the Demarka decision, the way it was made, and the learning that was gained during due diligence?
> What personal benefits come to mind that may motivate you to reassure him that you are the right consultant for the job?
> What initial questions do you have for Bill, and what do they reveal about you?
> What may your questions signal to Bill?
> What questions did you think of but decide not to ask? Why?

The First Meeting

The next morning, you arrive at the offices of Rampart Systems to meet with Bill Cavell, Rampart's president and founder. For the president of a $650 million technology company with nearly 3,300 employees, his office is modestly sized and decorated. His desk has that well-worn, unkempt look to it. It suggests he's a hands-on kind of president. Jan, a senior consultant with Summit with experience in information technology, has accompanied you. She worked with you previously on the engagement at Atlas technology.

"C'mon in. You guys want any coffee?" Bill asks as he juggles two files while signing several documents for his waiting assistant. After the formal introductions and exchange of pleasantries, you begin by summarizing what Bill described in his earlier phone conversation. Then, you ask, "Bill, tell us a little bit about Rampart, how things have been going the last couple of years and what led up to the decision to buy Demarka."

Bill obliges, "When we hit the half-billion mark three years ago, I sat back and thought long and hard about where I wanted to take this place. I honestly never thought we'd get this big this fast. I now realize that there are a lot of growing small businesses in the area, as well as throughout the Midwest, who can't afford to pay the huge costs of big technology companies but really need network and Internet solutions for their business. Now I've got these salespeople out there beating the streets and coming back with deal after deal. My installation teams are having to work almost round the clock to fill the service orders. Jeff Borgel is my right hand guy, been with me for about seven years. He came to me a few years ago and knocked me over the head, asking me, 'Do you realize what we're sitting on here? What happens when we hit a billion?' I was positively stunned. I'd never thought about it. I can remember starting this company with two other guys in my basement like it was yesterday!

"To make a long story short, our sales guys have been coming in over the last year or so telling us that our customers have been asking for ongoing support of the websites once they're up—page design stuff, marketing, retail transactions, et cetera. Well, we didn't do any of that stuff. I felt as if we were handing off our work to other vendors who were reaping the rewards of our work. Plus, we wind up getting called back on service calls when the vendor can't figure out a configuration or our customer wants to change something based on the vendor's recommendation. It was nuts. I don't have enough techs for them to be out on service calls for customers whose vendors come in and muck around with our stuff and also installing all the new orders coming through the door. I realized the only logical response was to figure out how to get in on the action. We toyed around with the idea of getting some people on board who did Internet marketing and support work, but we quickly found out that that talent is tough to come by, very expensive, and it would take too long to build up a team that could deliver a quality service and product. I'm not interested in selling the place, though I've gotten some pretty tempting offers. And I'm not going to go in debt to some venture capitalist to buy something big. So we started sniffing around to see if there was some small firm out there we could just buy. We put our lawyers on the hunt—their firm has a merger and acquisition practice—and they led us to Demarka.

"It took about four months to work out the deal. I lost a lot of sleep on this one, believe me. Maybe for some of your bigger clients, $65 million is small change. But I had to take some big gulps to get comfortable with this one. I'm still not all that comfortable; in fact, I'm scared, but we're here now and we've got to make it work."

Jan pipes in, "How do the rest of your senior people feel about the deal? Are they excited? Nervous?"

"Well, I think everyone is pretty excited about this. Like I said, many of these people have been with me for a long time. I'm sure most of them never dreamed we'd get this big. We have this building and the warehouse and plant a couple of blocks from here. I'd say they're behind the deal."

You continue, "You said on the phone yesterday that you weren't a big fan of consultants. How did that come to be? Have you had any bad experiences before?"

"Well, actually, we've never really used consultants before. I just know from what I've heard from some of our customers. They say people pay a lot of money for what you guys do and once you're gone, no one can really figure out what they got for it. I've always been a do-it-yourself kind of guy. I don't like going outside for help. I've always figured that if you can't do it with your own people, you probably shouldn't be doing it. But like I told you yesterday, Tim spoke highly of the work you did for him and said he really thought you could be helpful to us, so I called. So, tell me, who else have you helped with this kind of problem?"

A Moment of Truth

> How will you answer Bill's question? What factors are influencing your choices?
> How are you reframing Bill's issues for yourself?
> When you review the potential task, where do you see your strengths at this point—and your weaknesses?

The Agreement

This first meeting continues for another hour and a half. It is productive, informative, and you feel as though positive rapport is being established between you, Jan, and Bill. You explain to Bill how you prefer to engage, beginning with a process of discovery, including interviews with key employees and customers, as well as looking at performance data from the past four to six months. You and Jan determine that you will put together an engagement team that includes the two of you, three other consultants, and one junior researcher. Bill asks to have the proposal on his desk first thing next week. You agree to have it to him by then.

The Proposal

Now that you have made an agreement to deliver a proposal, you should ask yourself another series of questions:

> How will you position Summit, given your lack of solid merger and acquisition experience? What value could Summit genuinely provide?
>
> Would you consider walking away from the opportunity?
>
> What are your preliminary hunches, given what you know so far, and on what are they based? Do you detect the presence of any "consulting" biases?
>
> What additional information would you ask for at this point?
>
> How will you price the engagement? What length of time will you propose to stay engaged?
>
> How do you feel about Bill? What kind of client do you think he will be? Do you feel you've done everything needed so far to ensure your relationship remains healthy and productive?

The Negotiation

You have the proposal messengered over to Bill's office Monday morning after working on it most of the weekend. It's now Thursday morning and you said in your cover letter that you would call Bill today to see if he had any questions.

"Bill Cavell's office, this is Linda, may I help you?"

"Hi, Linda, it's (your name) from Summit. How are you today?"

"Fine. Bill got your package. I'm sure it's buried on his desk somewhere, but I can't promise he's gone through it in detail. Right now he's tied up behind closed doors. I think he's in there with the lawyers. Do you want to leave a message?"

"Just tell him I called to check in and see if he had any questions or needed any clarification."

"Will do."

The weekend passes. You check your voice mail early Sunday evening to see if any weekend issues came up with consultants on your engagement team or any of your clients. You hear, "You have one new voice-mail message, sent Friday, 10:45 p.m. . . . .

"Hey, it's Bill Cavell over at Rampart. I finally got through this proposal. I'll be home over the weekend so if you get a minute give me a call. I need to understand these fees a little better. I also want you to meet Jeff Borgel. I'm going to get him involved. I want him on top of this."

You call Bill at home, and agree to come by Monday afternoon.

At the meeting Monday, a well-groomed, bright-looking man in his late thirties shakes your hand as you walk into Bill's office. "Hi, Jeff Borgel, nice to meet you. Bill's running a little late. He said to start without him. I've read your proposal and we just had a few questions about the fees and some of the work you suggest."

"No problem," Jan reassures Jeff. "What can we clarify for you?"

Jeff raises some basic questions about the process, like: How will you propose actions and how do the fees correlate to the activities? Jeff asks you to go back and see if there is any way to trim down the fees to what amounts to about a 20 percent reduction. "Bill thought that you could simply cut out this . . . what did you call it . . . discovery phase. He said that there isn't any need to interview anybody, that whatever you needed to know he or I could tell you. Plus, we have a storeroom full of paper from the merger that the lawyers put together that has all kinds of information we could give you access to. We figured this could save us a nice little hunk of change and save you a lot of time. Does that make sense to you?"

You and Jan exchange a knowing glance, "Well, we'll go back and see if there are any opportunities to bring the costs more in line with what you were hoping to spend," you say rather cautiously. "I'm sure you can appreciate that I don't want to compromise the quality of the work or understaff the team and then not be able to deliver. The discovery phase is a critical part of our engagement process because it gives us a firsthand opportunity to get to know your organization. We often find that the perspectives of senior leaders differ from others in the organization, or from customers. We think this is an important opportunity for you to get to hear what's on the minds of some of your key employees and customers. I also appreciate you have other commitments and that you've just bet the farm on this acquisition, so resources are a particularly sensitive issue right now. We'll find the best balance we can among all these issues—I'm sure we'll be able to come back with a price that you'll feel is fair."

"I don't care what he said"—Bill can be heard bellowing out in the hall—"Just tell him I said to get the damn installation done by the end of the week or we'll be having a different conversation about his career next week!" Just then Bill walks in. "So, everybody getting to know each other? Where are we at, Jeff?" Bill seems to direct his attention more at Jeff than at you and Jan.

Jeff does a nice job recapping the conversation for Bill, including your agreement to go back and revisit the fee structure and your emphasis on the importance of doing the discovery phase.

Bill concludes, "Well, I don't see why you have to waste my people's time interviewing them when Jeff and I can tell you anything you need to know. But in any case, see if you can at least reduce how much time you have to spend in the front-end part so we can get to the meat of the process. I want you guys to work closely with Jeff on this. I'm going to depend on him to make this happen. So get us that revised proposal and we'll see if we can't get this thing moving."

On the way back to the office, you and Jan debrief the meeting.

"So how much do you think we can shave off?" Jan asks.

"I don't know if we can get all the way to where they want us. I have a feeling that if this goes, we're going to open up a few Pandora's boxes. I don't want to cut off our noses and wind up going in the hole. But I do want the project very much. The fact that they're willing to engage with us even though we didn't produce a long list of clients for whom we've done this type of work is great. And this will be a chance for us to learn a lot. So whatever we shave off I can consider an investment. But I'm certainly not going to walk away from collecting any data. He seemed a tad too anxious about giving us access to people for my taste. Could be typical CEO-entrepreneur, paranoia-control stuff, or in truth he may just not see any value in it. But I don't think we can do the work without our own data."

"Did you notice Jeff's face when Bill said he was going to depend on him to make this happen? He looked as if he was trying not to let on how surprised he was. How much do you think Bill has talked to him?"

"Not much. My gut says Bill may be one of this engagement's biggest challenges."

Establishing Healthy Boundaries

How will you handle the price-reduction request? What criteria will you use to make the adjustments? What, if anything, will you do to modify your discovery work?

What observations do you have about Bill and Jeff?

What concerns make Bill a potential challenge? How will you deal with the challenges?

What Pandora's boxes do you think will be opened?

Getting the Green Light

The weekend passes, and you get a message first thing Monday morning from Jeff Borgel's office. You call back.

"Jeff Borgel's office, Elaine speaking. May I help you?"

"Hi, this is (your name) from Summit Consulting returning Jeff's phone call?"

"Oh, yes, I think he's expecting your call. Just a minute please."

"Jeff Borgel."

"Hi, Jeff, it's (your name). I got your message."

"Oh, yeah, thanks for getting back to me. Bill and I went over your revised proposal over the weekend, and Bill's okay with the changes. He is still a little uncomfortable with this discovery work, even though you've narrowed the scope of it, but I got him to give a little. So I guess it's a go. What do we do next?"

"Well, that's great, Jeff. We're delighted that we'll get to work with Rampart. I think it will be a great opportunity for all of us. Thanks for the confidence in Summit—I know you'll be happy with our work. If you could just get us back a copy of the signed contract, we can get all of our behind-the-scenes project setup stuff under way here. The first thing we'd like to do is to come to Bill's next staff meeting to talk to your senior team about the work and begin to get them on board. When do you meet next?"

"Well, Bill doesn't really have staff meetings per se. He thinks they're a waste of time. When he needs to see somebody, he just walks to their office or calls them. We could have him send a memo out to people about the project—would that work?''

"Hmm. Well, Jeff, in my experience, people get on board much quicker if they're 'in the room,' so to speak, and have the chance to ask questions and meet the outsiders firsthand. Is there any way we could call a meeting—say for an hour or two—to do a quick update and project overview for people?''

"Oh, trust me," Jeff jumps in, "they won't have any questions. If Bill says he wants this to happen, it's a done deal. Bill's done a good job of raising loyal soldiers here!'' Jeff trails off the sentence with a laugh.

"Well, loyalty is a good thing. Just the same, could you check with him to see if we could get this brief meeting scheduled, say, just for your top ten to fifteen managers?''

"Sure, I'll run it by him. I don't think he'll have a problem with it.''

"Thanks, Jeff. Jan and I would also like to get on your calendar so you can meet the rest of our team assigned to Rampart, as well as to go over some basic project timing, to scope out some timelines and key milestones. We like to keep you involved along the way and make sure we keep the project on track. Are you free any time toward the end of this week?''

"Sure, Thursday morning works okay?''

"How about 10:30?''

"Great. And I'll run the staff meeting idea by Bill and get back to you on that.''

"Thanks, Jeff. We'll see you Thursday.''

The usual round of high-fives and congratulatory handshakes make their way to your office, as is customary at Summit when a new project is landed. The managing partner to whom you report stops by and gives you his characteristic "Nicely done.'' You can't pass on the opportunity to point out how this project will help put Summit closer to its revenue target for the year and how glad you are to have been able to bring it in. You also notice the conspicuous absence of acknowledgment from your peer who you suspect is also contending for the management committee promotion. *"Bad form,"* you think to yourself with a slight smirk.

Blank Stares and Murmuring

Bill agrees to the staff meeting, although he does say he would prefer not to make a habit of it, if at all possible. The meeting with Jeff on

Thursday goes very well; he's high-energy and the team clicks well with him. The work is scoped out for ten months, with key deliverables defined at bimonthly checkpoints.

You and Jan arrive early at Rampart for the staff meeting. You've tried several times to get to Bill ahead of time to prep him for the discussion, but he's been out of town. Jeff assures you that Bill is good on his feet. There are twelve managers coming to the meeting. The employee lounge had been converted for the afternoon, and chairs are set up around the room with the tables moved to the side. As they arrive, you can tell they've been talking among themselves about what this is about. They greet you and Jan a tad apprehensively, some looking cynical, some too immersed in their own world to be concerned, and one or two mildly enthused.

Bill opens the meeting by thanking them for taking the time out of their busy schedules to meet this morning. He continues for nearly a half-hour talking about the acquisition of Demarka, how important it is to the company's future, and how critical it is that the integration of Demarka not get screwed up. For some in the room, it is clear they were not in the loop about Demarka and that this is the first time they've received any detailed information. For others, this seems like Bill's stock spiel they've heard more than once before. Bill tells them that a few of them will be asked to spend time with you and Jan, and they are asked to be accommodating and responsive. There is definitely a "drill sergeant" tone to Bill's delivery. One interesting point of his speech is when he tells the group that Jeff will be spearheading the project. Jeff perks up in his chair, but the rest of the people in the room appear less than thrilled. Some actually roll their eyes. One whispers a sarcastic comment. Most look indifferent. Jeff seems strangely unaffected by their responses and Bill keeps right on going without a pause. You and Jan exchange another knowing glance—you both notice what just happened. The credibility of your key point-of-contact has just been publicly stamped with a seal of doubt.

Once Bill finishes, he turns the floor over to you and Jan. The group is absolutely catatonic throughout your presentation. You even throw some of your best one-liners at them and barely get a reaction in return. You and Jan maintain a very casual, conversational approach as you talk about the project plan drafted just days ago. You are careful to underplay Jeff's leadership role until you better understand the dynamic between him and the other managers. As Jeff predicted, when you finish, there are no questions. When you ask them how they feel, you get back one syllable answers like, "Sounds great," "Thanks," and "Take care." Bill and Jeff are huddled in the front of the room. Jeff has a list of the twelve managers from which Bill selects who should be interviewed. After everyone leaves, you and Jan walk over to Bill and Jeff.

"So, how do you feel it went?" you ask them.

Jeff starts to answer, but Bill beats him to the punchline. "Oh, they're fine. I've known these people for a long time, believe me. When you've been doing this for as long as I have, you learn to read people well. They're on board. Here's the list of whom you can talk to. I picked my six best managers. You can have my secretary set up the meetings if you want. I gotta run, I'm late for a dinner meeting tonight with a big prospect. Thanks guys—we're off to a great start."

"So Jeff, how do you feel it went?" Jan asks.

"Well, like Bill said, they seem like they're on board. Time will tell I guess, right?"

Building Relationships With Multiple Constituents

> What questions do you have at this point about Rampart?
>
> What dynamics stand out to you as interesting from the meeting, and to what would you attribute these dynamics?
>
> What new conclusions are you forming about Bill? What, if anything, might you be inclined to do based on these conclusions?
>
> What are your thoughts about the emerging role(s) Jeff is assuming?
>
> What might you suspect Bill means by "best" managers?

Let the Anthropology Begin

The six managers that Bill selected to be interviewed are:

Jack Ritchie	VP of Sales
Ann Lornsen	VP of Marketing
Parim Sakreth	Director of Operations and Installations
Al Cappoli	Director of Technology
Mike Goldberg	VP of Client Relations
Janice McDunnough	Director of Personnel

In Chapter 9, we continue our simulation and provide you with selections from the interview transcripts for each of these managers. These are simply portions of the conversations as they happened. At the end of Chapter 9, you will have the opportunity to determine how to sort the issues, as well as how best to report back your findings to Bill and Jeff. (Remember, this scenario and all of the people in it are fictitious. Any resemblance to real-life situations is purely coincidental.)

⑨

Pandora's Box

"Every man mistakes the limits of his own field of vision for the limits of the world."

—Schopenhauer

If you've been a consultant for any length of time, you've learned by now that until you get elbow-deep into the fabric of any organization, it's difficult to know what's going on. You also know that "things are not always as they seem" when it comes to diagnosing organizational issues, especially with regard to the perspective of the most senior leaders. The following sections continue the simulation from Chapter 8. You and your engagement team, as the consultants from Summit, have set out to conduct interviews with six top managers of Rampart Systems to surface numerous data points, opinions, questions, and issues. You will have to select what you believe are the most critical pieces of information and, more important, how to help Bill accept and address them.

Interviews With Six Managers

Jack Ritchie, Vice President of Sales

Summit: So, how long have you been here at Rampart?
Jack: I've been here about five years. I started as a salesman, worked my way up to regional sales manager, and took over sales about a year and a half ago. It's been an interesting ride, that's for sure.
Summit: What's been most interesting about it?

Jack: Well, first of all, we've grown so fast. It's hard to believe we've been averaging better than 20 percent a year since I've started. It's like being on a roller coaster around here. Never a dull moment. But it's been fun.

Summit: To what would you attribute Rampart's success?

Jack: No question, to Bill. He's definitely the engine behind this ship. He bleeds Rampart blood. He thinks up the products, has almost a sixth sense about the markets, and can anticipate what they'll want and what they'll pay for it. He has a passion for the work we do, and he could convince anyone about the value of our products and their superiority over our competitors. Whenever one of our salespeople feels like they've hit a wall with a prospect, all we have to do is get Bill to give a call to some senior person in the company, and it's like magic. Having him for a CEO is like our sales force's secret weapon.

Summit: Does the time he spends with prospects take away from his other responsibilities as CEO?

Jack: Well, I guess that depends who you ask. Obviously, for me, I'm grateful for the help he gives us. But others whine about the fact that he meddles too much and doesn't keep his eye on the big picture. Sometimes I wonder what would happen if Bill got hit by a bus tomorrow. Could we keep up the same growth? I don't know. Probably not.

Summit: Does Bill also get involved in pricing?

Jack: Oh, yeah. He approves pricing and credit on every deal, whether he's involved with the sale or not. That way the salespeople don't discount over what's reasonable, and we don't erode the margins just to get deals in the door. He's pretty strict. Once in awhile he'll make an exception, but not too often.

Summit: Do you ever worry that your salespeople won't develop into seasoned client-relationship managers who can build long-term relationships and face off with senior prospects?

Jack: Well, I guess that might be a risk. Although I think they learn a lot from watching and listening to Bill. Could they step into his shoes tomorrow? Absolutely not. Let's put it this way, I'm glad he's in good health.

Summit: Do you have any plans to invest in the development of your key salespeople?

Jack: You mean like train them? It will be a cold day in hell before

Rampart spends money on any meaningful training for employees. Bill has been an activist for self-development and on-the-job stuff, but he goes bonkers if you mention any kind of classroom training. He thinks it's a waste of time and money. Not to mention that it takes people out of the field.

Summit: So how do you feel about the addition of Demarka to Rampart?

Jack: I think it's gonna be a great boost for the sales force. We get so many requests from clients for post-installation support that we just can't provide. Some of the salespeople are nervous about learning the products well enough to be credible with prospects. After all, Internet marketing is not what Rampart has been known for. But once we get over that hump, we could start selling some pretty big deals. My guys are chomping at the bit to learn the products and to get out there and start selling them. I've heard some of them are already starting to generate leads. I just hope Ann Lornsen has some ideas on how to reposition Rampart to the market so that we'll be accepted as a real player. I think this acquisition has made her very nervous.

Summit: Why?

Jack: Well, since this is confidential, I might as well tell you . . . she and Bill haven't gotten along all that well since the deal was done. She had some strong opinions about how viable it would be, and Bill wasn't all that interested in being bucked. Now she's left facing the challenge of how to bundle the services and position the new offering as one, integrated solution, when we don't even know if our technologies are compatible, we don't know what kinds of networks their products can work with, and I've heard rumors that their key product development guy is thinking about bailing. I'm sure he's locked in for at least six months, but Ann doesn't know enough about their products to package the offering without his help. Especially if there are technology conflicts. So if he's unhappy for some reason, it's hard to say how much help he'll really be if he's got one foot out the door. I'm sure he expects to have Ann report to him, and he'll go nuts if he finds out that he may have to report to her. Either way, it could get ugly.

Summit: Do you think this is a major risk to the deal, or just some typical frustrations of any acquisition process?

Jack: Well, I don't know because I've never done this before. But I don't think I'd treat this as a little problem, that's for sure. It seems like we've bet a lot on this working out, and it all hinges on a more integrated offering. So the longer it takes for us to get there, the more revenue opportunities we'll miss, and the greater the risk of someone else getting to market with a competitive offering.

Summit: Do you think the rest of Rampart is generally excited about Demarka?

Jack: I'd say the jury is still out. A lot of people don't even know much about it. And I would say for the rank-and-file people, it's not really going to change much of their world. You're going to hear some people say that we're not ready for this, that we're still too much of a "small minded" company to do something like an acquisition. Many of the people that work here are still in college or recent grads, trainee technicians who get a few years of experience here and then move on, or part-time hourly order processors. I would say our top 100 people are really the ones who are going to be most affected by this, and among them, I'd guess that half are excited and behind it. The other half think Bill is out of his mind. They would much prefer to have seen the money put in our pockets in some type of long-term incentive plan.

Summit: What do you think the greatest challenge is going to be to make the Rampart-Demarka deal work?

Jack: Well, to be blunt, that's like the blind leading the blind. Don't misunderstand. I think it's a great opportunity, and I'm behind it all the way. But we don't really know what we're doing. In that top 100 group I mentioned before, maybe 30 percent would qualify as professional managers—people with solid managerial experience. The rest are homegrown. We're knocking on the door of becoming a billion-dollar company now, but we don't know how to act like a billion-dollar company. We still act like a $100 million company, making decisions by the seat of our pants. To pull this one off, we're going to have to grow up.

Ann Lornsen, Vice President of Marketing

Ann: So, you people are the white knights that have come to rescue us, eh?

Summit: Rescue you from what?

Ann: Our ridiculous naivete . . . that we actually think we can make this deal work.

Summit: It sounds as if your confidence is a little shaky.

Ann: Don't be so polite. We're delusional. I don't know what Bill has been smoking, but there's no way for this to end but to blow up in our face.

Summit: What makes you so sure it's going to fail?

Ann: First of all, have you seen an organization chart for Rampart?

Summit: Actually, not yet.

Ann: Well, don't hold your breath, because there isn't one. I have forty people that work for me in marketing, and they all essentially report to me. That's because we have absolutely no infrastructure in this place. It's one big free-for-all. We're all so busy running around like chickens with our heads cut off, what the hell makes him think we're organized clearly and efficiently enough to absorb a whole other company? We have spans of control that range from one-on-three to one-on-twenty with no logic behind them. We're very functionally minded. People live and breathe their silos, and yet we claim to provide integrated solutions. On the flip side of the coin, Demarka is structured around their client segments in multi-disciplinary teams—almost like mini-business units. How do we re-solve this little dilemma? And that's just one! I think the lawyers who worked out the details of this deal should have their fees with-held for a year until the dust settles. And then they should get paid based on how this thing really shakes out, as opposed to on what they projected, because I think they're being wildly optimistic.

Summit: Have you shared your concerns with Bill?

Ann: Of course I have, but he's not interested in hearing naysayers. Bill isn't the kind of guy you easily disagree with. He's so blind to the issues, and just can't accept the fact that he can't do every-thing anymore. The man is a one-man show, and he's got an audi-ence of about 3,300 employees cheering from the stands. He can't stand feeling like he's not in control. God forbid somebody makes a decision without checking with him first. So people have learned to game the system. They tell him what he wants to hear, and then they do what they want anyway. As long as you don't get caught, make your numbers, don't piss off the clients, you can be a hero.

Summit: How has Jeff managed to climb so high here? What does he do to be successful?

Ann: Oh, please, are you kidding? That man hasn't got a bone in his back. He can't go to the bathroom without Bill's approval. Bill loves him because he's a loyal soldier, will do whatever Bill asks, and he's just smart enough to get tactical things done, but not too smart where he can figure out he's just a puppet. Nobody around here respects him. They just put up with him. He's basically a nice guy, so he never tries to pull rank on anybody. I think he realizes that if he ever tried to push any weight around, everybody would sabotage him. He's kind of the company joke.

Summit: Let me switch gears here for a minute. We've heard some skepticism about whether or not Rampart's product set will be technically compatible with Demarka's products, and some concern that your department will be challenged to figure out the right bundling to produce an integrated offering. Your thoughts?

Ann: First of all, there's a couple of pieces of background data you should know. When Rampart first started offering LAN/WAN solutions nine years ago, everybody said it wouldn't work. When we started up our network support group and added on servicing to the deals, people said we'd never be able to compete. Two years ago, we did our first voice/data networking job and have done a couple of dozen since. This is a "show me" culture when it comes to change. But as far as our products and services go, we've come through every time. In the markets we play in throughout the Midwest and the mountain states, we are the leading provider of network services. And now we've had four or five pretty significant requests for additional add-on services to help support ongoing marketing efforts of websites we help build. Clearly there's an opportunity there that, if carefully pursued, could open up a lot of revenue streams and attract some larger clients. So, to answer your question, no, the problem isn't the product sets themselves. We can probably figure out relatively easily how to combine our products with Demarka's to build an integrated offering that's more end-to-end than we are today.

Summit: Than why are you so sure this will fail?

Ann: Has anybody answered the question for you, "How did we get to the decision to buy Demarka?"

Summit: We understood it to be a result of recognizing the opportunity these recent requests from clients represented.

Ann: Doesn't it seem a little spooky to spend $65 million just because some clients requested a service we can't currently provide? Talk about ready-fire-aim!

Summit: It isn't the worst criteria we've seen executives use to make decisions.

Ann: Look, my point is this: Where the hell is this place going? We have no articulated strategy that would suggest Demarka is a good decision or a bad decision. The only reason I can tell you we're leaders in the markets we play in is because I've had outside market research people benchmark our offering. Do you think Bill would have approved the money for that study if I'd asked? Forget it! If you polled every one of those twelve people that were in the room the other day on where they thought Rampart was headed, I swear you'd get twelve different answers. We don't have the appropriate MIS to help make management decisions, like how to emphasize or deemphasize products based on profitability or market performance. We don't pay any serious attention to competitors—if we lose a bid, we don't find out why. We never gather the senior leaders to talk about how to grow certain markets, penetrate more deeply into existing clients, or brainstorm new product and service opportunities. When it comes to running this place, we're basically winging it. Sure, we've been incredibly lucky. But to spend $65 million on a whim seems like lunacy to me. Do you see my point?

Summit: Yes, I certainly do. Are you the only one who has these concerns, or do any of your peers see what you see?

Ann: I got here two years ago from a very large consumer products company. I grew up in a seasoned, mature marketing organization with very sophisticated systems and processes for making critical decisions. I was told I was brought here to help Rampart "come into the twentieth century just in time to leave it." I've been frustrated since I walked in the door trying to help this place mature. Sure, others see it, but nobody is going to rock the boat. A few of us talk in the halls, but there's no real commitment to deal with these issues. Everybody's too scared of Bill.

Summit: How does Bill react to your concerns? Does he see you as a maverick?

Ann: I can tell he's struggling with what to do with me. You can always tell when Bill is upset. You get the cold shoulder. I've been getting the cold shoulder for a while now. He knows he can't fire me because it would look bad to the rest of the organization. Even though I can be a little in-your-face, he knows I've done a lot for Rampart, and whether or not he likes me, he knows he needs someone like me. It's not like I go out of my way to threaten him, he's just so used to being in total control.

Summit: If you could get him to take one piece of advice, what would it be?

Ann: Take the time to work with the senior leaders to establish a shared vision and strategy for Rampart's future—even if it's just the next three to five years. Then, start investing in creating the infrastructure, processes, and systems that will make us, well, more like a bona-fide company.

Parim Sakreth, Director of Operations and Installations

Summit: Tell us a little bit about your background, Parim, and how you came to Rampart.

Parim: Certainly. I finished my undergraduate work in computer science and my masters in information technology at Stanford. I worked in Silicon Valley for about five years doing the typical hop around from shop to shop on the leapfrog path to increasing my salary. Then I decided I wanted to settle down and stop the nomadic approach to my career. I got married and my wife has family here in the Midwest, so when I told her about the opportunity here at Rampart, needless to say she was very excited. I came about six years ago as a senior technician and two years ago became director of operations and installations. It's actually a really fun job.

Summit: What do you like most about it?

Parim: Well, we get to spend so much time with the clients. We get to see firsthand how well the solutions we provide meet their needs. When you see them get excited as their web pages go online, or their networks or intranets go live and they send their first e-mails and populate their first data sites, it's very rewarding.

Summit: What about when the clients aren't happy?

Parim: Fortunately, that doesn't happen too often, but it does happen. We're a pretty client-focused company, so when a client has a complaint or a need, people drop stuff and go running. We spare no effort to make our clients happy.

Summit: Does providing that level of service to clients cost a lot?

Parim: What do you mean?

Summit: Well, with other clients we've worked with, we find that sometimes, even with the best of intentions, companies are spending more money than their clients are actually paying on providing high levels of service. Does your pricing model allow for such extensive service levels? Are there different pricing models for different service agreements?

Parim: Heck, I don't know. We don't see the bills. We just respond to the requests. All I know is that if a client concern ever got all the way to Bill, there'd be hell to pay. We work very hard to get the installations right the first time, but we do make mistakes. And when we do, we work twice as hard to fix them.

Summit: What would you say was the greatest contributor to the mistakes?

Parim: The workload volume. We can barely keep up. The orders are coming in the door faster than we can get them set up. Clients don't want to hear that they have to wait three months to get their new technology up and running—they want it yesterday. But I also don't have time to get out there and hire more technicians that I need, because it takes too long to get approval for more headcount, find the candidates, pick the good ones—which are few and far between to begin with—then train them and get them up to speed. So I wind up going out on the installations myself. It's a catch 22. Then I get smacked for not being around the office when Bill calls with a question. Oh well, what can you do? And on the other side of the house, you've got the client service people booking service calls for clients when networks go down or servers crash. Because they don't like being on the other end of a screaming client, they just promise them whatever turnaround time they ask for, pass on the service requisitions to us, and we're left looking like the bad guys when we don't show up an hour after the client first called. It's crazy.

Summit: Do you have a lot of turnover among your installation and tech crews?

Parim: Not too bad. We pay our people really well, so the ones that come usually stay. Occasionally we get raided, or people decide this is a dead-end job, but for the most part we can hold on to our people.

Summit: Have you ever tried to work on these internal process issues between sales, client service, and your group? It sounds like there might be a pretty significant opportunity to improve some efficiency.

Parim: I've raised it with Mike before. I've asked him to have his people at least check our backlog before giving clients, especially upset clients, dates we simply can't hold to. When I ask, it works for a while, then they slip back into old habits.

Summit: How do your people feel about this Demarka acquisition?

Parim: All we've really heard is that we acquired this company in California. That's about it. I think it's a great idea myself. We can now stick around longer at our clients' locations and provide additional support. A few of our bigger clients have been asking for this support and we've had to refer them to other vendors. Now we can capture the opportunity ourselves.

Summit: What do you think will be the challenges to making it work smoothly?

Parim: Getting my operations people trained in the products. When we put together the customized hardware here in the shop before going on the install, there is a lot of precision design and engineering work that gets done. My guys are going to have to learn about a whole new set of technologies, and then they'll have to figure out how to make them work together. They're pretty smart, so I'm not worried that they'll be able to—I'm worried about *when* they'll be able to. They don't have time to breathe now. I just hope we don't start selling the new product right away, until my people are up to speed with how to integrate it into our current stuff.

Summit: Have you spoken to Jack in sales about your concerns on the timing?

Parim: Actually, I haven't. Maybe I should sit down with him and let him know that we'll need some time before we can actually deliver this thing. That's a good idea—thanks.

Summit: What is operations and installation's relationship with sales like? I would imagine your groups have to work pretty closely together?

Parim: You'd think so, wouldn't you? Quite frankly, the salespeople treat my guys like dirt. They'll send over boxes of candy when they need one of my guys to come on a sales call to help close the deal, but after that, they get barked at like servants. The salespeople are out only for their own commissions and couldn't care less what they have to do to get them. And Jack encourages it without even realizing it. He gets his guys so pumped up about pushing product, getting additional business and add-on services, that they'll do anything. Most of them barely know the products now, and they have to rely heavily on my guys to help them not look stupid in front of the client. But once the deal is sold, the contract is signed, the salespeople are nothing but a vapor trail, and my guys are left having to untangle all of the promises the salespeople made that can't be kept without huge heroics. Sometimes they can't be kept at all. Then we have to get the salesperson back involved, and they argue with us about why we can't do what they promised. They forget that we're still trying to deliver what they promised the last client, and that we're steeped in dozens of setups and installations at the same time. My guys actually resent all of the commissions they essentially earn for the salespeople.

Summit: Are your people rewarded when they help close a deal?

Parim: Yeah, like I said, they get the box of candy from the salesperson.

Summit: The reward system doesn't allow for them to share in the gain if they helped?

Parim: Around here, salespeople are royalty. Ops people and installers are the back-room people. So, no, we don't get any of the glory—or the money—that comes with closing the deals. On rare occasions, if a tech guy is really instrumental in getting new business, Jack will send him an e-mail and copy Bill on it. Bill is good about following up with another e-mail to the tech expressing his thanks. But like I said, that's rare.

Summit: So given this kind of relationship between your group and the sales force, how do you think it will impact the Demarka deal?

Parim: I can just imagine those salespeople foaming at the mouth now ready to sell, sell, sell the new products. I don't know how Bill is going to price it, but I'm sure the end-to-end support won't be cheap—which means the commissions will be sweet. I can also imagine that Bill will be very anxious to start making back the $65 million he spent, so he'll want orders coming in right away. So he's gonna be pushing the salespeople to sell the bigger deals. And who will get left holding the smoking gun if it all starts to unravel? You're looking at him.

Al Cappoli, Director of Technology

Al: Hi . . . Al Cappoli . . . nice to meet you . . . excuse me, I have to
get this phone call, it will just be a second . . . Al Cappoli here . . .
yeah, I signed it yesterday . . . well, then tell the purchasing people
if we can't buy parts, we can't make products. I don't care, we
need that stuff by the end of next week. I'm not letting some twerpy
little clerk who pushes purchase orders for a living dictate our product development schedule; I don't care what the policy says, tell
him to walk it to Bill's office himself and wait there for a signature.
I'll leave Bill a voice mail this afternoon and let him know it's for the
Addison project, he'll sign it. Thanks, Lisa. Bye. . . . I'm sorry, but
that's the way life is around here—always a battle to fight. You're
the people from the consulting firm, right?

Summit: Yes, nice to meet you, Al. Thanks for carving out time to
talk to us.

Al: No problem—if you can really help us, it will be worth it.

Summit: Tell us what exactly your job entails as director of technology.

Al: Somehow I think the list of what it doesn't entail would be shorter.
But seriously, there are two major buckets my people play in. One
group handles all of our internal IT needs, our own LANs, PCs, help
desk, telecom, software, MIS, et cetera. The other group, the larger
of the two, is really the closest thing Rampart has to an R&D function. They're responsible for developing new versions of our key
products, creating applications of our products for new platforms,
updating technical specs and documentation, and keeping their
fingers on the pulse as people find new uses for their networks,
creating additional network support needs. Right now, we're working on a brand-new intranet product that will enable easier transfer
between LANs and Internet traffic with some important security
features our clients have been asking for. I would say those make
up the bulk of my job.

Summit: Well, sounds like you're a pretty busy guy. I guess it must
be nice to be able to use your own products for internal use—I
assume your internal people are some of the first to get to use
products you develop and sell?

Al: Ever hear the expression, "The cobbler's kids have no shoes"?

Summit: So you're not using your own products?

Al: We haven't invested in our own technology in years. Sure, we're using our own products—the first ones Rampart ever invented when the company started!

Summit: You're kidding?

Al: I wish I was. I have my people working on the upgrades as fast as we can, but so many of the resources get poured into the product development efforts, there's hardly anything left for our own use. Some of these machines are being held together with chewing gum and prayer. The boxes on people's desktops are some of the earliest PCs that hit the market. The irony is that we're installing state-of-the-art servers at our client sites while our people are exchanging e-mails over dinosaur machines. Pretty sad if you ask me. We help our clients add speed and productivity to their organizations with cutting-edge network tools that give employees access to information, common databases, knowledge management tools, and fast transaction processing, like HR and finance transactions. Meanwhile, I've got a purchasing clerk running around the building trying to get a handful of signatures on a form that he'll process manually to purchase parts I need to invent new products. While we're networking our clients to their suppliers and customers, our people are using the telephone and U.S. Postal Service to stay connected to our suppliers and clients. It's pathetic if you think about it.

Summit: Why is it this way? Has anybody been advocating for more current technology? What's getting in the way?

Al: Well, we've always gotten by with minimal upgrading, minor adjustments, and getting the next revision of software only after four or five revisions have actually been released. Between you and me, most people wonder if it's not the fact that every dollar that doesn't go into new technology, or any investment for that matter, is another dollar that goes into Bill's pocket. And let's face it, we've been very successful. There's been no serious consequence because our internal technology stinks. At least not yet.

Summit: What consequences would you anticipate?

Al: Well, this Demarka deal should be interesting. I did one of the site visits out there last month. You know, wine and dine the owners, shake hands, make nice-nice with the new family members, that kind of thing. These guys aren't on the leading edge . . . they're on the bleeding edge of technology. There wasn't a piece of paper to be found. I asked if they had a photocopy machine in the building I could use to make copies of something. They looked at me as if I was from another planet. Everyone uses voice-recognition software for their document creation, they've all got video conferencing on their desktops, and they use the most recent releases of software. There are color scanners and color laser printers throughout the building. People fax right from their desktops. These people are like the ultimate Silicon Valley techies. They live and breathe pushing the envelope. Now, just how excited do you think these people are going to be working for Rampart when they see the sorry state we're in?

Summit: But wasn't all of this considered in the due diligence work? I mean, the implications are obvious—weren't they thought through?

Al: I know I raised the question. But I think their owners were anxious to sell and fed Bill some line like, "Don't worry about it, we can help you upgrade—it's one more piece of the value proposition of the deal—you get instant technology upgrades." Bill was feeling anxious about the deal and wanted to get it over with. I think he felt he'd gone too far down the path and couldn't turn back. So he convinced himself it would be no big deal.

Summit: Needless to say, you don't share that opinion?

Al: I think it's gonna be a *very* big deal. In fact, I've heard that their star development guy is looking to defect to one of Demarka's cross-town rivals. I don't know if he just feels disappointed that he didn't get a big enough piece of the pie, or if he got wind of what he's in for with our ancient technology. When you're a star developer, you can pretty much write your own ticket in this business. So if he's waffling about staying or going, even if we've locked him in for six months, our stuff will send him packing for sure. He'll never put up with this Mickey Mouse crap. And I can't say that I blame him.

Summit: Some people have expressed differing opinions on the compatibility of Demarka's products and Rampart's—that the potential "great combination" into an end-to-end offering may not be as achievable as everyone might hope. What's your take?

Al: Well, we can all rub lamps, light candles, squeeze our lucky rabbit's foot, whatever. It won't come easy. But I don't think the challenge is whether or not the products can work compatibly—I think we're smart enough to figure that out. What I think it's going to come down to is, are we willing to spend the dollars it will take to level the technical playing field so they can become compatible. And given the climate around here these days when it comes to spending money for even paper clips, Bill's not gonna swallow that kind of price tag without a major struggle.

Summit: What would it take to convince him that it is necessary to invest more in order to realize the leverage of the acquisition?

Al: A miracle.

Summit: What kind of miracle?

Al: Well, isn't that what you're here to figure out?

Mike Goldberg, Vice President of Client Relations

Mike: Hi, Mike Goldberg, how are you?

Summit: Hi, Mike, nice to meet you, (your name), Summit Consulting.

Mike: Let's see, the note here says we're talking about "my thoughts and ideas about how best to make the Demarka acquisition most productive and efficient in terms of integration and performance"—sounds like you wrote this for Bill, am I right?

Summit: We gave him some input, yes. But it's his note. Why do you assume it came from us?

Mike: Bill doesn't write notes. In any case, no matter. What do you want to know?

Summit: Well, maybe you could start by talking a little bit about your role as vice president of client relations, what that entails, how long you've been in this role, the major challenges.

Mike: Okay. Well, I've been at Rampart for about eight years, started out as an installations tech. Spent a few years working there, then came over to client relations. Managed a team of CRRs—client relations reps—and took over as head about a year and a half ago. We have three teams of reps, each managed by a team leader and segmented by products. So one team handles client contact for intranet and network support, another does Internet, and the third is for e-commerce. The boundaries are a little blurry because some of our clients have more than one of our products, and in those cases we have dedicated reps to those accounts for all client interactions. The reps mostly handle routine questions, account issues, schedule service calls, relay technical questions to the operations people, renew service contracts, things like that. Most of them come out of operations and installations, so they are fairly familiar with the products. Some of them aren't the most interpersonally talented, but we've given them some coaching. No major liabilities on any of the teams.

Summit: What's the most common complaints they hear from your clients?

Mike: Gosh, I don't know if there's any one particular type of issue that comes up more than others. But I know getting service calls scheduled and done quickly has always been tough. Clients want someone at their site within an hour, and we just don't have the resources to respond like that. Sometimes our techs can get online to correct a minor issue; sometimes they can troubleshoot over the phone. But when the problem is major, sometimes we can't get a crew there until the next day. Now, for a few clients that isn't a major problem, but for most of them who live and die by their technology, that's significant downtime. And it doesn't matter that some bozo in their company did something stupid to cause the network to go down or the website to become inaccessible or the server to freeze, they just want us there to fix it right away. I can appreciate their urgency, but you can't get blood from a stone—I can only do what I can do with the resources I've got.

Summit: Are you understaffed? Could you use more techs to get the work done more responsively to clients' urgent needs?

Mike: That's a matter of opinion. I certainly think we're very lean. Getting headcount added around here is like pulling teeth. Most of our clients are pretty flexible, and we've never really had a client fire us because we couldn't be there when they wanted us. They get all heated up in the moment, but once the issue is resolved, the relationship remains pretty solid.

Summit: Have you ever had a client fire you because of chronic service issues?

Mike: No, not really. We've had a few occasions where we had to credit their accounts or waive fees because we just didn't deliver on time, but that's more the exception than the norm. I'd say for the most part we've got pretty strong client service.

Summit: How do you know? Is it just the absence of complaints that tells you that, or are there metrics in place that help inform your hunches?

Mike: We started a couple of years ago doing a client satisfaction survey. We did it every six months and after new installs, specifically about the start-up process. But for the most part, the data weren't all that helpful. Sort of middle-of-the-road. Places we knew we'd not done our best got us okay to not-great ratings, and places we knew we'd done well got us excellent ratings. After a while, the process was more of a bureaucratic exercise than a valuable one, so we just stopped it.

Summit: Do you ever worry that just getting mediocre or indifferent reactions from clients may not be good enough over the long term?

Mike: Nah. I mean, we're the best game in town and most people know it, so it's not like they've got loads of options to choose from. Even if a client hated us, which I don't think any do, where are they gonna go?

Summit: So if we went out and polled a random sample of your clients across your product lines, you believe that the majority of their responses would be favorable?

Mike: Yeah, I'd have to say so. This is a service business, and Bill is pretty open about his commitment to clients. We take our cues from him. He gets out there and visits clients, is more than generous when resolving their issues, and actually talks about them a lot—you know the typical rhetoric about "they pay our bills." I think he really means it, too.

Summit: Do you and your team share his passion and commitment?

Mike: Well, nobody could ever match him. I think we're committed for the most part. Remember, these are not MBAs from Harvard here. With the exception of a few high-priced MIT-types, these are high school and tech school graduates making very good money in jobs that would not pay this much anywhere else. So I'm just glad when they come to work, get the work done, and don't give me a hard time about anything. Now I don't know exactly what commitment would look like coming out of this type of employee, but to the extent these people can be committed to anything, I'd have to say they are.

Summit: How are you feeling about the Demarka acquisition?

Mike: Well, we haven't heard too much about it. It sounds like a pretty good opportunity.

Summit: Is their client service organization fairly comparable to yours?

Mike: I don't know, I've only read reports and seen organization charts of how they're set up. It's hard to tell from just that information. But I can't imagine it will be significantly different. Just smaller.

Summit: Have any of your people approached you with questions about how their roles might be different now that they'll be servicing a new set of clients with new products?

Mike: No, they haven't. It's actually not been established as to whether or not Demarka's clients will continue to get serviced from California or if that work will move here. I would imagine it will stay out there for a while.

Summit: Do you have a preference?

Mike: I haven't thought about it much, but I'd probably say I'd prefer for it to stay out there for as long as possible. The less we do to rock the boat here, the better we'll all be.

Summit: Rock the boat?

Mike: Yeah, you know, shake things up, make big changes. I think things have been going fine for a long time. I'm sure this Demarka thing is a good idea, but let's face it, it's gonna be very disruptive. I don't like disruption. I have a well-oiled machine here that's working just nicely. I certainly don't need to topple the whole apple cart trying to figure out how to service clients on the West Coast who don't know us, don't know our products, and whose questions nobody here will be able to answer. So I'd be just as happy to have this take a long time.

Summit: I'm a little confused. Earlier you said you thought the Demarka acquisition sounded like a good opportunity. But it doesn't sound like you're all that thrilled with the idea of them joining forces with Rampart? Am I missing something?

Mike: I think it is a great opportunity—for Rampart. But for me, it's going to be a pain in the rear. Not only am I going to have to deal with the clients, my CRRs, and Bill, now I'm going to have a new crop of people whining at me for stuff. So you're right, I'm not thrilled with the idea of having to listen to more whining.

Summit: Why do you think . . .

Mike: . . . I mean, how easy do you think it is to have a boss constantly breathing down your neck, watching every penny you spend, always telling you you're not pulling your weight, and then

slamming you from the other side when you don't service the clients properly. It's a vicious cycle. You spend money to meet client
needs, you get smacked! You don't meet the client's needs, you
get smacked! You try and motivate your people to remain service
oriented, then the salespeople and the techs are yelling that we
aren't including them enough in resolving client issues or that we're
overpromising on what the techs can do. So then I tell my people
to make sure they play team ball, to keep their peripheral vision up,
to be good business partners with their colleagues, and throw
every other stupid cliché at them to remind them of their internal
clients, and *wham!* We're getting kicked for being too internally focused and not paying enough attention to the clients. Everywhere
we turn, it's another brick wall!

Summit: Well, Mike, I wonder if . . .

Mike: . . . Can you see how this is a no-win job? What the hell makes
anybody think I'm gonna be thrilled about another opportunity to
disappoint more people?

Summit: Mike, does Bill know how frustrated . . .

Mike: . . . Oh, please, don't go there! Believe me, whether or not Bill
knows how tough any of us have it is irrelevant. He'll be the first to
rant and rave about how he's done every job in this company, and
how he could still do every job in this company. He'll preach about
how much he appreciates a can-do attitude and how he really can't
stand whining. "Don't come to me with a problem, come with solutions," he says in one breath, and in the next breath, you're hearing, "Do you have any idea how much that'll cost?" when you
propose your solution. Look, I wasn't looking to go off on a Bill-
bashing spree here. I think Bill's a great guy. I admire him a lot for
how he's built Rampart, and for how dedicated he is. I guess all
I'm really saying is that he doesn't have a clue what it's like for us
down in the trenches. But since he's sure he does, there's really
no benefit to trying to convince him otherwise.

Summit: I imagine this must be very discouraging for you sometimes.

Mike: I guess. I hadn't thought of it that way, but you're right. All of
us want to do a good job. We really do. I guess I seem like I'm one
of those about-to-blow employees whose burned out with stress.
But the real issue is that we all do care a lot about Rampart, and
we're scared that this Demarka deal could crater the place. The

one thing I think we all have in common is that we're all barely hanging on and keeping together what we've got. It's like a house of cards. It's always that last card that brings the whole thing down. The problem is, you never know which is the last card until the whole thing falls apart. I think some of us are afraid Demarka is the last card.

Summit: I can see how you would feel that way.

Mike: I apologize for venting so much, that really wasn't my intent.

Summit: No problem. We're used to having clients use these interviews as a catharsis. We understand.

Mike: Have you been sensing similar frustrations from my colleagues?

Summit: I would say there are some clear themes emerging.

Mike: Do you think you can help us?

Summit: We're certainly going to try our best. As you acknowledged yourself, this is no small challenge Rampart is facing.

Mike: What odds would you give us for succeeding?

Summit: That depends.

Mike: On what?

Summit: On whether or not every leader in the place believes you have no other choice but to make this succeed.

Janice McDunnough, Director of Personnel

Summit: Hi, Janice, it's nice to meet you.

Janice: Likewise. So how can I help you today?

Summit: Well, as you know, Bill has brought us in to help your firm try to make the Demarka integration process go as smoothly as possible. We're spending time with a few of the senior leaders to get a more informed point of view about where things are today, so we can hopefully make more insightful recommendations.

Janice: Well, you've got your work cut out for you, I can tell you that much.

Summit: How so?

Janice: Well, so far, I wouldn't exactly call this a hand-in-glove fit. The culture of Demarka is almost a complete opposite to Rampart's. From an HR perspective, our compensation and benefits structures are very different, our beliefs about assessing and rewarding performance are different, and we have almost opposing philosophies with respect to developing employee talent.

Summit: Talk a little bit about the specific differences.

Janice: First of all, their benefits package is far more generous than ours. Better carriers with lower employee contributions, a higher employer match in the 401(k), and a whole lot more perks—car allowances, health-club subsidies, the works. From a compensation perspective, our total packages are pretty comparable, but they have larger portions at risk, which means their bonuses are much larger and tied to company performance. We do annual plain-vanilla performance appraisals; they have an online 360-degree feedback process that is integrated with a substantial development program. We're lucky if we can order books for our people to read. In case you haven't heard, Bill isn't a big fan of formal training.

Summit: So we've heard.

Janice: But I'd say the main difference is stock ownership. While neither of us is public, Demarka was considering an IPO before we approached them. A few years ago they started one of those phantom stock programs that issued shares to employees. It was a great retention tool since their Silicon Valley rivals are known for raiding talent. We don't have anything like that, but I can tell you that some of our more senior people have been mumbling for a long time about how they've been very tempted to leave for opportunities that offered long-term ownership. Bill is very generous sharing profits with employees, but it could never compare to having a piece of the action. Now, as part of the deal we agreed to keep Demarka's people on their plans and programs for at least a year. I think that may prove to be a big mistake. It's gonna take about four nanoseconds for our people to get wind of what Demarka's people are getting, and my worst nightmare is a mutiny. At our size and in our industry, we're just not competitive, and with Demarka coming into the fold, that's going to be more obvious than ever. Sure, we look great if you compare us regionally. But across the industry—that's a different story. And on the other side of the equation, their key employees are only under retention contracts for six months to a year, depending on the individual. If we try and convert them to our plans and programs the way they are today, we'll have a mass exodus on our hands. But other than that, the deal oughta work fine!

Summit: Well, I'd say you've got your work cut out for you, too. Where will you start?

Janice: My first approach will be to outline a long-term plan to build a comp and benefits program that is not only competitive, but comparable enough to Demarka's that they won't all bail out after the year grace period. Then I'm going to do a ton of homework to find carriers and vendors who can deliver low cost to us, so I can put an accurate price tag to the plan. The one good thing about the year grace period is that it buys me some time to research and plan. I'm going to look at outsourcing, too. As for the development and assessment programs, where Demarka is clearly way ahead of us, I'm going to propose a plan that adopts a modified version of their processes. That's just good business sense. Technology pcople who feel like they're not continually learning usually flee pretty fast.

Summit: Given all the obstacles in the way, HR and otherwise, do you think the Demarka decision was a good choice?

Janice: There's no doubt in my mind that if we can pull this off—and I realize that will be no small feat—it could give Rampart a point of differentiation that we've just not seen other network systems companies have. It's unique. It will broaden our offering in a way competitors wouldn't expect. But the distance between here and there is big. And the cost to get there has yet to be fully determined, much less accepted. Yes, I think it was a smart bet, but a big bet nonetheless.

Summit: All of the interviews so far seem to suggest that Bill will have to fundamentally change the way he leads this organization. Would you say that's accurate?

Janice: In a big way! But to be perfectly honest, I'm not sure he's up to it. He's done things the same way for a long time, and it's worked—damn well, in fact. He's an interesting man. I think he's brilliant. His mind never stops working. He can see things others can't. But Rampart is his life. His family life is in shambles. I can't believe he's stayed married this long. His kids can't stand him because he tries to run them the way he runs Rampart—like a navy ship. I've been with Bill for a long time. I know his heart's in the right place. He would never consciously hurt someone. And when our people have been in trouble, he's there. Last year he paid for one of our people's husband to have an experimental cancer treatment at the Mayo Clinic when the insurance declined to cover it. He did it quietly. Just told me to have the bills sent here. He cares about Rampart and our people a lot. Sometimes he cares too much. And I just think at his age, it's too painful to face up to the fact that maybe his baby has outgrown his abilities and may well be better off in the hands of a different leader. I know if I'd dedicated practically my entire career to building my own company, it would be painful for me, too.

Summit: Have you talked about succession with him? Does he have someone in mind?

Janice: He gets very tense when I bring it up. He knows he has to pick someone to groom, but that's a tough reality. Right now he's got Jeff to lean on, but Lord knows he's not the answer. Jeff's a nice guy—don't get me wrong. But not CEO material, that's for sure. And Bill knows that, too. Unfortunately, he's never told Jeff that. And I'm worried that Jeff may soon start to think he's the heir apparent. I'm pushing Bill to have that talk with Jeff sooner rather than later. Bill realized it two years ago when Jeff made a major blunder with a client. He's tried to give Jeff chances to grow into executive skin, but Jeff isn't wired that way. In fact, there was a time when Bill was thinking of making Jeff COO, but I talked him out of that. He and Jeff are very close, so it will be hard for Bill to initiate that conversation. Some employees make sarcastic comments like, "Jeff is the son Bill never had." There really isn't anybody else internally who comes close to being ready to step into Bill's shoes anytime soon. This is highly confidential, but I'm sure Bill will tell you eventually . . . we have a search out now for a COO. We started it right after we signed the Demarka deal. Nobody knows but Bill and me. Personally, I think Bill is scared that he's bitten off more than he can chew having bought Demarka. He wants help. The fact that you people are here is evidence of that. Filling the COO job is a different story. You people will be gone one day. A new COO is a symbol to Bill of his eventually having to pass the reins to someone else. For someone like him, that's really tough. He's rejected every candidate he's interviewed so far. But at least he's interviewing them—small steps still count. He and I are pretty close, and I can tell when he's anxious. It may not be obvious to the naked eye, but trust me, he is. If you guys only accomplished one thing, I would hope that it would be to help Bill recognize that the greatest legacy he could leave Rampart, whether he leaves tomorrow or in ten years, would be to invest in its future. Build a plan that allows for the place to mature into a robust, viable enterprise that can compete in the twenty-first century. Right now, without Bill's passion and force of will, we'd sink pretty fast. I sure hope he'll listen to you, because the rest of us haven't been able to get through to him.

Summit: What advice would you give us on how best to approach Bill with what we're hearing?

Janice: Be straightforward. Don't pull your punches. And be compassionate—remember, you're talking about his entire life. There's a lot at stake for him. And for the rest of us, too.

Translating Data Into Value

Well, there's the data. Needless to say, on a live engagement, you would have the opportunity to gather a lot more data in both quantitative and qualitative forms. For the purposes of the Rampart simulation, we'll treat this as a springboard from which to determine what additional questions and data you might want to pursue. We've provided a format for you to follow that might serve as a useful way to initially sort the data. We've also asked you to identify places where potential bad habits may creep in if a consultant were so inclined, and where the value-creating roles described in Chapter 3 may be particularly effective. After that, your next steps are to see what client of choice characteristics Bill may be displaying—in the right amount, too much, or too little—and to identify any sources of organizational reverence for which a consultant's irreverence might apply.

Initial Reactions

- What are some of your early conclusions about Rampart after these six interviews?

- Do you see any patterns emerging among the data?
- What are the top two or three most critical issues based on the data you have so far?
- Go back and look at your responses to the above three questions. What, if any, evidence do you see of your own discipline or expertise influencing the lenses through which you view Rampart? What issues did you not list as critical? Why?
- How are the conclusions you drew about Rampart also informing you about your own consulting biases? Looking back over your career, can you see what experiences and training helped form these biases?

Expanding the Anthropological Hunt

- Based on the data you have, and your initial conclusions, what additional data do you think would be helpful?
- What new questions do you have now that you didn't have before doing the interviews?
- What is prompting the desire for this specific information?

Priorities

- If you had to prioritize a list of critical issues based on what you know, which issues would be on the list and why?
- On what do you base these priorities? What evidence do you have to support your conclusions that these are the vital few areas Bill should focus on?
- Which issues have the potential to be very urgent, but not particularly important? That is, which issues, if pursued, could consume considerable energy and resources, but not yield a significant degree of value? How would you help Bill distinguish these from the issues you identified as most critical?

Bad Habits Die Hard

How might each of these bad habit consultants react to Bill and Rampart, given the data provided? Give specific examples.

Messiah	Dependency Builder	Colluder

How might the situation at Rampart provoke these negative motives?

Missionaries	Mercenaries

Enacting the Value-Creating Roles

How might each of these value-creating consultant roles contribute to the Rampart engagement, given the data provided? Give specific examples.

Partner	Capability Builder	Truth Teller

Organizational Reverence and Opportunities for Irreverence

- What evidence did you detect of Rampart having misplaced reverence (e.g., undiscussables and untouchables)? List as

many examples as you observed, and explain the potential drain this misdirected energy is having.
- Next, prioritize your list. Which source(s) of misdirected reverence do you think are the most destructive to Rampart right now?
- As an irreverent consultant, what message do you need to deliver, to whom must it be given, and how? What are the risks of drawing attention to this issue? What are the risks of not drawing attention to this issue?
- How might each of the irreverent characteristics help create value at Rampart? Give specific examples.

Self-Reflection	*Gutsiness*	*Tough Love*

A Closer Look at Bill

Considering the criteria for a client of choice, and given the data provided, how would you rate Bill with regard to the five characteristics. Give specific examples. (It isn't necessary to have a response for every criteria—just react to those you believe are readily apparent.)

Criteria	Examples of Right Amount	Examples of Too Much	Examples of Too Little	Positive/ Negative Consequences
Results Orientation				
Intellectual Curiosity				
Self-Confidence				
Optimism				
Ambition				

Considering Potential Interventions

Based on the conclusions you've drawn so far about Rampart, and about Bill, make up a list of the actions/interventions/possible solutions you might initially consider as part of an action plan to recommend to Bill and Rampart. This is just a preliminary list, not necessarily what you might actually propose. For each item on your list, rate its potential impact on specific issues (e.g., high-medium-low), how receptive or ready Rampart will need to be for the action to "stick," and how ready the client organization is now, based on the preliminary data. Indicate some sense of sequencing (e.g., some actions may be predicated on the completion of others) and an importance level based on the priority of the issue being addressed. Here's a formatted table you can use to create the list:

Action Item	Issue(s) It Addresses	Potential Impact	Required Readiness	Readiness Now	Sequencing Concerns	Importance

Preparing for the Heart-to-Heart Talk With Bill

Needless to say, whatever the results of your analysis so far, any next steps must obviously be preceded by a difficult talk with Bill. If you contracted with him upfront to be able to offer less-than-pleasing data, then the conversation may be slightly easier. If you never had the conversation with him early on about the sensitivity and challenge of the kinds of issues you might raise, then your job will be that much more difficult, because he may not be expecting, or even desiring, to hear what you have to say. That said:

- Think about how you would prepare for such a conversation, what approach you would take, and what alternative approaches you should consider before choosing.
- Evaluate the potential risks and benefits of each approach, and choose the one you feel would work best in this situation, even if it's not what you would most naturally be inclined to do.

In Chapter 10, we will provide you with our "take" on Rampart, our view of the data, and what approaches we might take given the data provided. This is not meant in any way to be the "right" answer. It's not even the "expert" answer. We're confident that we could put ten management consultants from different backgrounds and experiences in a room with this case and they could each produce a viable approach to helping Rampart, and they would differ significantly from one another. The point is that each would have merit. Unfortunately, we're equally as confident that for every ten management consultants that could produce a viable, value-creating approach, there are fifty or more that would, inadvertently though it might be, produce a value-eroding, destructive approach that could take a very painful situation and make it insufferable. None of us is immune to the temptations of the bad habits. We each must struggle against whatever instincts might lure us toward them. We hope this activity has heightened your awareness of which of these habits might be lurking, waiting to trap you and your clients into a value-eroding engagement.

10

Epilogue

"People only see what they have been prepared to see."
—Emerson

Using the same queries and tools we presented for your participation in the Chapter 9, we will provide you with our point of view on the simulated company, Rampart Systems. Keep in mind that these observations and questions reflect our biases and approaches to consulting as much as your observations and questions reflect your biases.

First, you should know some of the reasoning behind the design of the Rampart simulation. We believe that there is a growing number of "Ramparts" in the United States today run by many "Bill Cavells." Many entrepreneurs who began companies within the last two decades are now faced with leading maturing, complex organizations whose needs are drastically different from the small, often family-owned businesses they began. What makes these transitions very difficult for entrepreneurs is that the very skills and abilities that enabled them to blaze the trail often become obstacles to making the kinds of changes needed to forge the organization into a viable, competitive enterprise. The bias for action, accompanied by a paternalistic treatment of employees who "stuck it out" with the entrepreneur, often turn into an aversion for needed processes and structures that the entreprenuer disdains as "too bureaucratic." Entrepreneurs who came out of a negative experience in a large, corporate environment must now confront the dilemma of having to construct the very types of corporate mechanisms and processes they so vehemently renounced. Unable to intellectually

distinguish healthy, productive process and structure from bureaucratic nonsense, they resist the need to implement infrastructures
as long as possible. The inability to let go of total control in order
to develop leadership throughout the organization is equally challenging. Psychologically, the entrepreneur's identity is often deeply
rooted in the organization. The notion of beginning a process that
distances the entreprenuer from the organization creates an identity crisis and a series of knee-jerk reactions intended to regain
control and reassert authority.

Despite how common this pattern may be, we believe there
are many corporations in America and abroad facing this crisis of
maturity. For the right consultant, the problems of growth present
an extremely viable market niche and an opportunity to be especially helpful to leaders who might otherwise preside over their
own demise.

Because of the numerous and complex issues presented in situations such as Rampart's, our first consulting principle is that the
organization must be viewed systemically. Single interventions applied randomly throughout the organization cannot catapult Rampart into competitive sustainable viability, nor is there a quick
solution. Organizations are complicated, dynamic systems in which
change is inherently difficult. Uncovering where the system is vulnerable to change, mobilizing the leadership to do all the things
needed to bring about the change, and establishing the right mechanisms to sustain the change are all part of the formidable challenge facing any consultant entering the organization. Keep this in
mind as you review our analysis of the situation at Rampart. You
might find it helpful as a backdrop against which to consider the
approach you initially laid out in Chapter 9.

Initial Reactions

What are some of your early conclusions about Rampart after your
six interviews?

- Rampart appears to be an organization facing a maturity crisis. The founding entreprenuer is in great turmoil over the

situation but is ineffective in confronting it, since he appears not to have surfaced the issue consciously as yet.

- The system is approaching a state of "overload." There is insufficient infrastructure in place to accommodate the growth Rampart is experiencing. It is at risk of collapsing under its own weight.
- People are choosing unproductive ways of coping with the system stress; collusion, "siloism," apathy, anger, and resentment are emerging.
- People both respect and fear Bill simultaneously, which sets up unhealthy dynamics of dependency, paternalism, and idolatry. The employees appear to have regressed to an adolescent state in which they view Bill as a father figure who is part mythic, part resented authority.
- Rampart appears to be directionless.

Do you see any patterns emerging among the data?

- There is a great deal of frustration and "panic" in the organization, especially with regard to Demarka.
- The Demarka decision is getting mixed reviews.
- People seem to view Bill as both cause and solution to the dilemmas facing Rampart, a pattern that has been in place since Rampart's inception. The organization's collective capacity to identify and solve its own problems appears limited.
- Bill's openness and capacity to change is questioned, even doubted.

What are the short-term, most critical issues based on the data you have so far? (in priority order)

- The lack of a comprehensive integration plan for the Rampart-Demarka acquisition that includes a shared understanding of all the concerns held by the senior leaders
- The organization's fear and confusion about Demarka
- The lack of a strong COO
- Understaffing in key customer contact functions

What are the long-term most critical issues based on the data you have so far? (in priority order)

- The lack of a well-crafted and shared vision and strategy for Rampart
- The dramatic lack of infrastructure (processes, systems, structures, governance) to support Rampart's current and impending growth
- Rampart's corporate culture and the unproductive norms that have emerged throughout the years (e.g., dependency, seat-of-the-pants decision making, conflict avoidance, "not invented here" thinking)
- Leadership crisis—specifically, Bill's need to more clearly define and carve out his role as CEO, hire a COO/successor, and develop his direct reports into competent executive leaders
- Lack of enterprise-wide managerial capability or talent
- HR issues—the inability to renew, identify, retain, develop, and reward top talent

On what do you base these priorities? What evidence do you have to support your conclusions that these are the vital few areas Bill should focus on?

- The separation into long and short term may make the issues more digestible to Bill.
- The conclusions seem representative of the organization's shared concerns.
- The "Bill" issues are raised, not covered up. But they are not dealt with immediately upfront, which could shut Bill down if approached too quickly.
- There is a sequencing issue; resolving some of these issues is predicated on first resolving others.

Which issues have the potential to be urgent but not particularly important? That is, which issues, if pursued, could consume energy and resources, but not yield significant value?

- Training and development consultants might be easily seduced by the numerous staff development issues, which would be a twofold mistake. First, Bill is clearly averse to this work, and second, it will only put a small plug in the bursting dam.

- Operations and specialist consultants may be drawn to the many process issues and want to dive right into repairing the infrastructure mess (i.e., HR, technology, the front-end processes associated with client acquisition, setup, and service). While these are all needs that must be addressed, in the absence of clear strategy and better-defined, more productive operating norms, the proposed solutions will encounter great resistance and may create more problems than they solve.
- Consultants with a psychological bent will find all of the Bill dynamics, as well as the Jeff issues, very appealing. While these matters must be dealt with, there are two major cautions: One consideration is Bill's and Jeff's individual and collective readiness to deal with these issues—premature attempts to open them for deep discussion could prove damaging. Second, there is a danger of dealing with these issues to the exclusion of the systemic, organizational, and strategic issues. If this turned into a purely "behavioral" engagement, the organization's performance would likely remain unchanged.

Expanding the Anthropological Hunt

Based on the data you have, and your initial conclusions, what additional data do you think would be helpful?

- All of the due diligence data from the Demarka deal
- Rampart's performance data for the last three years
- Interviews with Demarka employees and owners
- Interviews with customers
- An interview with Jeff
- Interviews with a small handful of next-level employees

What new questions do you have now that you didn't have before doing the interviews?

- What were some of the driving assumptions that led Bill to buy Demarka? Did he have misgivings during the deal? What were they? (This would help understand the potential role that "deal fever" and Bill's ego may have played in the decision. Whether or not Rampart is truly ready for the acquisition is a relevant question, although water under the bridge at this point.)
- How much of the "letting go" issue is playing into Bill's controlling behavior? Is he aware of any of the unproductive consequences? How does he justify his biases about employee development, expense management, headcount management, staff meetings, and other basic organizational processes (each of which may be a symptom of a larger issue)? Are his decisions mainly financially driven—related to the impact on his personal gain? (Access to this information could indicate the degree to which Bill may be open to change and where his openness is or isn't.)
- Who is Rampart's most immediate and formidable competitive threat? What data exist that might track their competitors' moves, recent deals, and victories in the market over Rampart? Are there any detectable patterns in their behavior that could provoke Rampart to action? (Finding such information might be a challenge in the face of Rampart's insularity, but worth a shot.)
- Where do Rampart's senior leaders see leverage opportunities for change? Do they have any sense of ownership of Rampart's future, or do they feel powerless given Bill's tendencies? (This perspective might help calibrate how much leadership and support for change they can provide as Bill awakens to the need for change.)
- Who does Bill respect and listen to, either within or outside Rampart, that he might talk with, and who might help him accept the need for significant change? (Knowing this could help uncover needed allies.)

Bad Habits Die Hard

How might each of these bad habit consultants react to Bill and Rampart, given the data provided? Give specific examples.

Messiah	*Dependency Builder*	*Colluder*
• Uses examples of failed acquisitions to frighten Bill. • Tries to play on Bill's fears by reinforcing his lack of M&A experience in comparison to own extensive experience.	• Exaggerates the data to emphasize the negativity about the Demarka deal. • Presents the integration process in excessively complex ways to advance feelings of inferiority.	• Presents Bill's team as the major obstacle to Demarka success while positively reinforcing Bill's "courageous" decision to do the deal. • Plays up the organization's concerns about Jeff in order to assume the "right-hand man" role.

How might the situation at Rampart provoke these negative motives?

Missionaries	*Mercenaries*
"I'm going to show Bill and Rampart how to become a real company!"	"Boy, did we underprice this engagement, or what? There is an endless revenue stream here given how screwed up they are!"

Enacting the Value-Creating Roles

How could each of these value-creating consultant roles contribute to the Rampart engagement, given the data provided? Give specific examples.

Partner	Capability Builder	Truth Teller
• Involve Bill, Jeff, and the team in problem-definition phase to build commitment and ownership. • Discuss boundaries with Jeff—clear definition of his "project manager" role and consultant deliverables.	• Work with Bill to identify leaders who could be tapped to lead integration activities as a way of building their leadership capability. • Create cross-functional forums to address Demarka integration issues that will simultaneously build collaboration and conflict resolution capability among key functions like Ops, Client Service, and Sales.	• Openly discuss the need to provide candid feedback to Bill. • Be direct with Bill about people's perceptions of his leadership and contribution to the issues. • Candidly discuss with Jeff how the credibility gaps may affect his leadership of the project, or be an opportunity to close the gaps.

Organizational Reverence and Opportunities for Irreverence

What evidence did you detect of Rampart having misplaced reverence (e.g. undiscussables or untouchables)? List as many examples as you observed and the potential drain this misdirected energy is having on members of the organization (in priority order).

- *Bill's leadership and management.* Bill's need for omnipotence leads him to believe that he can manage nearly every aspect of his rapidly growing company. He fails to recognize and accept that Rampart is no longer the fledgling start-up company he could once control. A cycle has been set up in which the employees revere him for his storybook success, thereby reinforcing his omnipotence-seeking behavior. Unfortunately, when people are in awe of their leaders, they tend to conceal unpleasant truths from them. Not surfacing and dealing with these issues directly causes conflict avoidance and people to defer problem ownership.

- *Insufficient resources to get the job done.* This is an outgrowth of the first issue regarding Bill. The issue is being addressed on a one-off basis as people plead their cases in hopes of garnering Bill's support. By dealing with Bill in a way in which he is comfortable, they avoid the root issue, which is that resource allocation decisions seem to hinge on Bill's mood and not objective business criteria.
- *Jeff's questionable ability in the eyes of his peers as Bill's right-hand man.* Employees resent Jeff's seemingly arbitrary appointment to a top position for which he is clearly unqualified. The issue of his competence is secondary to the fact that his "siblings" are jealous of his "favorite child" status. This undermines teamwork and productive decision making at the top at a time when it is especially needed.
- *The conflict between Ann and Bill.* This is symptomatic of the concern with Bill's leadership as well, but because the conflict is playing out publicly, it needs to be addressed. The real question is, how open to outsiders and outside thinking are Bill and the homegrown Rampart leaders? Ann is the victim of Rampart's not-invented-here culture, and her abrasive style isn't helping.
- *The tug-of-war between sales, operations/installations, and client service.* The three leaders seem to be engaging in denial about the potential negative consequences Rampart could suffer as a result of this issue. Instead, they are each bolstering their own positions to appear blameless while pointing the finger at the others. The root issues are numerous, and again they stem from Bill's tight resource control, as well as the organization's inability to manage conflict. Because this workplace war is center stage to many of the employees, the three managers' modeling of collusion pervades the organization.

How might each of the irreverent characteristics help create value at Rampart? Give specific examples.

Self-Reflection	Gutsiness	Tough Love
• Manage biases attributable to one's professional lens that might lead to suboptimal or inappropriate recommendations. • Monitor motives and impulses that are pushing or avoiding certain issues.	• Help build Bill's and Rampart's courage to take some of the bold actions required to make change. • Take on the tough issues rather than avoiding Bill's inevitable strong emotions that need to be surfaced and dealt with.	• Help Bill understand and accept the unproductive consequences of his leadership style. • Push Bill to hire a competent COO and find a more appropriate assignment for Jeff. • Help Bill shift the accountability for leading the enterprise to his senior leaders.

A Closer Look at Bill

Considering the criteria for a client of choice, and given the data provided, how would you rate your client, Bill, with regard to the five characteristics? Give specific examples.

Criteria	Examples of Right Amount	Examples of Too Much	Examples of Too Little
Results Orientation	• Instinct to grow Rampart by buying Demarka	• Imbalance between extensive workload and insufficient resources	
Intellectual Curiosity	• Contribution to product innovations		• Lack of current technology and openness to external thinking
Self-Confidence		• Maintenance of excessive control	
Optimism	• Obvious passion for Rampart's abilities	• Oversimplification of how complex integrating Demarka may be	
Ambition	• Rampart's historical growth • The Demarka deal		

Maturing Rampart's Thinking

While not explicit in the data, inherent in the conversations with the six Rampart managers is a serious lack of mature business thinking. Think about it. If they thought differently about their organization, the markets in which they compete, the customers they serve, the competitors against whom they vie for market share, and the market spaces they may one day play in, then isn't it likely that their infrastructure would look different? The many issues to be

addressed organizationally are yet symptoms of a greater problem—Rampart's crisis of maturity is one of intellect as well as organization.

For example, the director of operations had no idea whether
Rampart's pricing allowed for the service levels being provided.
There could very well be cases in which Rampart is losing money
on the clients they are serving. How would you imagine any of the
senior leaders answering the following questions?

> What is Rampart's value proposition?
> Where in Rampart is value created for its clients?
> Of the many options Rampart had to expand its offering into
> contiguous market space, how was Internet marketing cho-
> sen as the most viable?
> Who are Rampart's most threatening competitors, and what is
> Rampart's point of differentiation?

Our hunch is that the responses would be less than impressive. Not
because Rampart's leaders are unintelligent, but because they have
never been required to know the answers to such questions. But
moving from a $650 million dollar organization to a billion-plus-
dollar organization successfully will most assuredly require them
to not only know the answers, but to insightfully and creatively
act upon them. We've seen many bad-habit consultants, especially
dependency builders, who create unimplementable solutions for
clients whose thinking severely lags behind the complexity of the
solution. Providing brilliant new organization designs, technology
solutions, process innovations, governance models, and cultural
values for organizations in the absence of the mature intellect
needed to assimilate such solutions is of no value. The next generation of consultant must help mature an organization's thinking
while advancing the effectiveness of its various components.

A Heart-to-Heart With Bill: From Analysis to Feedback

Clearly, there are a host of issues that must be discussed with Bill,
many of which will distress him. His inevitable defensiveness and
strong emotional reactions should not deter you from the obliga-

tion to present all the data you have unearthed. We have heard many consultants excuse their avoidance of such conversations with their feelings of inadequacy, fear of the emotional reactions, concern over risking the engagement, the discounting of the severity of the data, or relegating the delivery of the bad news to their client's therapist. Frankly, we don't buy any of these excuses. If you were qualified to take on the assignment, you should be qualified to do all that it entails. Playing on the fringes of the organization—concentrating on the technical, structural, process, and developmental issues at the expense of the hard and painful problems with Bill's leadership—not only erodes value from the engagement, it perpetuates the bad-habit reputation from which our profession now suffers. With all of your clients, have the courage to take the high road and do what will ultimately serve the client and his organization best. Say what needs to be said, and help set the organization on the course to becoming what they envision themselves to be.

Well, that concludes our time with Rampart Systems, but our hope is that from this experience you will take away one or two new insights about yourself and your profession, as well as your clients. Remember, our conclusions are not necessarily the "right" conclusions, they are just ours. Yours may be very different and equally valid. However they differ, if you exit Rampart rethinking some deep-seated assumptions or rules of thumb you've never tested before, then we'll consider our time together very worthwhile. We hope you will as well.

Our Final Hope

If you recall the original tale of Pandora's box, then you remember that in her haste to prevent the world's evils from escaping from the box, Pandora shut the lid before the last remaining element could break free . . . and that was "hope." We realize this book, in some respects, is like Pandora's box in that we have opened up new ways of thinking and enacting the role of consultant. These may be intimidating, even overwhelming, thus tempting you to dismiss or avoid the need for change. Our hope is that enough of us will resist this temptation and, together, build a critical mass of consultants willing to transform our profession. We are hopeful that in doing so, we will form a new generation of consultant who will restore our profession to the once-admirable work of helping, advising, and serving others.

Today, the consulting profession is on a trajectory. A negative one. All someone has to do is mention the word *lawyer* and instant disdain, distrust, frustration, and skepticism are conjured up. Without change, the word *consultant* will soon produce the same reactions. We can prevent this. But if we want the mention of our profession to elicit positive reactions such as "tremendously helpful," "insightful advice," "caring support"—"lasting value"—then we must change.

Lest we consign our profession into the hands of a generation prepared only to mimic what they have seen, we should start now.

Bibliography

Bellman, Geoffrey. *The Consultant's Calling: Bringing Who You Are to What You Do.* San Francisco: Jossey-Bass, 1992.

Block, Peter. *Flawless Consulting.* San Diego: Pfeiffer, 1981.

Champy, James. *Reengineering Management: The Mandate for New Leadership.* New York: HarperBusiness, 1995.

Kennedy Research Group. *The Global Management Consulting Marketplace: Key Data, Forecasts & Trends.* Fitzwilliam, N.H.: Kennedy Research Group, 1998.

Kouzes, James, and Barry Posner. *Credibility: How Leaders Gain and Lose It, Why People Demand It.* San Francisco: Jossey-Bass, 1993.

Micklethwait, John, and Adrian Wooldridge. *The Witch Doctors: Making Sense of the Management Gurus.* New York: Times Business, 1996.

O'Shea, James, and Charles Madigan. *Dangerous Company: The Consulting Powerhouses and the Companies They Save and Ruin.* New York: Times Business, 1997.

Scherer, John. *Work and the Human Spirit.* Spokane, Wash.: John Scherer and Associates, 1993.

Index